Nostradamus
in the 21st Century

Nostradamus

in the 21st Century

AND THE
COMING
INVASION
OF EUROPE

PETER LEMESURIER

PIATKUS

© 1993, 2000 Peter Lemesurier

First published in 1993 as
Nostradamus – The Next 50 Years
by Judy Piatkus (Publishers) Ltd of
5 Windmill Street, London W1T 2JA
www.piatkus.co.uk

Reprinted 6 times

This revised edition 2000

The moral right of the author has been asserted
under the Copyright, Designs and Patents Act 1988

A catalogue record for this book is available
from the British Library

ISBN 0 7499 2163 3

Set in 11/13 Sabon by Action Publishing Technology, Gloucester
Printed & bound in Great Britain by
The Bath Press, Bath, Somerset

CONTENTS

Notes

1   For cross-references please refer to the **Index of Predictions Quoted** on page 314. Asterisked predictions are those added since the first edition of this book was published in 1993. Any dates listed against the right-hand margin are those either indicated by Nostradamus himself (whether calendrically, astrologically or via his 'liturgical' count) or arising directly from the author's astrological application of the 'Janus hypothesis' to identifiable historical events.

2   Superior numbers refer to items listed in the **Reference Bibliography** on pages 311–13.

NOSTRADAMUS BY A LEADING CONTEMPORARY

Be it Great God beyond all space and time
Roused Nostradamus' rapture into rhyme;
Be he by daemon good or evil stirred,
Or gifted with a soul that like some bird
Soars up to heavens no mortal man may know
To bring back auguries for us below;
Be his a mind so gloomy, dark and dim,
Crammed with gross humours, as to cozen him –
Whate'er he is he is: yet none the less
Through the vague portents that his words express
Like some old oracle he has foretold
For many a year what fate for us shall hold.
I'd doubt him, did not heaven, that to men
Imparts both good and evil, guide his pen.

PIERRE DE RONSARD
(tr. from the *Elegie sur les Troubles d'Amboise*, 1560)

'Before us –
Stands yesterday.'

– Ted Hughes from 'Climbing into Heptonstall'

INTRODUCTION

MUCH HAS HAPPENED SINCE THIS BOOK was first published in 1993, both on the world stage and in the field of Nostradamus research. As might be expected, some of this has redounded to the prophet's credit – and, as we shall see, in the most fascinating of ways, at that – while some of it almost equally fascinatingly has not. It was ever so. Given the vast cloud of credulous misinformation that has surrounded Nostradamus in the past (not least in respect of his celebrated '1999' prediction, which will be considered at length in Chapter 3), some whittling down of the alleged 'facts' is only to be expected. And, as the smoke clears, it is almost inevitable that new, more reliable and, frankly, more interesting facts should emerge into the light of day. The absolutely fundamental 'Janus hypothesis' outlined on page 3 should serve as a case in point.

First the bad news . . .

Nevertheless, some unpalatable facts have to be faced first. In that same year of 1993, for example, the late Pierre Brind'Amour, of the Department of Ancient Studies at the University of Ottawa, Canada, published his ground-breaking

Nostradamus Astrophile[8] – in which he analysed the sixteenth-century French seer's published horoscopes and other astrological works in unprecedented detail – and came to the conclusion that, as an astrologer, he had been quite astonishingly incompetent. This was nothing new. Even the professional astrologers of Nostradamus's own day had long since reached the same conclusion, and said so loudly and often. But then Nostradamus himself had never claimed to be an astrologer as such, much preferring the term *astrophile*, or 'star-lover'. The very word appears to this day on the plaque beside the door of his house in Salon-de-Provence.

Besides, to all such attacks the wily prophet simply replied that he was 'divinely inspired' – which effectively put paid to the argument.

In 1999, Bernard Chevignard, Professor of Language and Communication at the University of Burgundy in Dijon, published a massive further work entitled *Présages de Nostradamus*,[14] in which he reprinted and analysed books one to four of the huge, newly-restored twelve-book manuscript by Nostradamus's latter-day secretary Jean de Chavigny entitled *Recueil des Presages prosaiques de M. Michel de Nostradame*. This contained no less than 6,338 dated predictions by the seer, religiously assembled by this first and keenest of his disciples from Nostradamus's annual *Almanachs* and *Pronostications* – international bestsellers for which the latter was far better known in his own day than for the *Propheties* with which he is more normally associated today. Since these predictions were all for his own century, it is now of course possible, thanks to Chevignard's work, to analyse their success-rate against the historical record of what actually happened. And, unfortunately, the analysis is not encouraging: for this type of prophecy, at least, Nostradamus's identifiable success-rate seems to have been extraordinarily low – in the order of 5.73 per cent.

. . . then the Janus hypothesis

However, also in 1999 a further important piece of research was published. This was the historian and classicist Roger Prévost's *Nostradamus, le mythe et la réalité*.[49] Unduly sweeping and sometimes factually careless though this intriguing study proved to be, Prévost successfully demonstrated that many, if not all, of Nostradamus's better known *Propheties* were based on *past* events drawn from ancient histories and medieval chronicles that can quite easily be identified not merely by the events they describe, *but by the fact that Nostradamus often quotes from them virtually verbatim!*

This highly original piece of research in turn helped to add a great deal of force to what by then was starting to become known as the 'Janus hypothesis'. As you will no doubt recall, Janus was the two-faced Roman god who looked backwards and forwards at once – and the suggestion was that Nostradamus, in a sense, had been doing the same.

Whence, conceivably, the fact that when, in 1594, Chavigny published the first of his four books on Nostradamus (based on his copious written research notes) he entitled it *La premiere face du Ianus François*, or 'The First Face of the French Janus'.

On this model, Nostradamus would have arrived at his more major prophecies by looking back at significant ancient events (or even relatively minor recent ones), then establishing in which signs or houses the various planets were at the time, and finally working out when some at least of these would be in the same positions again in the future. There was absolutely no difficulty about this: numerous sets of planetary tables for doing so had been available since the 1540s (some of which we know for a fact he possessed). Additionally, there was even a set of cardboard disc-based computers for achieving the same result (published by the Emperor Charles V's chief mathematician Peter Bienewitz, better known as Apianus, in his lavish *Astronomicum Caesareum*, or

'Astronomy of the Caesars' of 1540). This procedure would then have given the seer a date when the same event, or something very like it, was theoretically likely to occur again.

I say 'theoretically likely to' because astrology has always expressly denied that celestial events actually *cause* specific earthly ones. The theory has always been that, at best, they provide conditions propitious for them – as the contemporary astrologers were always reminding Nostradamus. And I say '*a* date' because astrology is, of course, cyclic, and consequently the potential for any given event's theoretical recurrence is liable to be there every time the particular planetary pattern recurs again in the future.

The cyclic view of history

This point is important because, by calling them *vaticinations perpetuelles* or 'perpetual prophecies', Nostradamus acknowledged in his original preface that his prophecies were of this type. We know this because other booklets similarly calling themselves *Propheties perpetuelles* posited just such a cyclic model of human destiny – some of them proposing a twenty-eight-year cycle on the basis of which they offered a whole series of prophecies extending up to the present day.[42] Rabelais was already parodying the genre in 1533.

Nostradamus's model was not nearly so simplistic. His planetary cycles were far longer ones, and not as regular, either. But the principle was the same. History was essentially cyclic. The notion was basic to the very Renaissance in which he played so prominent a role in France. Just as it was widely believed that the golden age of classical Greece and Rome was about to dawn again in Europe by sheer effort of human will, so – in terms of the Janus effect – what had happened at any time was quite likely to occur again, given the right planetary and human conditions. And given that nothing was going to change the planetary variables, the only thing that could avoid or bring about the event in question was human behaviour itself.

4

The underlying principle may or may not have been scientifically valid, but this at least seems to have been the gist of the idea.

The *Propheties* thus take on a perfectly useful function. Far from being mere forecasts of inevitable doom, they become a communal project in which humanity can either co-operate or not, their function being to warn, to guide, to encourage. But, by the same token, all prospect of tying the fulfilment of any prophecy down to any particular date flies out of the window. The event *may* happen in any given year or month: on the other hand, the potential for it may be avoided, and its fulfilment put off until *next* time the relevant planets are in position.

Possibly that is one reason why most of the *Propheties* are undated – since they can never have been for any one particular date in the first place. The fact that this also allowed Nostradamus and his followers constantly to say 'Well, it hasn't happened *yet*' was a pure bonus that enabled the prophet to avoid ever being proved wrong.

The Islamic threat

The upshot, then, is that past and present events that loomed particularly large in Nostradamus's mind tended to resurface in his prophecies for the future, too. By way of a case in point, Western Europe had for centuries been menaced by militant Islam. In the east, the Ottoman Empire had been advancing westwards across Europe even since the mid-fifteenth century, arriving before the very gates of Vienna in the self-same year as the young apothecary enrolled for his doctorate course at Montpellier. In the south, powerful Muslim pirate fleets continually ravaged the Mediterranean coasts. In the west, the Moors had been finally expelled from Spain only a decade or so before Nostradamus's birth.

Unsurprisingly, therefore, not only his annual *Almanachs*, but his *Propheties* too, continually warn of further Muslim attacks and invasions. So insistent are these warnings in the

Prophecies that it is possible to cobble together a whole potential scenario out of them. According to my admittedly speculative reconstruction of this, we have (it seems) to expect a massive invasion of Mediterranean Europe by hordes from the East who will be Asiatic, Muslim *and red* (whatever Nostradamus means by the term). Reaching Italy by around the year 2000, the insurgents will also spread along the North African coast and, via Spain, into southern France. The Pope will be forced to flee to the Rhône valley, where he will be pursued, captured and eventually killed: *moreover, he will apparently be the present Pope* (this detail alone cannot help but emphasise the imminence of the events described). The Vatican will subsequently be destroyed. From southern France the invaders – looting and raping, as well as persecuting the Catholic church in particular – will advance steadily northwards in their millions. With the aid of some kind of aerial fire-weapon, they will overrun major defence-lines on the rivers Garonne and Loire, until they eventually reach the English Channel coast. Only at the last moment will an invasion of England be averted, and then more as a result of dissension in the Asiatic ranks than of any efforts on the part of the defenders – always assuming, of course, that the West plays its cards wrongly.

But then there are currently signs that we may have got some at least of the answers right. The projected invasion is already overdue. Either that or (as we shall see) it is taking some rather surprising forms.

Then Second World War history will repeat itself (the idea of prophetic repetition, as we have seen, is implicit in the Janus hypothesis itself), as a massive allied counter-invasion is launched. In this case, though, it will set out both from Britain and from Germany. Thanks partly to brilliant invasion-tactics, the invaders will be chased out of a now desolate and largely depopulated France, then out of Italy and finally out of Spain. Later they will be pursued to the Middle East by a charismatic new Western leader who will go on to become ruler of most of Europe after the manner of the Emperor

Charlemagne. An era of unprecedented peace and prosperity will then ensue that will last for over half a century.

So, at least, Nostradamus seems to be saying – and he says it repeatedly, vividly and in immense detail. The picture is dramatic, even horrific at times, yet it is by no means all gloom. Moreover, it has next to nothing to do with the one that emerges from most of the existing accounts.

Facing the facts

Fact or fiction, then? Is such a scenario even remotely possible? Even as I write, it is easy to assume that it is not. And yet extraordinary things are starting to happen. In Central Asia, the newly-independent Muslim republics of the former Soviet Union are steadily finding their feet, aided by Turkey and other Muslim countries. Their combined potential oil-wealth is already considerable, their store of armaments (left over from the Cold War) immense. Islam is recovering its former power by leaps and bounds. There is a longing for a new, charismatic leader who will set everything to rights. Already there is talk of founding a new 'United States of Central Asia'. Meanwhile, in the Middle East and the Caucasus, the conditions are becoming ever more ripe for some kind of ultimate confrontation between militant Islam and the West, while in the former Yugoslavia the temptation is growing for the Arab world to intervene in the very heart of Europe itself ...

And what then? Are we really in for some kind of Armageddon? Or is the strikingly apocalyptic flavour of many of Nostradamus's prophecies merely a result of the fact that, once again, both he and his Catholic French contemporaries – assailed as they believed themselves to be by the Four Horsemen of the Apocalypse in the form of War, Famine, Plague, and Death, to say nothing of the Antichrist (in the form of Calvin) sitting in Geneva – assumed that they were living in the long-predicted Last Times?

Are his apparent predictions for our times once again merely projections of his own times?

They could very well be. Yet the answers, clearly, lie not in what we believe about them, but in what we do about them. We have been warned. If we respond to those warnings appropriately, the prophecies – this time around at least – will fail. And so Nostradamus will be proved wrong – which, of course, is the fate of all good prophets.

This current volume

It seems to me to be of the utmost importance, then, to establish just what it is that Nostradamus predicted, whether for the coming years or for a more distant future. I have therefore rendered his prophecies in the clearest and most appropriate way that I can – namely in rhymed verses of the same type as he himself used. So far as I know, this is the first time that this has been done in English.

True, in the very nature of things, rhymed verse translations necessarily have to take poetic liberties at times – paraphrasing somewhat here, padding out a little there, rearranging as necessary. But then we have both a model and a splendid validation for this. *For Nostradamus himself wrote and published such translations* (in his case from the Latin) – and in almost every case the results were *far* freer than anything you will find in this book! Moreover, to the connoisseur it is very evident that, even when writing his own original verses, the prophet himself often distorted what he was trying to say merely in order to make it rhyme, especially when he was running out of space at the end of a verse – which, paradoxically enough, he often seems *not* to have seen coming!

At all events, the result is, I believe, the first accessible English translation of Nostradamus of recent years. But then, if Nostradamus is right in anticipating the events he does, it may well need to be.

To start with, I propose to look briefly at Nostradamus the man and to tell the story of his life. Following this, I shall examine his prophetic and writing career and some of his

8

working methods. In Chapter 2, I go on to look at how inter-preters and commentators have struggled to make some sort of sense of the baffling riddles left by the Prophet of Provence. I will also outline my proposed principles for interpretation and explain briefly how I arrived at the sequence suggested. Chapter 3 will take a look at some of the seer's predictions that are widely regarded as having been fulfilled already, and in Chapters 4, 5, 6 and 7 I shall set out in verse his astonish-ing prophecies for the coming years. Finally, Chapter 8 will summarise my findings.

For this book the translations have been newly rechecked against the original texts – for quatrains I.1 to IV.53 the 1555 edition, for quatrains IV.54 to VII.42 the September 1557 edition, for quatrains VIII.1 to X.100 the 1568 edition, and for the *Presages* and *Sixains* the 1605 edition. In most cases the original French will be found reprinted in my *Nostradamus Encyclopedia*,[34] as will a brief Nostradamus dictionary. Starred verse-translations are new to this book, most of them prepared especially for this edition.

★

> *Up! Flee far, far across the land!*
> *And let this dark, mysterious tome*
> *From Nostradamus' very hand*
> *Suffice to guide you as you roam.*

GOETHE
Faust (I. 1)

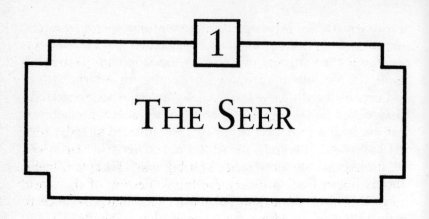

THE SEER

Seated, he studies secretly at night
On tripod bronze, the quiet eremite:
A tiny flame amidst the lonely night
Bids fair to bring what none should doubt to light.

Century I.1

UNEASE, FEAR, FATALISTIC DREAD – these are among the most usual reactions of people today when the name of Nostradamus is mentioned. The mysterious medieval doctor and seer has acquired something of the aura of a magician, a dark and threatening master of the occult, a delver into unspeakable realms of astrology and witchcraft. Many have come to class him with Mephistopheles himself.

Not because he was necessarily anything of the kind, but because that is how his crabbed and curious verses have come to be seen – especially by those who have never read them.

It is almost as though this eminent sixteenth-century physician and occultist – the contemporary of his English near-equivalent, Queen Elizabeth I's celebrated court astrologer Dr John Dee – were, through his verses, not only predicting the future, but actually controlling it from his grave, dead though he has been now these 400 years and more.

Certainly, the leaders of Nazi Germany seem to have believed as much. Either that, or they were determined cynically to exploit popular superstition to that effect. Not only Dr Goebbels's ministry of propaganda, but also Himmler's SS delved into the prophecies in a big way. Their aim seems to have been first to descry the future destiny of the world in general and of the Third Reich in particular, and then to convince that world of their conclusions. The British and Americans, no less cynically, retaliated in kind. So, much more genuinely, did one of the best-known French Nostradamus-scholars of the day, Dr Max de Fontbrune. His book on the prophecies of Nostradamus, published in 1938, admittedly foretold the German invasion of France, but it also predicted – if in general terms – the subsequent victories of the Allies in North Africa, their invasion of Italy, the disgrace of Marshal Pétain, the triumphant return of General de Gaulle to France and the defeat and partition of Germany. Not surprisingly, the occupying German forces banned the book almost as soon as they arrived in France in 1940. De Fontbrune himself was persecuted by the Gestapo. It was as though they believed that attacking the prophetic conclusions – blaming, as it were, the messenger for the message – would somehow alter the world, too. And strangely enough, there is actually more than a grain of truth in the idea. Prophecies do seem to have a role in conditioning events.

But if so, then it is literally vital that we should not draw the *wrong* conclusions. If we somehow manage to convince ourselves – as many have – that what Nostradamus foretold for our immediate future was an era of nuclear war, widespread genocide and general hell on earth, then just possibly that is precisely what we shall inherit. Equally possibly, if we discover that his original oracle foretold nothing of the kind, then that realisation, too, may have its tangible, practical consequences. Whence, of course, the urgent need for a new and more cool-headed investigatory book such as this.

Student and physician

Michel de Nostredame came of humble Jewish-French stock. Born in St-Rémy-de-Provence on 14 December 1503 (Julian) to a local merchant's wife, he was brought up in the Roman Catholic faith, to which his paternal grandfather had converted from his ancestral religion some forty years before out of understandable concern for survival amid an age of growing religious bigotry. The strange, adopted family name was a direct result of this, apparently commemorating the saint's day on which the conversion had been celebrated.

The eldest of seven or eight sons, he seems to have been educated initially by his maternal great-grandfather, a local doctor and herbalist, who no doubt taught him Greek, Latin, Hebrew, mathematics and astronomy/astrology (the two were indistinguishable at the time). He then went on to study at Avignon, and after eight years as a wandering apothecary joined the Montpellier Faculty of Medicine. However, he was expelled from the student body a fortnight before his course even began for having, as an apothecary, been rude about doctors – and we do not know whether he ever rejoined it. Certainly there is no record of his eventual doctorate either at Montpellier or at any other known medical faculty, even though that of François Rabelais (who would have been his illustrious contemporary there) is duly recorded. His celebrated 1552 medical cookbook (the *Traité des fardemens et confitures*, finally published in 1555) is clearly the work of an apothecary rather than a doctor, and is prefaced by a *Proem* admitting quite frankly that he was a self-taught, if well-read, healer who had been 'unable fully to attain the summit of this perfect doctrine'. Moreover, in Chapter 27 of Part I he refers to *messieurs les docteurs de la faculté de medecine* – some of whom he would subsequently cite as references and authorities – in terms which suggest that he didn't actually think of himself as one of them.

This would fit the circumstantial evidence, too. At Agen and Marseille he would later go on to work under the local doctors Scaliger and Serre – just like the traditional apothecary – while at Lyon he would admittedly be placed in sole charge, but only after what seems to have been a bitter row with the city's medical establishment. If, by contrast, he was positively welcomed in a plague-stricken Aix-en-Provence, it may well have been for no better reason than that all that city's doctors had already fled in panic, in accordance with the plague-prescription famously offered to his fellow physicians by the celebrated Augier Ferrier of Toulouse: 'Get out fast, stay well away, come back late.' Possibly, in other words, it was the very plague itself that would offer the gifted apothecary from St-Rémy the opening he needed to play the role of physician, and consequently lead quite fortuitously to his enduring fame as a leading plague-specialist, and as an established 'doctor' to boot. It was a high-risk strategy if so – but the absence of competition of course meant that he could charge virtually anything he liked for his services.

Could this, then, be how Nostredame came to be accepted as a physician – even eventually by the French royal family? In view of his acquired fame, certainly, it is extremely unlikely that anybody would have thought to check up on him. Perhaps it was simply that, in the end, he felt he had to live up to the public perception of himself as a 'plague-doctor', backed up by subsequent publisher's hype, even to the extent of posing for the engravers in suspiciously pristine doctor's garb (*see* Frontispiece).

Certainly, fake degrees were not all that uncommon at the time. The contemporary 'Doctor' John Dee has always been so called, even though he never in fact acquired a doctorate, while the equally contemporary Paracelsus, though immensely influential in medicine, never did so either.

Whatever his actual credentials at the time, however, Nostredame had by 1531 taken up a regular medical career. By 1533 he was working with the well-known doctor and philosopher Julius Caesar (or Jules César) Scaliger at Agen, where he prospered and married one Henriette d'Encausse. They had two children, whose names are unknown to us. His good fortune was to be short-lived, however, for soon either the plague or some other epidemic visited the town and both wife and family promptly died from it. This personal disaster not only nearly destroyed Nostradamus himself; news of it all but destroyed his practice too. What price, after all, the medical expert who himself survived, but could not even save his own nearest and dearest?

Further calamities followed. He quarrelled with Scaliger, was apparently persecuted by his late wife's family and, to crown it all, found the Inquisition of Toulouse starting to take an interest in him because, as a man with reformist Franciscan sympathies, he had allegedly made some sacrilegious remark about the then-prevalent idolatry of the saints. His reaction was predictable. He took to the road again. During the next six years he travelled Europe, everywhere gathering material from local apothecaries for the medical cookbook mentioned earlier. He also undertook some academic translation-work. Most of his life at this time, however, is a complete blank to us, and so almost inevitably raconteurs and romancers without number have been drawn to fill the vacuum with fanciful tales of startling personal predictions and pieces of almost magical precognition. You may believe them if you wish, though I am afraid that you will have to look elsewhere to find them.

By 1544 the wanderer had returned – this time to Marseille, where that winter's unusually severe floods, flushing out the rodents from their nests, brought renewed plague in their wake, and consequently more work for Nostredame too, who (as we have seen) placed himself under the command of the renowned local physician Louis Serre. By May 1546, it was the stricken town of Aix-en-Provence that

was appealing to him for help. As ever, Nostradamus will-
ingly – perhaps eagerly – responded, subsequently becoming
the acknowledged hero of the hour, despite his own admis-
sion in his *Traité* that none of his cures worked, not even
the regulation blood-letting. Having subsequently settled at
Salon, he was next sent for by the city of Lyon, where a
quite different epidemic – possibly whooping cough – was
raging. Then, laden with gifts, he returned to his new home
again.

His second marriage followed in 1547, this time to a rich
widow by the name of Anne Ponsarde, known as 'Gemelle' (the
Twin). Their house in Salon, which stands to this day, has
recently been renovated in his honour. Now, however, he
largely abandoned medicine in favour of writing. Long aware
that he was one of a line of natural clairvoyants – though always
careful (for obvious reasons) to describe his skill as a gift from
God and to link it with the Bible's prophecy that 'your old men
shall dream dreams and your young men see visions' – he
started as early as 1550 to produce at least one *Almanach* or
Pronostication a year, using the name 'Nostradam*us*' for the
first time. Now, having converted part of the top floor of the
house into a study, he launched into a more all-embracing work
altogether. This was a vast collection of general prophecies that
was designed to consist of ten books of 100 four-line verses each
– 1,000 quatrains in all – predicting in some detail all the major
events leading from Nostradamus's own time to the end of the
present age and the inception of the expected millennium. These
comprised the celebrated work that would subsequently be
published as the *Propheties*.

Working methods

Nostradamus's exact working methods are fairly obscure.
The very first quatrain (quoted at the head of this chapter)
suggests a divinatory approach akin to that of the Delphic
oracle in ancient Greece. The second quatrain (I.2), which in
my translation reads:

15

Wand placed in hand as once in Branchis' fane,
He dips in water both his hem and feet.
A dread voice shakes him in his gown amain,
Then light divine! The god assumes his seat.

is similarly redolent of the former oracle of Branchidai (now Didyma in Turkey), once consulted by Alexander the Great in person. Yet both verses are simply paraphrases of the well-known account (*De Mysteriis Aegyptiorum*) by the third/fourth century neo-Platonist philosopher Iamblichus of the divinatory practices of the ancient world – and on a number of other occasions Nostradamus merely says '*as though* on the bronze tripod'. It is fairly clear, then, that these verses indicate not so much what the seer actually did, as the way in which he wished people to view his work. He wanted them to see him, in other words, as a prophet in the direct tradition of the oracles of the ancient world.

In his private correspondence, on the other hand,[2,18] he paints a quite different picture. Here he meditates, goes into trance with the aid of 'magic' herbs, practices ritual incubation (basically, dream interpretation), and even resorts to a form of automatic writing (writing while in trance).

But Prévost's evidence in particular, backed up by my own research, suggests that this was merely the icing on the prophetic cake. Much more basic was the process that I have dubbed 'comparative horoscopy'.[34,35,36] As I have outlined it under the terms of the 'Janus hypothesis' in my Introduction, Nostradamus seems to have conceived it as his basic task to predict, with the aid of the astrological tables available to him (to say nothing of Apianus's cardboard computers) just when and on what latitudes the major events both of ancient history and of the recent past might strike again.

Not that he was normally prepared to say exactly when that would be. As we have seen, this would actually have been outside the terms of reference of the technique. Being astrologically based, the events were liable to return again and again. It was human attitudes and actions that, ultimately, would decide the issue. Besides, undated prophecies have a much longer shelf-life than dated ones!

So, Nostradamus simply completed his task by imposing on the resulting visionary scenarios the discipline of working them into rhymed quatrains of a type that would not only render them memorable and difficult to tamper with, but also lend them a fine, incantatory air such as was formerly associated with the ancient Sybilline oracle.

Disguising the prophecies

Astrology being astrology, of course, the recurrences of past celestial patterns came in no particular order – and neither, consequently, were the recurrences of the associated ancient events likely to do so. The subsequent tradition that Nostradamus deliberately scrambled his verses, therefore, seems to have little basis in fact. With the ever-watchful Inquisition in mind, though, and with the risk that he might be accused of witchcraft by the authorities if he were suspected of using magic rather than astrology, he not only burned his written sources, but also took good care that his own predictions would not be too clear or specific – 'written in terms that are cloudy rather than plainly prophetic', as he himself was later to put it. We shall see in Chapter 2 just how he achieved this and how in consequence we might hope to decode them.

However valid the original insights, there were a whole host of dangers inherent in the subsequent 'tidying-up' exercise. One particular risk was the contamination of the original vision (if vision it was) with established religious expectations and eschatological beliefs. Indeed, the more Nostradamus's conscious mind became involved in the exercise, the more was this potentially the case. Certainly, when in 1555 he concluded the first part of his *magnum opus* by writing a preface in the form of a straight, prose letter to his new son César (presumably named after his former host at Agen), the preconceptions took over almost completely.

There were to be untold catastrophes, plagues, famines, revolutions, floods and holocausts 'more terrible than there have ever been'. As had already happened with the plague itself only some 200 years before, humanity's numbers would be so reduced that there would be scarcely anybody left to work the fields. Only then, after all this period of doom and gloom, would the final golden age or millennium arise.

Which was all very well, but it had all been either said or done before. The Bible's Revelation of St John was full of it. History, equally, was full of it. Moreover, in terms of the 'Janus hypothesis' it was a fair bet that the future would be full of it, too – possibly on a repeated basis. Indeed, much of it has already come true once again in our own time. Whether the letter's gruesome end-time scenario has anything to do with what either Nostradamus's original 'Janus' approach or his nightly visions actually revealed, consequently, is something that we shall need to establish on our own account by looking carefully at what the quatrains themselves say, while making due and cautious allowance for the seer's subsequent exercise in 'tidying up'.

End-time calculations

Moreover, we shall not need to take too seriously Nostradamus's claim in the same letter that the prophecies were intended to cover only the period up to the year 3797 – almost as if this was destined to be the date of the 'End of the World' – nor indeed the constant attempts by modern interpreters to connect this idea with the year 2000 or the early years of the new millennium.

True, there was (as we have seen) a pronounced feeling in his day that the End of the World must be at hand. Conditions in Europe were so gruesome – with plague, starvation, war and death all rampant – as to make it difficult to avoid any other conclusion. Consequently, attempts were constantly being made to calculate its supposed date.

But, curiously enough, round centuries and millennia had

virtually nothing to do with it. Most contemporary attempts
to calculate the date of the End of the World focused on the
ancient idea that the world was destined to last for 7,000
years from the date of the biblical Creation – and since this
date apparently fell in an embarrassing no-man's-land *in
between* round millennia as calculated on the reigning Julian
calendar (Nostradamus himself was to offer no less than five
different dates for it, at least two of them in the self-same
document!), the supposed 'End of the World' seemed
destined to fall at some point between 1800 and 1887. Even
the attempt by the astrologer and cleric Richard Roussat to
extend the system somewhat in his influential *Livre de l'estat
et mutations des temps* of 1549/50[53] – a source much used
and even plagiarised by Nostradamus – merely came up with
an 'End of the World' date of AD 2242.

Now Nostradamus, you will remember, originally made his
'3797' forecast in his *Preface to César* of March 1555 – and it
so happens that the sum of 1555 and Roussat's date of 2242
is ... 3797! Possibly, then, this indicates at least some
measure of mental confusion on the prophet's part – and one
that we shall do well to take into consideration whenever we
are tempted to wonder whether or not he might have had
some fiendishly clever scheme for encoding, scrambling
and/or dating his predictions!

Fame and fortune

The great project, however, was never to be published in full.
The text first published in 1555 consisted of only the first
three *Centuries*, plus part of the fourth (the old French word
centurie here designates a group of 100 verses, and has
nothing to do with hundreds of years), together with the
prefatory letter to the seer's young son César, mentioned
earlier. Even the 1568 edition lacked fifty-eight of the seventh
Century's intended quatrains – though it did contain an odd,
imprecatory quatrain in Latin doggerel at the end of *Century
VI* (see translation at the head of chapter 2), plagiarised from

a work by Petrus Crinitus of 1504 entitled *De honesta disciplina*, which we know that Nostradamus owned.[8] Also included was a bafflingly symbolic prose synopsis of his predictions: this took the form of a rambling screed entitled *Letter to Henri King of France the Second*. In addition, 141 *Presages* (Portents) and 58 *Sixains* (six-line verses) were incorporated into various subsequent editions, as were a couple of dozen additional quatrains that were probably discarded drafts that Chavigny had found lying around after the seer's death.

Completed or not, however, the effect of the whole compilation was both immediate and electric, at least in ruling circles. At once Nostradamus was summoned to the royal court, where he was fêted and consulted by every man and his dog, and not least by Queen Catherine de Médicis herself. He was required to draw up horoscopes for all the royal children – a difficult and delicate task in view of the ill-fortune that (unbeknown to the Queen) he had already seemingly predicted for almost all of them in his *Propheties*, albeit in his customary covert form. If he had been unsure before of just how personally dangerous for him his chosen task might turn out to be, no such doubts could now remain – especially when news suddenly reached him that the Justices of Paris were starting to make serious enquiries about his alleged magical practices. Nostradamus reacted in his usual way. He simply went back on the road. Hurriedly he returned home to Salon, where his newly-acquired fame easily swamped any darker suspicions that might be circulating about him. Indeed, despite more serious interludes when his reputation was attacked by literary and astrological critics, or when his life was threatened by civil and religious unrest – and a brief spell in prison for publishing his 1562 *Almanach* without the required approval of a bishop at a time of acute national religious sensitivity – that renown steadily increased as prophecy after prophecy now apparently started to come true, especially in respect of the French royal family.

So impressed by now was the Queen that she even called on the seer at Salon with her son, the adolescent King Charles IX, during a major royal progress in 1564. Word has it that he used the occasion to identify among their vast retinue the young prince, who would subsequently become the future King Henri IV. A few days later, Nostradamus was again summoned to attend them at Arles, where he was appointed Privy Councillor and Physician in Ordinary to the King, and awarded a grant of 300 gold crowns to match. His triumph, clearly, was complete. True, he was becoming increasingly ill with gout, arthritis and dropsy. Such afflictions have ever gone with growing age. But with the *Almanachs* and *Propheties* already being reprinted both at home and abroad (indeed, the latter have rarely been out of print since), at least he could die rich, famous and content.

And this he duly did, at the age of sixty-two, during the night of 1–2 July 1566, just as he had predicted to his secretary Chavigny the evening before, and in exactly the manner that he had apparently already described in *Presage* 141:

> *Once back from embassy, once garnered in*
> *The kingly gift, all's done: his spirit sped,*
> *The dearest of his friends, his closest kin*
> *Beside the bed and bench shall find him dead.*

Unfortunately, however, we now know (on the basis of a contemporary Italian translation of the *Almanach* in which this verse first appeared[14]) that this verse was almost certainly 'doctored' by the over-eager Chavigny after his Master's death. The original had actually read more like:

> *Th' ambassadors, returned, repaid shall be,*
> *The King in honour of his life be shorn:*
> *His friends, his kin, shall lack posterity,*
> *Blood-brothers too, as I do truly warn.*

Such, it seems, are the hazards of blind adulation!

Nevertheless, it had been a remarkable, if turbulent life, and one that would reverberate around the world for centuries to come. As he lay dying amid the silence of the night that he so loved, Nostradamus may well have allowed himself a secret smile at the thought that the world had yet to hear the last of him.

2

FISHING IN THE DARK

Think on this, reader, sagely as you may,
But shun my verse, you mob profane and shallow.
Astrologers, barbarians, fools, away!
Or else yourselves to rites satanic hallow.

Century VI.100 (the Latin quatrain)

NOSTRADAMUS REALLY HAD NO choice in the matter. The message must be deliberately garbled – or at very least made ambiguous, arcane, obscure. The whole thing must be written (to recall once again his own words on the matter) 'in terms that are cloudy rather than plainly prophetic'. Not only was he under constant attack from the astrologers for claiming that the stars predicted what they could not – whence the above riposte, misquoted from a critique *of lawyers* by Petrus Crinitus (b. 1465) that had been republished in Lyon in 1543. He was also under attack from poets and scholars for his clumsiness, by Catholics for being in league with the Protestants, and by Protestants for being in league with the Devil. Yet somehow, with a growing family to support, he still had to sell his prophetic books. And so his very survival

23

as a prophetic 'authority' depended on not being proved wrong, which, of course, meant being as vague as possible.

The *Propheties* show the results of this. They are arcane to the point of bafflement. Often they seem to be all but devoid of meaning. Frequently they are difficult to square with normal French syntax – even though Nostradamus is nearly always extremely careful with his grammatical agreements (a good deal more so, it has to be said, than most of his would-be interpreters). The words themselves are little better. It is not just that they are often archaic, or borrowed from Greek or Latin. It is not even that their spelling (not unusually for the period) is inconsistent and chaotic. Quite often they are wilfully distorted and mangled, whether to fit the demands of Nostradamus's rhymed decasyllabic lines or merely to hood-wink the reader. A favourite trick is to disguise words as their homonyms, rather as in English 'tiers' might be substituted for 'tears', or even 'wear' for 'where'. Thus, *dame* ('lady') is sometimes spelt *d'ame* ('of soul'); *d'eux* ('of them') or even Latin *duces* ('leaders, generals') becomes *deux* ('two'); and in verse II.62 *sang humain* ('human blood') takes on a surprising new life as *cent, main* ('a hundred, hand').

If, that is, they are tricks at all – for the truth is that, for purely practical reasons, typesetting at the time was normally done by dictation from another typesetter (or possibly even an apprentice), with the result that printers tended to spell more or less as they wished or were accustomed to, unless the author had carefully spelt out the desired lettering in capital letters beforehand (as Nostradamus occasionally did). If they were unsure of which word or spelling was involved they tended to be guided purely by the sound, as their contorted renderings of unfamiliar place-names so often makes only too clear.

But that is not the half of it. In Nostradamus's *Propheties* names of places are frequently replaced by ancient, unfamiliar equivalents. Names of people are equally frequently disguised under abstruse mythological or biblical pseudonyms – then, for good measure, sometimes scrambled into anagrams. Except in a handful of cases, dates are either entirely lacking,

24

or (occasionally) encrypted into astrological patterns. The whole thing is presented in fairly crude rhyming verse rather than plain prose (and even Nostradamus's prophetic *prose* is generally far from plain), with all the strange, elliptical constructions and other unfamiliar turns of phrase which such an approach allows. And the predictions, as we have seen, are not even presented in chronological order.

Moreover, to cap it all, Nostradamus (in the scholarly manner of his day) was from the start evidently thinking in Latin rather than French and phrasing his ideas accordingly, rather as though he were a Virgil or an Ovid.

'They will be neither too obscure nor too clearly revealed', wrote the sage rather optimistically to his son César. The latter, thanks to his closeness to his father, obviously had the advantage of us. To modern readers, who live at a much greater cultural and temporal remove from the great man, they can seem only *too* obscure. At which point, of course, it apparently becomes permissible – if not irresistible – for commentators to read almost anything they like into them.

As, indeed, they repeatedly have.

Yet, even on the basis of the familiar biblical maxim 'By their fruits ye shall know them', it soon becomes clear that this is totally the wrong approach, as weary readers of this type of literature will by now be only too well aware. If there is one characteristic that stands out above all from the masses of would-be interpretations that have appeared in print since the seer's death, it is how naive, infantile and often hilariously wrong nearly all of them have been, despite the occasional lucky hit – as not only professional sceptics such as James Randi[50], but also learned critics such as David Ovason[47] have not been slow to point out.

Enter the interpreters

Nostradamus himself seems to have been well aware that this would happen. 'Be alive to the fact,' he wrote to his son César, 'that men of letters will make grand and for the most

part overblown claims about the way in which I have interpreted things.'

Neither antiquity, nor modernity has very much to do with
it. If anything, many modern interpretations have turned out
to be even more ludicrous than their predecessors – quite
catastrophically so, in fact, as today's critical press often
points out with such evident and justified glee. With
Armageddon allegedly looming on the horizon, modern interpreters have felt driven to cram the fulfilment of all the
still-outstanding prophecies – well over 500 of them, even at a
conservative count – into a matter of a few decades. The
tighter the cramming, inevitably, the less convincing the
resulting scenario. Yet now (if the interpreters are to be
believed) there are only a few years left. And with the clock
ticking inexorably down to zero-hour many of the would-be
interpretations are turning out to be, if anything, even
wronger than before, rapidly exposing for all to see the
unwitting self-delusion that so often underlies them.

Thus, French commentators tend to site many of the
allegedly predicted events confidently in France, American
ones equally confidently in America and British ones in some
uneasy space between the two. One of my Canadian Internet
correspondents insists that they are largely about Canada,
another – from Malta – that they are substantially about . . .
yes, Malta! The religiously-minded persist in interpreting the
predictions in largely eschatological terms, the scientifically-
minded in terms of advanced technology, the ufologically-
minded in terms of awesome visitors from outer space. Nearly
all of the resulting offerings – as has long since become all too
obvious to an increasingly critical public – seem to be
outstanding for their historical glibness, their geographical
ignorance, their philological amateurishness, their childish
naivety, their awful schoolboy French, or even all five at
once.

All of which merely tends to give Nostradamus an even
worse name than he would have if he were simply allowed to
stand on his own two feet.

But why all this self-delusion? Why the desire to read into the prophecies what manifestly is not there? Presumably because, in attempting to make sense of any unknown quantity, we always try to make *our* sense of it. We attempt, in other words, to relate it to what we know. And so, if we are keen observers of the current world-scene, we tend to see future events as mere extensions – however improbably – of present ones, forgetting that there may be no discernible links between them at all. In Arthur C Clarke's words, 'The one fact about the Future of which we can be certain is that it will be utterly fantastic'.

And so, to take one example, the published commentaries on Nostradamus of only a few years back were full of Third World Wars and nuclear confrontations between the Soviet Union and the Warsaw Pact on the one hand and West Germany and its allies on the other. Little had the commentators foreseen that none of the countries or organisations just mentioned would now exist to take part in their colourful scenario in the first place.

Which is odd because, if their interpretations of Nostradamus were really as reliable as they purported to be, one would somehow have expected them to anticipate the fact.

Again, those who are conventionally religious may be inclined to see the future foretold by Nostradamus exclusively in terms of the biblical apocalypse as described in St John's Revelation – famines, pestilences, holocausts, Armageddon, Last Judgement and all. That, indeed, was how Nostradamus himself, as a devout Catholic, clearly saw that future when in full waking consciousness. Yet the results of such an approach are likely to turn out to be no more reliable than those wonderful Last Times scenarios dreamt up by well-meaning fundamentalist Christians who are convinced that the events predicted refer to *present-day* powers and alliances, and interpret them accordingly. Amid the curiously comforting certainties of the former Cold War and the murderous, if reliable, confrontation between communism and capitalism, such expectations may have seemed reasonable enough. Now, however, things have changed – and not necessarily for the better. Ever and anon, consequently, such ideas will have to be drastically revised as the map of world politics constantly changes, dissolves and reconstitutes itself into new and totally unexpected configurations.

And always the excuse will be, '*Then* we were wrong. *Now* we are right.'

You can believe that if you like.

Reading Nostradamus in context

Any valid interpretation of Nostradamus, therefore, has to avoid these obvious pitfalls. Eschewing preconceptions, avoiding all past or present assumptions, it needs to decode his quatrains purely in terms of what is known about Nostradamus himself – his working methods, his arcane literary tendencies, his keenness to condense and veil his prophecies 'somewhat obscurely' in order to protect both them from the ignorant and himself from the hands of his enemies.

Above all, it needs to interpret Nostradamus as a man not only of his age, but of his place and creed as well. The seer, after all, was not merely a Renaissance scholar, imbued through and through with classical mythology. He was also something of a medieval mage, a contemporary of both John Dee and Paracelsus. His sixteenth-century mind inevitably contained an extraordinary mixture of the educated, the everyday and the purely fantastic. Medically enlightened as he undoubtedly was to a degree, he was every bit as prone as his contemporaries to see the future in exclusively biblical terms – and overwhelmingly dark and threatening ones at that: he lived, after all, amid an age of plagues and pestilences that had decimated Europe's population only a couple of centuries before, and constantly threatened to do so again. As a Jew, he was possibly privy to many of the ancient secrets of Jewish occultism, and not least the Kabbalah. As a Catholic, he was naturally liable to relate his insights into the future to Catholic apocalyptic teaching, as well as to the fate of the Church and its leaders. He was also prey to every kind of religious superstition in an age when such superstition was rife – rife enough, in particular, to fire the revolutionary Protestant initiative of Martin Luther. Above all, as a Frenchman, he was prone to relate world events mainly to his own country and those bordering it, while also casting a wary eye on the Muslim threat from North Africa and the East.

And so we should positively expect him to write in terms of alchemical notions, hermetic symbols, kabbalistic insights, biblical doctrines, mythological entities, plagues, epidemics, famines, floods, conflagrations, Armageddons, Second Comings and Last Judgements. If he did not, it would actually be surprising. For obvious reasons, too, we should expect him to describe future national leaders as 'kings' or 'princes', to disguise their names even when he anticipates them, to use classical or contemporary – rather than modern – names for countries and cities and to set his ultimate predictions within the framework of some kind of Last Times scenario.

And of course we should expect him to draw a further veil of obscurity over the insights that he was seeking to convey, by casting his predictions in rhyming verse rather than clear, straight prose – and rhyming verse of a particularly obtuse kind, at that.

Principles of interpretation

From all of which three major interpretive principles seem to follow:

1   Since all translation relies for its success on an awareness of overall context, it will be no more possible to interpret individual stanzas *in isolation* than it is possible to interpret individual pieces of a jigsaw puzzle. In the absence of the original 'picture on the box', we have no option but to reconstruct it gradually for ourselves from

first principles, piece by apparently meaningless piece. Preconceptions as to what the outcome will be are likely actually to get in the way. Possibilities can of course be adumbrated, but only as possibilities among other possibilities, and then only insofar as is warranted by what Nostradamus actually says.

2   It then has to be our major objective to relate each quatrain, once roughly decoded, to other decoded quatrains so as to establish roughly what the correct sequence is. In this way it should then become possible gradually to discover what the true overall context is, too, and thus eventually to put ourselves in a position to interpret Nostradamus *in terms of himself*.

3   Finally, the usual, literal, word-for-word type of translation will actually be counterproductive, since it merely reproduces the original surface lexicon without giving any flavour of its sense, shape, vigour or flow, still less of the former complex semantic associations which have long since become lost to us. In short, it is not translation at all, but semi-legalistic nonsense – and anybody who has ever attended a court of law will know what travesties of justice such insensitivities to linguistic nuance can produce.

The present book

In view of this, I propose in the following chapters to render Nostradamus's verses in just the same memorable, rhythmic form that he himself adopted – rhymed decasyllabic lines (i.e. pentameters) of almost exactly the type that were also being written in English at the time by the immediate precursors of Shakespeare. Not that Nostradamus was himself in any sense a Shakespeare. His verse is generally terse in the extreme, often telegrammatic, sometimes clichéd, even crude at times. Much of it is so bald and garbled as to read rather like semi-dyslexic newspaper headlines. Nevertheless, it follows its own distinct (if Latinate) grammatical rules, generally scans,

religiously observes a *caesura* or hiatus after the fourth syllable of almost every line (so religiously, indeed, that
Nostradamus habitually treats it for metrical purposes as if it
were the end of a line), and virtually always rhymes – and any
true translation will therefore need to do much the same.

Though the *caesura* itself deserves to be treated more as a
useful guide to analysis and interpretation than necessarily as
a strict model for English translation!

I do not propose, though, to reprint the original, sixteenth-
century French text here, or even an edited version of it, since
most readers (who, after all, would not expect their Homer or
Plato to come with the original Greek, still less their
Dostoievsky to wave the Russian text at them) are in any case
linguistically unqualified to benefit by it. Those who *are* so
qualified (scholars of sixteenth-century French, say) are of
course always welcome to compare the resulting English with
the easily-available versions published in any number of existing compilations – though to access all the *original* words, the
only reliable English-language publication currently available
is my own *Nostradamus Encyclopedia*.[34] As ever with serious
translation, meanwhile, it is to be hoped that such readers
and critics will have an eye more to the overall gist and style
than to particular words and phrases. Nostradamus's prophecies, after all, are poems, not legal documents, and translation
is not, and can never be, a matter of crude word-for-word
equivalents.

In this way I would hope to put readers in the best possible
position to assess the various prophecies for themselves, first
checking the claimed accuracy of those that are supposed
already to have come to pass, and then matching those that
are still unfulfilled with actual events as they unfold. But
actually *anticipating* those events is something that will
depend heavily on just how far it turns out to be possible to
reassemble into its original sequence the prophetic jigsaw-
puzzle that either Nostradamus's inner visionary source or his
crude application of the 'Janus hypothesis' to historical events
itself so determinedly disassembled all those years ago.

3

A SHORT COURSE IN PROPHECY

On numerous occasions and over a long period I have predicted well in advance events that have since come to pass in particular regions.

NOSTRADAMUS
Preface to César

IF THERE IS ONE THING for which Nostradamus is more widely renowned than for the fearsomeness of his predictions concerning our future, it is the uncanny and unerring accuracy of his predictions of events that now belong firmly to our past. If popular mythology is to be believed, almost every event of any note that has happened since his death has been found to have been already foretold in his enigmatic verses. That, indeed, is often seen as his prime qualification for offering himself as a guide to our future in the first place.

To take the *Centuries* proper, for example, out of a total of some 942 quatrains, around 420 have been identified by one commentator or another as having already come to pass – which means, incidentally, that rather more than half of them are still awaiting fulfilment.

However, this figure – and with it, consequently, the implied success-rate – is actually far from being what it seems. For the fact is that, out of the 420 or so proposed 'hits', *only some fifty* meet with any measure of general agreement among the commentators. Of the other 370, different interpreters frequently disagree over which events should be linked with which verses. Any two commentators may well apply a given verse to quite different countries and even centuries.

But that is not the last of the surprises. *On only a dozen or so of the allegedly 'fulfilled' predictions do* all *of the commentators seem to agree.*

Taken with Chevignard's already mentioned research into the 6,338 other prophecies[14] and my statistical analysis of it, this fact is something of a bombshell. It means that Nostradamus's alleged past accuracy has far more to do with popular belief – perhaps even with a popular *need* to believe – than with actual fact. You may insist, of course, that the commentators – or some of them, at any rate – must be wrong. Alternatively, you may deduce, possibly with a sigh of relief, that it was Nostradamus himself who was wrong.

What the figures really suggest however, is something much less satisfying to those who like final answers. It is the sobering thought (sobering, that is, for would-be commentators) that the seer's predictions, interpreted in isolation, are in most cases cast in far too vague a form to permit much in the way of positive and final identification even of events in our past – to say nothing of events in our future.

Not that this would necessarily have been a bad thing from Nostradamus's point of view – for the already-mentioned possibility always needs to be borne in mind that history is in some degree cyclic, and that the same or similar events actually do tend to return again and again, much as Nostradamus clearly believed, and as the author of the book of Ecclesiastes (allegedly King Solomon himself) likewise suggests:

To everything its season, and to every activity under heaven its time ... Whatever is has already been, and whatever will be has already been, and God recalls each event in its turn.

In this chapter, then, I propose to quote a selection of what are generally supposed to be the more strikingly successful of the predictions (Roman numerals will refer to the number of the *Century*, or book; Arabic ones to that of the quatrain quoted). The reader will note that a common feature of many of these is the mention of specific times and place names – the latter especially being a feature which Nostradamus himself recommended to his son César as a vital key to interpretation. I propose also to include one or two others which commentators have all too easily consigned to a familiar eschatological future, but which seem to me already to have been fulfilled in terms at least as clear as those applying to most of the other agreed 'hits'.

On this basis, hopefully, readers will then have a much clearer idea in their minds of the kind of predictive features to look for in the as yet unfulfilled prophecies, and so may stand a better chance of using them, if not actually to anticipate future events, at least to recognise them when they come.

What follows, in other words, may be regarded as a kind of short course in prophecy – or at least in prophetic decipherment – conducted in terms of practical examples from Nostradamus himself.

I.35   *The younger lion shall surmount the old*
        On martial field in duel man to man.
        Two fleets combined, eyes pierced in cage of gold,
        Death shall come hard as only dying can.

It is with the alleged success of this quatrain that

34

Nostradamus is usually said to have made his name as a seer. During the combined marriage celebrations for two of his daughters in the summer of 1559, King Henri II of France insisted on tempting fate by taking part in a series of three jousts – despite warnings by the astrologer Luca Gaurico that he should avoid all such combats during his forty-first year – and was fatally wounded, dying in agony some ten days later. The tragedy was to prove all but fatal for France itself, too, for it was torn apart by religious feuds and wars over the next few decades more or less as a direct consequence.

There is a problem, however. The beginning of line three simply does not fit this scenario, and most commentators have consequently roped in the Greek word *klasis* ('break, fracture') to explain the French word *classes* ('fleets'). I, too, have to admit to having flirted with the suggestion. But it has now been established that it never occurred to anybody to connect the verse with the event at all until the seer's son César did so in his *Histoire et chronique de Provence* of 1614, some fifty-five years later. Nostradamus's secretary Chavigny, writing in 1594, had evidently never heard of the idea, either, or he would have grabbed this wonderful piece of propaganda for his master with both hands. As for Nostradamus himself, in a subsequent letter to one Jean de Vauzelles, he linked the event with a different verse entirely – namely III.55 – though only by dint of retrospectively changing one of its words from *grand* to *grain*, to fit the fact that the killer's name was *Lorge* ('barley')![8]

According to Prévost[49], verse I.35 refers back to the deposition of the old emperor of Constantinople, Isaac II Angelus, and his son Alexius IV, by the younger Alexius V Ducas Murtzuphlus in 1204, just as the Crusader and Venetian fleets were allying themselves to attack the city. The planetary tables reveal that in January of that year Saturn was in Aries, Jupiter in Pisces, and Mars, Venus, Mercury and the sun all in Capricorn. On the basis of the 'Janus hypothesis' referred to earlier, the next time something similar has the astrological potential to occur will be on or about 19

December 2027, when all except the sun (which will follow six days later) will be in the self-same signs at similar celestial latitudes.

On the other hand, Brind'Amour[9] refers the verse back to the vision of a 'celestial battle' that was seen in the skies over Switzerland in 1547, as reported both by Conrad Lycosthenes and by Gerolamo Cardano, who describes it in the words, 'In Switzerland (so they say) two lions were seen fighting each other in the air, of which each cut off the head of the other'. As I do not know the exact month when this happened, however, I can offer no alternative 'Janus' calculation in this case.

Sixain 52 *Another blow, great town, half-starved anew,*
The feast of blessed Saint Bartholomew
Shall grave into the bowels of your heart.
At Nîmes, Rochelle, Geneva, Montpellier,
Castres and Lyon, Mars on his Arian way
Shall take on all for noble lady's part.

Allegedly found among Nostradamus's papers on his death in 1566, this prediction was to come horribly true six years later in the form of the now-infamous Saint Bartholomew's Day Massacre. Apparently carried out at the Queen's behest, this was an attempt to massacre all the Protestant leaders in France at one fell swoop. In the course of it some 8,000 died, not only in Paris, but in other towns and cities as well – though not, it seems, in Geneva. Note that it is the specific details of time and place that ultimately validate the prediction. However, prior knowledge of this prediction by the Queen cannot be ruled out. I know of no 'original event' in Nostradamus's past that would allow us to use the 'Janus hypothesis' to calculate a possible date for the event's future repetition.

III.51   *Paris shall plot grand murder to commit.*
Blois shall contrive to bring the deed to pass.
Orléans would restore its leader's writ.
Angers, Troyes, Langres shall make them pay, alas!

Here again, it is above all the place names that seem to make it possible to identify the prophecy – this time with the celebrated murder of the Duc de Guise on the King's orders in the royal château at Blois on 23 December 1588. (Tourist guides at the castle still lovingly recount the gory details to this day.) This bloody event was to prove a crucial event in France's sixteenth-century wars of religion. Its immediate effect was to produce general unrest throughout the country, during which the citizens of Orléans replaced their governor with a Guise supporter. Only the predicted reaction of the three towns in the last line is at fault: Nostradamus apparently failed to foresee that Angers and Langres would support the Guise cause, while Troyes would stay neutral. However, Prévost[49] is confident that the prediction refers to a different Guise murder entirely – namely that of the famously scarred Duke François de Guise before Orléans in February 1563. Certainly the details fit better. But then, since the verse was first published in 1555, presumably its historical original lies even further back in time.

IX.49   *Brussels and Ghent shall march against Anvers*
And London's parliament its king shall slay.
Wine shall be ta'en for wit a thing perverse
With government in deepest disarray.

This quatrain, it is generally agreed, constitutes a clear prediction of the death of Charles I of England in 1649 – though once again the lack of specific dating means that Charles

himself would have had the greatest of difficulty in taking
warning from it, even had he been inclined to. Nevertheless,
Brussels, Ghent and Anvers (Antwerp) were indeed all in
contention between the three great powers of France, Holland
and England in 1648/9, so that it could be said that the
warning signs were there, however indistinctly. Not too much
should be read into the fact that the verse itself is numbered
'49', however. Attempts to turn such connections into a
general principle have so far proved extraordinarily uncon-
vincing. Once again, no historical original immediately
suggests itself as a basis for applying the 'Janus hypothesis'.

II.51   *Though no just blood they'll spill in London town,*
                 Bolts from the blue'll singe six times twenty-three.
                 The ancient dame from high shall tumble down.
                 Of the same sect shall many murdered be.

Numerous commentators have managed to identify this
prediction with the Great Fire of London in 1666, thanks
mainly to a deliberate twisting of the words of line two. As
can readily be seen, however, the verse fails to fit in a number
of ways. Prévost[49] argues convincingly that the original
historical reference in this verse is in fact to the Affair of the
Templars in 1310, when the English Templars, having
confessed, went unpunished, but 138 (6 times 23) were put
on trial in France (Nostradamus is clearly enjoying the fact
that *fouldres* means not only thunderbolts but excommunica-
tion or anathema!). Nor is this the only verse that refers back
to this event. I.81 (*see* page 54) – often said by the inveterate
'twisters' to refer to the *Challenger* space-shuttle tragedy –
clearly refers back to it, too. Given exact details of dates,
then, it should be possible to calculate possible dates for the
event's recurrence.

VIII.76 *More cudgeller than ever English king*
Base-born, by force the wretch in power shall sit.
Sans law, sans faith, blood from the land he'll
    wring.
His time's so close I sigh to think of it.

Nostradamus's description of a non-Catholic commoner seizing power in England seems to offer a more or less perfect fit with Oliver Cromwell, who was born only thirty-three years after the death of the French seer. Prévost[49] traces the historical original back to events surrounding King John and the Emperor Frederick Barbarossa in the late twelfth century.

IV.89 *Thirty from London secretly lay schemes*
By sea to act against their king anointed.
His circle has no taste for death, it seems.
From Friesland a fair-headed king's appointed.

Here it is the place names that give the game away. In 1688 a group of leading noblemen (whether thirty in number or not is not recorded) left England by sea to seek the assistance of the Dutch William of Orange against their King, James II. The latter conceded defeat with remarkable alacrity, first fleeing, then accidentally captured by William's forces, and finally gratefully accepting the chance that he was offered to escape again to France. And to crown Nostradamus's evident prediction of England's so-called Glorious Revolution, William had indeed been born, if not in Friesland, at least in the region corresponding to the modern Netherlands. No historical original immediately springs to mind, however.

> *. . . And starting in that year there will be greater*
> *persecution of the Christian Church than ever took*
> *place in North Africa, and it will last until the year*
> *1792, which will be thought of as the beginning of a*
> *whole new order.*

Quite what the beginning of this extract from Nostradamus's *Letter to Henri King of France the Second* refers to is anybody's guess, but his pinpointing of 1792 as the start of a new dispensation seems to be an accurate prediction of the beginning of the anti-religious French revolutionary republic in that year. But then, on the basis of a major planetary conjunction in that year, leading astrologers had already been predicting a major social turnabout at this time for around a century before Nostradamus's day. Perhaps it is significant, then, that this prediction comes not in one of the quatrains, but in Nostradamus's fully conscious prose writings.

IX.20 *Through woods of Rheims by night shall make her*
        way
        Herne the white butterfly, by byways sent.
        The elected head, Varennes' black monk in grey
        Sows storm, fire, blood and foul dismemberment.

Of the numerous predictions that seem to apply to the future French Revolution of 1789 onwards, none is more famous than this apparent bull's-eye. The surprising mention of the insignificant town of Varennes (the one near France's eastern border, presumably) immediately points to the sole historical event of major note that ever seems to have happened there – namely the celebrated night-time arrival of Louis XVI and his Queen, Marie Antoinette, on 20 June 1792, in the course of an attempt to flee the country that was to prove the final nail

40

in the coffin of the French monarchy and its credibility. It is this identification in turn – and this alone – that then makes it possible for us in retrospect to decode the rest of the quatrain. 'Herne', via the form 'Ierne', decodes anagrammatically as 'Reine' (Queen). The route to Varennes had indeed been largely circuitous ('two parts devious', as the French puts it), taking the royal couple through the forest near Rheims (suggestively spelt 'Reines' in the original). The King, who (unusually) was an elected one, and a Capet to boot – the French has *cap* which could as easily be short for this as for the Latin *caput* ('head') – is said to have been wearing grey, while the Queen (certainly a frivolous butterfly at the best of times) is said (on almost equally slender evidence) to have been clad in white – the same colour that her hair allegedly also turned following the incident. Despite determined efforts by some commentators to explain the kingly 'black monk' as an 'impotent aristocrat', though, this expression seems to be yet another demonstration of Nostradamus's endearing fallibility.

The last line is just as difficult to decode – though not, in this case, because its meaning is entirely inaccessible. It is merely that it is so cryptic – more a list of disconnected words than a sentence. Consequently, a measure of hindsight has to inform the final line of the translation. Dismemberment (my admittedly free interpretation of the French *tranche*) is certainly what awaited the kingly 'head' and that of his consort, in the form of the guillotine. It is also a fair description of what was to befall countless numbers of their subjects, too, during the next few years. However, Prévost (who accuses commentators who arrive at conclusions such as the above of 'linguistic acrobatics', and points out that there are and were numerous 'Varennes' in France) argues that the historical original actually refers to the grisly exploits during the contemporary Wars of Religion of one Antoine du Plessis in the region around the city of Tours in the early 1560s. This is probably too late to act as a 'Janus' link, however.

I.60 *Near Italy an emperor is born*
Who'll cost the Empire dear; and ever since
Those even who his hand decline to scorn
Shall say he is more butcher than a prince.

As in the case of the French Revolution, Nostradamus seems to devote an extraordinary number of quatrains to the Corsican-born Napoleon Bonaparte, at least if the popular commentators are to be believed (Erika Cheetham[11,13] lists no less than fifty-five references to him, plus a further nineteen devoted to the Napoleonic wars). In one of them (VIII.1) the seer apparently even tries to spell out, by way of one of his customary geographical puns, the future emperor's name in the capital letters that he tends to reserve for such exercises in literary clairvoyance: PAU, NAY, LORON – which resolves anagrammatically into 'Napaulon Roy'. Given Nostradamus's main prophetic concerns (king, country, religion), this emphasis on Napoleon – whom he seems to regard as some kind of Antichrist, though he never actually uses the word of him – would not be too surprising. Nevertheless it has to be said that few of the proposed identifications are as detailed or consequently as convincing as they might be.

The above verse could be seen as a case in point: it fits, but it could equally well fit any other major leader born in the Mediterranean area. Prévost, for example, convincingly identifies the original figure in question as the Emperor Frederick Barbarossa. But then, under intense pressure to identify quatrains that predict such major events as Trafalgar, Waterloo or the Retreat from Moscow, a good many commentators all too readily retreat into flagrant dishonesty, forcing meanings onto quatrains that patently cannot bear them – mainly by dint of totally ignoring or even blatantly misrepresenting Nostradamus's syntax (he may have been deliberately devious, but he was certainly not illiterate!). This naive tendency to corral his quatrains around favourite, pre-selected themes – especially present-day ones that for obvious reasons loom much larger in our own consciousness than they are likely to do in that of posterity – is a common one against which we shall need to be constantly on our guard when attempting to decipher what appear to be Nostradamus's predictions for our future.

I.25   *For finding what was lost for many an age*
Shall Pasteur be as demigod acclaimed.
Then, as the moon ends her great pilgrimage,
Shall he by wishes contrary be shamed.

On the face of it, this piece represents an extraordinary prophetic bull's-eye. According to Nostradamus's major source Richard Roussat,[53] the last Age of the Moon ran from 1533 to 1887 – though Cheetham[11,13] 'tweaks' this slightly to make it read 1889. And true it undoubtedly is that the years 1888–9 marked the establishment by Louis Pasteur of his famous Paris institute, dedicated as it was to his discovery that many diseases were partially caused by micro-organisms. The prediction (if that is indeed what it is) suggests that this was known about in ancient times, too. Modern medicine has since rather gone overboard in this direction, almost as though Pasteur had suggested that infectious diseases were caused by nothing else – when in fact he adduced environ-mental, emotional and psychological factors as well. As in the case of Nostradamus himself, in other words, the guru was more or less turned into a god, and his words taken by devo-tees to ridiculous extremes. Not so Pasteur's immediate contemporaries, however. As always, the reigning establish-ment opposed his views. Hence, presumably, the last line. But then all this is to assume that Nostradamus was really talking about Pasteur in the first place. My guess is that, had he been asked, he would have taken the view that the word 'Pasteur' in fact referred to a future pastor of the church – or even a

simple shepherd – who would rediscover some ancient arte-
fact or holy relic (he frequently addresses the theme of buried
treasure and classical artifacts, for example). In which case
we should have an example of prophetic intuition – or, more
likely, some little-known historical precedent – producing a
fascinating prediction for the future. Even more importantly,
however, we have an example of a quatrain that offers us
both a name and a date as a means of identification. For our
current purpose, such things are worth a ton of general specu-
lation.

VII.25   *Long-drawn-out war the army's strength so saps,*
               To pay the soldiery shall nought remain.
               Instead of coins they'll issue parchment-scraps.
               French bronze shall face the crescent flag again.

Among the various quatrains that commentators commonly
assign to the First World War, this one is little more specific
or convincing than most (one or two of the others will in fact
be listed as predictions for the future in the next chapter).
Nevertheless, it does seem to reflect the enormous drain of the
war, both in men and in materials. Indeed, Nostradamus
seems to imagine that this is why people are starting to be
paid in paper money rather than coinage ('gold and silver', as
he puts it) – a detail which certainly does seem to date the
prediction to the fairly recent past rather than to the future,
even though it is a fairly safe bet that the prediction is actually based on some historical precedent, probably during a
known military campaign. If the term 'parchment' (*cuir* in the
original) seems slightly odd, one only has to ask oneself what
paper money looks like once it has acquired a goodly layer of
grime. Line four also seems accurately to anticipate the use of
French cannon in the war against the Turks in the Middle
East – a detail presumably based, in this case, on earlier

battles against the Ottoman Empire, which thus provide the probable context of the historical 'leather money' episode, too.

... In the month of October a great upheaval shall take place, so profound as to convince people that the earth has ceased to move naturally and has descended into everlasting darkness. In the preceding and follow-ing springs extraordinary changes shall occur, kingdoms be turned upside down. There shall be great earthquakes, too. And all this shall be accompanied by the spawning of the New Babylon, that miserable wench pregnant with the abomination of the first holocaust. This shall last no more than seventy-three years and seven months. At that time, from the stock that has so long been barren, originating in the 50th degree, shall come one who who shall restore the entire Christian Church. Then a great peace shall ensue ... The countries, towns, cities, kingdoms and provinces, having quit their original paths in an effort to set themselves free – but having thereby imprisoned themselves all the more firmly – shall experience a secret rage at the loss of their freedom and religion, and shall start to strike from the left to return once again to the right.

This extraordinary piece of prediction from the *Letter to Henri King of France the Second* – which in the interests of readability I have been forced to render fairly freely – imme-diately begs to be identified with the Russian Bolshevik Revolution of October 1917, which had indeed been preceded by a preliminary rising the previous spring. Seventy-three years and seven months from that date takes us up to the early summer of 1991, when the emergence of the new order in the Soviet Union was in full swing, and was about to lead on to the sudden rightward lurch that Nostradamus had predicted over 400 years before (however he may have understood the idea). Since the fiftieth degree of latitude passes almost directly through Krakow in Poland, the great restorer of the Christian Church (in Eastern Europe especially, presumably) begs to be identified as Pope John Paul II, who was formerly the city's archbishop – even though in those days religion in the Eastern bloc had, as foreseen, perforce been something of a 'barren plant'. He also, of course, played a large part in the Soviet Union's eventual downfall, though the 'Great Whore' I shall have to leave readers to identify for themselves.

Allowing for the seer's customary exaggeration, however, it has to be said that the accuracy of the whole forecast, especially for a 'clear consciousness' one, is astounding – always assuming that we have identified its correct fulfilment. (The prediction, after all, is immediately surrounded by others that seem to refer to nothing recognisable at all. Indeed, the groups of predictions contained in the letter seem to be both scrambled and inserted back-to-front, almost as though Nostradamus was determined not to reveal his hand too clearly even in his letter to the King. As he himself writes: 'In this discourse I am putting everything predicted confusedly as regards its timing ... ')

This problem of identification is always where the danger lies. The actual words of the prediction, after all, say nothing whatever about Russia, still less about Communism. Even with the text in front of them, nobody could have used it to forecast the events in question until at least the year 1917, when they had already started to happen, simply because the identification of any prophecy has to depend on whether details can be found to fit it – but then actual events are so complex that it is nearly always possible to find details that do, however obscure they may be. The chief merit in the present identification is that the details are not obscure at all, but large and plain for all to see – and consequently it is for similarly large and plain facts that we shall need to look as we attempt to identify Nostradamus's most important predictions for the future. Meanwhile, we can at least gain from the current exercise a better idea of the scale on which to interpret Nostradamus's use of such familiar apocalyptic notions as the 'Great Whore of Babylon', for example – presumably a much less vast and even cosmic concept than religious tradition might have led us to suppose.

IX.16   *From Castile's council Franco shall set out:*
The legate, loth to please, shall split away.
Those of Riviera shall join in the bout
And entry bar to the great gulf that day.

Albeit translated with the benefit of a fair amount of hindsight, this quatrain not only magnificently pinpoints Franco's epic Spanish coup of 1936, but seems to name several specific names – not only Franco himself, but the former dictator, Primo de Rivera, and Castile too, in whose ancient capital of Burgos the original revolutionary *junta* named Franco head of government. The last line seems to refer either to his exile in the Canaries or to his difficulties in getting his forces across the Mediterranean from Morocco at the time of the coup. Either way, however, the prediction is a devastatingly effective one, even in the absence of dates: if enough names are openly named, it seems, a prediction can be a useful pointer to events even in the absence of other information.

X.22   *For lack of will to let divorcing be*
Which aftertimes unworthy should be deemed,
The Islands' king shall be constrained to flee,
Replaced by one who never kingly seemed.

Widely regarded as predicting the abdication of Edward VIII in 1936, this quatrain once again gets it slightly wrong – which immediately suggests a slightly different historical original. It was the British government and Church who objected to the King's marrying the divorced American Mrs Wallis Simpson, not the young monarch himself. The last line well describes his unwilling brother who was to become George VI as a result of the abdication. Here, once again, Nostradamus shows his extreme sensitivity to any threat to what he seems to regard as the 'divine right' of monarchy, even in a foreign country. No doubt there was some past 'Janus event' – but if so I am unaware of it at present.

III.35   *In occidental Europe's deepest heart*
To poorest folk a little child is born.
Such throngs he shall beguile by speaker's art
As even Eastern kingdoms to suborn.

It seems to be widely agreed that this quatrain predicts the birth and life of Adolf Hitler. On the other hand, it is so general that almost any great central European orator would fit: he would not even need to be a dictator. In the event, it is the man's clearly nefarious nature that tends to clinch the issue. As a guide to the future, however, the prediction – even as I have fairly freely translated it with the benefit of hindsight – would have been valueless, lacking as it does either names, dates or (except in the vaguest terms) places.

V.26   *By accident of war the Slavic race*
Shall come to be raised up to high degree.
One rustic-born their leader shall replace.
His forces, mountain-raised, shall cross the sea.

With its evident reference to Russia, this quatrain seems to predict the rise of Stalin to world power largely as a result of the Second World War. In this case, though, the last line is somewhat dubious. Even where Nostradamus does apparently get it right, it seems, we cannot expect him to be correct in every detail. But then this is not so very surprising, since once again he is presumably basing his prediction on a quite different historical original.

X.100   *For all-commanding England there shall be*
More than three hundred years' imperial sway.
Great armies shall go forth by land and sea.
The Portuguese shall sorely rue the day.

Nostradamus's very last quatrain in the original collection of ten *Centuries* is a perfectly clear and unambiguous prediction for the future British Empire. The fact that the Empire finally collapsed around the middle of the twentieth century would suggest that he foresaw it as having its origins around or shortly before the year 1650 – some half-a-century or more after his own death, say. This ties in well with the founding of England's first successful colonies in North America in the early 1600s. The rather more dubious last line might then refer to colonial rivalry between England and Portugal. For Nostradamus's day, of course, the whole idea was a quite extraordinary one: England was then little more than a medium-sized power on the fringes of Europe. Note, though, that the dating of the prediction can, as usual, only be established *after* the event.

Sixain 54 *Six hundred, fifteen, twenty then again,*
Great Lady dead, a long and deadly rain
Of fire and iron shall hurt those countries sore.
Flanders is of their number, England yet:
Long shall they by their neighbours be beset
Until to them constrained to take the war.

This verse has been identified by some commentators as predicting the Second World War and the so-called Blitz mounted by the German Luftwaffe on Britain in the early stages of it: certainly the details are evocative, if somewhat skewed. However, as I have shown in my *Nostradamus: The Final Reckoning*[33] and *Nostradamus Encyclopedia*,[34] the dating reference is almost certainly based on an 'ecclesiastical reckoning' derived from the date of the foundation of the Christian liturgy, and involves adding 392 to the figure given. This in turn would refer the verse to the years 2007 to 2012 (*see* Chapter 5). However, the original reference is no doubt to the sixteenth-century wars between France and the Holy Roman Empire to the east.

IV.15 *From thence where famine shall be thought to hang*
Shall come instead recovery long-sought:
By ocean king with avaricious fang
Shall oil and flour from land to land be brought.

This quatrain has for some time now been widely identified as describing the Atlantic convoys of the Second World War bringing supplies from America to a beleaguered Britain. The rather obtuse line three has often been supposed (not least by me) as referring to the 'sea-wolf's eye' – apparently an inspired prediction of the submarine periscope – and since the Germans themselves were to refer to their U-boat fleet in terms of packs of sea-wolves, the line naturally begs to be so applied too. On the other hand, it is not at all certain from the French that Nostradamus did not foresee the submarines – if, indeed, he really foresaw anything at all – as actually doing the bringing, rather than desperately trying to prevent it. But then Brind'Amour[9] reads the verse – quite correctly, in the light of more recent research – as simply describing the sabotaging of a sea-blockade by a maritime ruler (*oeil* – a word used by Nostradamus to mean 'king' on other occasions, too, not least at the beginning of his *Letter to Henri King of France the Second*) who has much to gain by continuing to trade.

X.89	*Brick walls they shall in marble reconstruct:*
	Of peace seven years and fifty shall there be.
	For humans joy, rebuilt each aqueduct;
	Health, honeyed times and rich fecundity.

In his *Letter to Henri King of France the Second*, Nostradamus explains that his predictions are largely based on the periodic return of given planetary configurations. In view of this celestial 'Janus effect', they are of course subject to multiple fulfilments. The current verse is no exception. However, the historical origin of this verse is well known. It is a direct reference to the statement of the Emperor Augustus at the end of his reign that he had 'found Rome brick and left it marble'. Consequently, we can not only date the start of the period involved to 27 BC (the date when Augustus officially ascended the Imperial throne – which, by his description, Nostradamus seems to have confused with that of his much earlier accession to power), but we can use comparative horoscopy to calculate when it should theoretically recur. Not only was there a good match in 1945, but a further match is due in 2037 (*see* Chapter 6).

And indeed, this verse is particularly reminiscent of the period of post-war reconstruction that started in 1945. In devastated city centres all across Europe, bomb-damaged brick buildings were being widely rebuilt in gleaming white concrete – which to the sixteenth-century seer would have looked remarkably like the marble with which, as a man of his times, he was so familiar. After an initial period of severe austerity, much more affluent times did indeed then ensue, with vastly improved health-standards, restored public utilities and a huge increase in world population, much as the verse seems to envisage. But there is a sting in the tail. The period of peace is to last only fifty-seven years. By implication, then, Nostradamus seems to expect ghastly war once more to descend on his homeland (always the prime subject of his prophecies) in or around the year 2002.

II.89   *The two great masters from the yoke they'll free,*
          Yet greater power on great brows seen to sit.
          The new-leased land – in his high tower he'll be,
          The bloody one who'll keep accounts of it.

Once upon a time this quatrain was confidently applied to Mussolini and Hitler (the 'bloody one'). Nowadays it is more fashionable to apply it to the revolutionary series of summit-meetings between Ronald Reagan and Mikhail Gorbachev that started in November 1985, and which certainly led eventually to a major realignment of world power and an enhancement of American influence at the expense of the then Soviet Union and her allies. The prominent red birthmark on Gorbachev's brow then becomes a real gift for the interpreters. However, it can readily be seen from the above that line three's *terre neufve* is not, after all, necessarily a reference to the 'New World', as I and others have previously assumed – and the last line, too, makes the case even less certain.

II.28 *The last but one the prophet's name to bear*
Shall take Diana's day to rest in peace.
He'll roam, frenetic, here, there, everywhere
And a great race from tribute shall release.

This is one of a number of stanzas that have been widely taken by apocalyptically-minded commentators to refer to the expected Antichrist. This is mainly because they have read the verse to mean that the figure described is determined to replace the accepted Sabbaths of the three major Western religions with a secular one of his own – this time Diana's day, or Monday (until, that is, the death in a car-crash of Diana Princess of Wales brought a whole flood of new, skewed 'interpretations' by ill-informed Anglophones to the effect that the verse referred to the incident – even though the French doesn't really fit the idea at all!).

In fact, though, nothing so drastic is suggested by the verse. The figure involved is merely described as taking Mondays off – and I have to say that I can see little that is particularly satanic about that, especially as thousands of Christian priests, having spent all Sunday hard at work, regularly do the same. The fact that he travels frenetically all over the world to release a 'great people' from financial bondage does not seem particularly sinful, either. My own suggestion is that the verse could well be applied to the present Pope, John Paul II, especially if line one is taken as a reference to the fact that his next-to-last adopted name (*surnom*) is indeed the name of that well-known Prophet of the Messiah, John the Baptist.

I.70 *Rain, hunger, endless warfare Persia knows:*
Faith overdone the monarch shall ensnare.
What starts in France there to its ending goes.
To him it touches, so the Fates declare.

Nowadays, this quatrain is widely applied to the Iranian revolution and the overthrow of the Shah by the forces of Islamic fundamentalism ('faith overdone') in 1979. In this case, the moving force did indeed come from France, where the Ayatollah Khomeini, who was the revolution's inspiration and figurehead, was in exile at the time.

I.81*   *Of human flock nine shall be set apart,*
From judgement and from counsel separated:
Their fate shall be decided at the start,
Kappa, Theta, Lambda dead, banned, isolated.

Despite almost manic efforts by commentators ever since 1986 to link this verse with the *Challenger* space-shuttle tragedy, clearly neither the numbers nor the initials fit. Nor were the seven crew 'banished' in any way. As Prévost[49] points out, the original event referred to is once again clearly the Templar affair of 1307 to 1314 – and particularly the execution at Senlis of the nine Templars whose trials had been discontinued. As for the *Kappa, Theta, Lambda* (the original text gives the actual Greek letters), these, he points out, are ancient gematric code (based on the fact that Greek letters also formerly stood for numbers) for 20 + 9 + 30 – which makes 59, the exact number of Templars who, having retracted their confessions, were burnt to death in two carts in Paris in 1310. (Nostradamus's evident predilection for number-games in both verses of this 'pair' suggests that he was reluctant to reveal his prophetic technique too openly in this case.) Any future fulfilment therefore has to be in terms of a similar series of events – a fact which of course, has in turn to inform any attempted translation.

VIII.15   *Great efforts by a northern woman mannish*
Shall Europe vex and nearly all Creation.
She'll hound failed leaders till they're fit to vanish,
With life and death facing Pannonia's nation.

Most of this stanza seems uncannily, if wryly, predictive of Britain's so-called Iron Lady, former prime minister Margaret Thatcher – as popularly perceived, at least – yet only recently has it been possible to decode it satisfactorily. This is partly because, on the basis of the Latin word *dux* ('leader' or 'general') Nostradamus has – not for the last time – characteristically disguised the word *ducs* in line three as *deux*, thus contriving to fool generations of astrologically-minded interpreters into imagining that he is talking about 'two eclipses' instead of 'failed leaders'. (Well might we recall his warning words quoted at the beginning of Chapter 2!) Puzzles of this type nearly always indicate that Nostradamus is, for the moment at least, writing in code. Pannonia was the classical name of the whole region centred on Hungary – including much of Yugoslavia – and in classical times was inhabited mainly by Slavs.

VIII.70   *Wicked and vile, a man of ill repute,*
The tyrant of Iraq comes in apace.
With the Great Whore all then shall plead their
suit.
Horrid the land shall be, and black its face.

Until quite recently, nobody had managed to decode this prediction satisfactorily. With the recent advent and rapid passing of the 1991 Gulf War in Kuwait and Iraq, however, its fulfilment seems all too obvious. Despite the intervention of undisguised biblical imagery, everything seems well-described – even the almost apocalyptic scenes of darkened skies and oil-covered desert which filled the world's television screens for days on end. As usual, though, there is some ambiguity in the text – this time as to whether the country that the 'tyrant' is entering is Mesopotamia (Iraq) itself or some other country. At the same time the word translated above as 'land' is in fact *tertre*, not *terre* – a word meaning 'mound', and typical of Mesopotamia's 'tells', or city mounds – so unless this is a misspelling (deliberate or otherwise), the fit may not be as convincing as perhaps it seems at first sight.

VI.33   *Through bloody Alus shall his final fight*
         Fail to ensure his status oversea.
         Between two rivers, fearful of armed might,
         The furious Black shall make him bend the knee.

Here the enigmatic 'he' (an apparent indication that the verse has a 'pair' somewhere in which the figure in question is in some way identified) is once again widely assumed to be a future Antichrist. On the other hand, the text itself says nothing of the kind. By some it is even assumed that 'Alus' is that figure's actual name. In fact, however, it seems more likely that 'Alus' – whose name, removing the Latinate ending, could well be 'Ali' – is merely a military ally of whoever is being referred to, and possibly one who lets him down either overseas or on the naval front. The familiar phrase 'between two rivers' immediately suggests, once again, the area of modern Iraq.

Whether any of this (possibly like VIII.70) is of relevance to the Gulf War of 1991 is thus rather dependent on whether Saddam Hussein had a senior military associate called Ali. *In the event, he did.* Alaa Hussein Ali, a former senior officer in the particularly bloody Iran-Iraq war, and subsequently in charge of Iraq's anti-missile programme, was appointed to head the puppet government in Kuwait following Iraq's invasion but, as apparently predicted, was unable to hang on to the country on Saddam's behalf. Assuming, then, that Nostradamus was as psychic as he liked to claim, he could thus have picked up on either the first or the last name. As for the 'furious Black' (*le noir l'ireux*), the curious construction makes it look almost as if the first two words were meant to be a name such as 'Lenoir' – hence my capital – unless, of course, the double article half-implies a double subject (i.e. 'the Black and [the] furious one'). As it happens, the 'avenging angel' whose furious assault forced Saddam to his knees during the course of what was specifically code-named 'Operation Desert Storm' was one general Schwarzkopf, the allied commander whose *German name actually means 'Blackhead'* – and who was nicknamed 'Stormin' Norman' for good measure.

As if all this were not enough, behind the 'furious' Schwarzkopf stood his own commander-in-chief, General Colin Powell, who was indeed black in his own right. It seems fairly reasonable *a priori*, then, to treat this quatrain as a continuation of quatrain VIII.70. With black skies, black seas, black desert, a black commander-in chief and a local commander whose very name incorporated the very word for 'black', small wonder that Nostradamus should have picked up particularly on blackness in both stanzas. Whether, however, this pair of quatrains might have any future – and still less any apocalyptic – significance for us largely depends on how valid Nostradamus's 'Janus hypothesis' proves to be over the longer term.

VI.74   *Once hounded out, she shall return to power,*
Her foes revealed conspirators to be:
More than before above her age she'll tower,
All too assured till death from seventy-three.

Formerly applied (albeit with some difficulty) to Queen Elizabeth I, this quatrain was recently discovered by the British media, who promptly assumed that it, too, applied to Margaret Thatcher. They may or may not have been right. It is the last line that determines the date of fulfilment of this quatrain – and, fortunately or unfortunately, that date (1999) has now safely passed!

V.92   *Once he for seventeen years has held the see,*
       They'll change the papal term to five years' time,
       What time another shall elected be
       Who with the Romans not so well shall chime.

We now turn to unfolding events in the Vatican, in which Nostradamus always showed a keen interest, almost as though they were a kind of index of future world events. However, in his day the Vatican also exercised a tight control over European thought and opinion. This may account for the strange mangling of the second line in the original. Once it is restored, however, the meaning becomes clear. After some seventeen years, the reigning pope asks to resign. He is refused, but is offered a new law whereby popes, like many lay presidents, will in future reign for only five years at a time – with himself automatically appointed as the first of them.

Thus, if the pope in question happened to be the present incumbent, John Paul II, he would (having been elected in 1978) have tendered his resignation in October 1995, but been asked to continue for a further five years. This would place the end of his pontificate in the year 2000, when he would be eighty – a fact which, as we shall see, would help to date various other contemporary developments too. And indeed, rumours have recently been circulating in the Italian press to the effect that just such an initial consultation did occur, though the date is not generally specified. However, only actual events – which may possibly not be revealed to the world at large until many years later – can possibly reveal the accuracy or otherwise either of Nostradamus's apparent prediction or of its interpretation as presented above.

Sixain 14*   *More crimes the mighty siege shall bring,*
              Worse than before redoubling,
              In '605 'midst verdant land.
              Recaptured shall be what was ta'en,
              Soldiers afield till frost's at hand,
              Then, afterwards, afield again.

Nostradamus does not name the site of his great siege, which culminates in 1997 by his 'liturgical' count (as will be explained more fully under VI.54 below, this involves adding 392 – the date of the official imposition of St Ambrose's Catholic liturgy throughout the Roman Empire – to the figures offered), but he does seem to refer to it again at *Sixain* 3 below. If so, then the latter, too, can be dated.

Sixain 3*   *A thousand cannon-shots the town*
            Shall turn, remorseless, upside down,
            With strong emplacements underground.
            Five years she'll hold against such blows,
            And then be handed to her foes;
            Then, after war, with water drowned.

The siege, it seems, is one that has started in 1992 and is destined to end five years later in disaster. The only 'great siege' that seems to fit is that of Sarajevo in the former Yugoslavia, though the actual dates seem none too accurate.

Sixain 16 *October '605 appoint*
With royal chrism to anoint
Sea Monster's Steward, or exult
Should '606 in June befall
Great joys for lords and commons all:
Great deeds shall from that rite result.

Here much hinges on the exact identity of the 'Sea Monster' and its 'Steward'. Typically, it is to Britain that expressions such as the former tend to refer in Nostradamus, while the word 'Steward' or 'Provider' often seems (as we shall see) to indicate the future United States. On the other hand, while the verse *could* refer to the inauguration of a future American President – apparently in mid-term, in that event – the vocabulary makes it seem more likely that, in this particular case, it is a *British coronation* that is envisaged – and, as the apparently 'liturgical' dating seems to indicate, in 1997 or 1998. If so, Nostradamus proved wrong on both counts – though it has to be said that, at that particular time, President Bill Clinton was very much at risk of impeachment and dismissal, and there was also much talk of the possible abdication of Queen Elizabeth II in the wake of the British royal family's perceived out-of-touchness in the wake of the sudden tragic death of Diana Princess of Wales in a car accident. But then, tempting though it is to try and tie the seer down to a set list of symbols, he is quite liable to vary their significance on a whim, sprinkling them around with complete abandon. Alternative dates, meanwhile, are something of a feature in the *Sixains* – a fact which, once again, follows more or less automatically from Nostradamus's underlying divinatory mechanism of recurring planetary configurations.

Sixain 18* *Considering the sad, Greek Nightingale*
Who shall her woes with cries and tears bewail
And in such wise consume her earthly days,
Six hundred five she shall deliverance see
From all her pains: so does fate's web decree.
By means sinister she shall succour raise.

The spotlight now turns on Greece, apparently with special reference to continuing troubles along its frontier with Turkey (the 'Nightingale' in question is named as the mythical Athenian princess Philomel, violated by a Thracian prince, who accidentally caused the death of her own nephew and, as a nightingale, has mourned him ever since). Evidently, some unexpected, even sinister development was theoretically set to divert Turkey's attention to other matters in 1997, possibly on her eastern borders. Whether this could be said to have any connection with her troubles with the Kurds is a matter for debate.

Sixain 19* *In '605 and six and seven we*
Until six hundred seventeen shall see
The ire, hate, loathing of the Firebrand spread.
So long beneath the olive tree concealed,
The Crocodile that lurks in fen and field
Shall rise to life, though he before were dead.

On the basis of later symbolic references, this verse inevitably refers to the inexorable rise of North African Muslim militancy (the 'Crocodile') against the former colonial regimes and their puppet successors – and against France in particular – during the last years of the twentieth century and the early years of the twenty-first, with (as subsequent verses will reveal) the grimmest of eventual results for France and southern Europe

61

generally. Subsequent events both in Algeria and in mainland France have indeed borne out this prediction in the most dramatic way. The dating in line one is evidently yet another of Nostradamus's 'liturgical' deadlines based on the year 392.

V.25   *Mars, Venus, sun in Leo: to Arab Khan*
        Shall Christendom at length by sea succumb.
        Some million men from round about Iran:
        To Nile and Istanbul coiled snake shall come.

There can be no doubt about it. This verse represents a summary of the initial stages of what Nostradamus now foresees as a major Muslim invasion of Europe. Having mobilised a huge force of around a million from the area around Iran, the 'coiled snake' who is evidently the Muslim overlord finally despatches it westwards, with two major spearheads heading for Istanbul (and thus Europe) on the one hand and Cairo (and thus North Africa) on the other. However, it needs to be remembered that this is a summary verse. A large-scale invasion such as that described inevitably takes a long time, starting from quite small beginnings. It is this starting date that line one seems to pinpoint astrologically to 21–22 August 1998 – until, that is, the planets once again take up the same positions in the future.

It is perhaps sobering to note that on the morning of the 21 August I duly warned the members of the Internet Newsgroup *alt.prophecies.nostradamus* that the next two days would no doubt reveal how much credence should be attached to Nostradamus's prophecies – quite expecting a resounding failure. There were, after all, no signs whatever of such an invasion, despite the ever-threatening presence of Saddam Hussein, who had indeed been described in the British media as a 'coiled snake' – *and who had just announced his intention of raising a citizens' army of a million!*

My exact words, posted at 10.56 BST on 21 August 1998 (and still accessible via independent Usenet archives such as *www.deja.com*), were:

> Seriously, though, folks, today/tomorrow is the 'window' for the start of the alleged Asiatic invasion of Turkey and Egypt by the 'coiled snake' with 'near a million men' (V.25), unless the astrological date applies not this time but the next time around (in 2006, I believe) – or, of course, the time after that ...
>
> OK, typically the date would refer to the astrological causation, rather than to the event itself – and present events on earth would of course neatly correspond to that causation – but if something of the kind hasn't shown signs of happening by, say, the end of September or middle of October, then either the astrology isn't for this time at all ... or Nostradamus was WRONG!!
>
> In this particular case, there's no room for saying that it must be the interpretation that is at fault.
>
> So hold your breath!

Nobody was more surprised than I was, then, when something quite dramatic *did* happen ...

Within hours of my posting the announcement, the Western media were flooded with stories that the Muslim world was in uproar. By 09:07 EDT (14:07 BST) Reuters was reporting blood-curdling threats against the USA from all across the Arab quarter, the Stars and Stripes was officially burned in Libya and Pakistan, cries of 'Death to America' resounded at Friday prayers in Teheran University and the American embassy in Khartoum was stoned. The leader of Egypt's Muslim Brotherhood warned that the flame of extremism and instability had been ignited in the Middle East, and Lebanon's Hizbollah predicted world-wide attacks on American interests.

And the reason for all this?

It was the stark fact that the Pentagon had just taken it upon itself to launch cruise missile attacks on an alleged chemical factory in Khartoum and a guerrilla encampment in Afghanistan. Both, it was revealed, belonged to the exiled Saudi Islamic dissident and terrorist Osama bin Laden, who was claimed to have been responsible for an earlier brutal bombing of the American embassy in Nairobi, Kenya.

And so it was no surprise that, to cap it all, Bin Laden himself now promptly redeclared *jihad* (holy war) on Israel and the West. As a result, America and much of the West have been on a state of high security alert ever since, only wondering where and when the inevitable blow will fall.

This astonishing development appeared to back up Nostradamus's apparent dating to the hilt – even though, on the face of it, the event itself was smaller than the prediction seemed to envisage. Here much depends on how subsequent events develop. If Bin Laden deploys the suitcase chemical, biological and/or nuclear weapons that he is widely alleged to have at his disposal, who knows what horrors might be in store? If he allies with a threatening figure such as Saddam Hussein of Iraq, or if subsequent Western attacks add further power to the elbow of the many powerful groups who are already proclaiming a general *jihad* against the West throughout the Muslim world, Nostradamus's prophecy of a Muslim invasion of Europe may yet come to some sort of fruition – unless, that is, Europe and the West remain alive to the dangers and take appropriate counter-measures.

Nostradamus's warning function, in other words, will once again be very much in evidence.

Sixain 25* *Six hundred six or nine are for*
A great ox of a Chancellor,
A Phoenix old and full of years.
He'll shine no more where once he shone:
Oblivion's ferry bears him on.
On Champs-Élysées he appears.

At this point, Nostradamus appears to see a leader who looks uncannily like Helmut Kohl, former Chancellor of Germany, journeying to Paris to hold his final international talks before retiring at the end of his term in 1998. So, at least, I suggested some years back, when assembling my notes for a subsequent edition, duly incorporating the idea into my *Nostradamus: The Final Reckoning* of 1995. In the event, Kohl did indeed fall from power in 1998. True, he did not conclude his term of office with a visit to Paris – but, curiously enough, such a visit was the very first diplomatic act of his successor, Gerhard Schröder.

VI.54*   *At dawn, the second time the cockerel calls,*
From Tunis, Fez and Bougie they appear:
Morocco's King to Arab captors falls.
Of Liturgy 1607 the year.

Here the 'year 1607 of the Liturgy' seems to refer directly to the year AD 392, when (on 8 November, to be precise) the emperor Theodosius I finally issued his decree making Christianity not only the official state religion of the entire Roman Empire, but the only religious cult permitted whatsoever. It was from this date, in other words, that the Church became for the first time not only Roman but truly Catholic (i.e. universal) too. It was also at around this time that St Ambrose first promulgated a version of the sequence of texts since known as the Canon of the Mass, which was to provide the basis of the Church's eucharistic liturgy for the next 1,600 years. The upshot is a striking one, for on this basis the dating in line four brings us to the year 1999, when (it seems) Muslim fundamentalists are predicted as being on the march all across North Africa.

To an extent, of course, this duly happened – but the King of Morocco was not taken prisoner. *Instead, King Hassan II died!*

VIII.71*   *Astrologers in droves so great shall mount*
        That they'll be hounded, banned, censored their
           work
        In year 1607 by Church's count:
        At sacred rites danger for them shall lurk.

Once again, Nostradamus uses his 'ecclesiastical count' to date an event to 1999. By then, it seems, astrology will have become so popular and so threatening to public morale as to alarm Church and political establishment alike. Nevertheless it has to be said that, to my knowledge, no such ban was in fact imposed, whether in France or elsewhere.

IV.18   *Of those most learn'd of facts celestial*
        Some shall by ill-read princes be impeached,
        Proscribed, then hounded as though criminal
        And put to death where'er they can be reached.

In view of its obvious similarity of theme, this verse may also belong at this point. Nostradamus's prophecies often come in 'pairs' of this kind. Nevertheless, whatever the verse's original – for VIII.71 above, Prévost[49] suggests a link with Pope Pius IV's campaign against heresy, and his foundation of the *Index Librorum Prohibitorum* (the 'Index of Forbidden Books') in 1557 – nothing of the kind in fact happened in 1999.

X.72   *When 1999 is seven months o'er*
        Shall heaven's great Vicar, anxious to appease,
        Stir up the Mongol-Lombard King once more,
        And war reign haply where it once did cease.

This translation of what is possibly the most celebrated – and feared – of Nostradamus's predictions was first published in my *Nostradamus Encyclopedia*[34]. No doubt this aura of terror arose in recent years partly because the date was both so specific and so imminent, and partly because in most translations the term *Roy deffraieur* ('defraying King') in line two had been incorrectly rendered 'King of terror', on the basis that later editions erroneously printed it as *Roy d'effrayeur*. This, of course, suggested that it might refer to the expected Antichrist, while most commentators assumed that line three referred to a Mongol invasion (*see* the French text below). True, possibly Nostradamus actually intended at least the former ambiguity. Dark clouds are seldom without their silver linings, nor silver linings without their dark clouds, apocalyptic or otherwise. But then the prediction was quite likely, as usual, to turn out not to be truly apocalyptic at all.

Transcribed into modern lettering, the original 1568 text of this verse reads:

> *L'an mil neuf cens nonante neuf sept mois*
> *Du ciel viendra un grand Roy deffraieur*
> *Resusciter le grand Roy d'Angolmois.*
> *Avant apres Mars regner par bon heur.*

My original application to this verse of the familiar technique of comparative horoscopy suggested (via no less than a five-planet match) that the figure in question was to be not some kind of Antichrist, but merely a latter-day version of Pope Gregory the Great – a 'heavenly prince' who indeed came from Rome's *Mons Caelius* (*du ciel*, as Nostradamus archly puts it) and was, as the verse also requires, a great public benefactor as well as a notable appeaser. His intervention would, it seemed, be no more than a re-run of Gregory's efforts to buy off the pagan invaders of Italy (the Langobardi, who indeed were allied to a tribe with Mongol connections) during the fourth century of our era. His modern equivalent thus begged to be identified as the current Pope, who in July

1999 (as I repeatedly suggested on the Internet beforehand) would fly (*du ciel* again!) to Sarajevo (the latitude is specified by the astrology) to attempt to buy peace.

Much to my surprise, there was indeed a major meeting of heads of government in Sarajevo (of all places!) on 30 July 1999 to attempt to regulate and finance the peace in the Balkans in the wake of the war in Kosovo. Unfortunately either for me or for Nostradamus, however, the Pope was not one of them.

Meanwhile, new linguistic evidence was starting to emerge. For a start, the word *deffraieur* at the end of line two did in fact turn out to have been a known one at the time. Under the heading *Parochus* in Estienne's *Dictionarium Latinogallicum* of 1538, the meaning of this Latin word was defined as *Ung deffraieur, qui nous fournist de tout ce qu'il nous fault par les chemins* – 'A defrayer who furnishes us with everything that we need for the road'. As the English Cotgrave was to put it in 1611, it meant 'A Cater, or Steward; one that in a iourney furnishes, and defrayes the prouision, and expence of the whole companie'. The word *deffraieur* thus meant 'defrayer', 'host', 'steward' or even 'provider'. And soon, on this basis, the research came up with a match that was much more direct and convincing.

For Nostradamus, after all, 'the great King from Angoumois', of which Angoulême is and was the capital, was by definition the magnificent King François I of France, who reigned right up until the time when the seer moved to Salon. After a brilliant early reign, he was captured by the Imperial forces of the Holy Roman Emperor Charles V in February 1525 at the disastrous battle of Pavia (when Nostradamus was still wandering the countryside as an apothecary), and was imprisoned in a dismal tower in Madrid, where he moped, wrote songs and poems, and became gravely ill with an abscess in the head. There were national prayers for his recovery, and the Archbishop of Tournon even came and said mass over him. Eventually a treaty was signed for his release in January 1526, on terms which included the handing over of his two sons as hostages (one of them the future Henri II), a promise to send troops to help the Emperor wage war on the Muslim Ottomans, and the payment of a huge ransom amounting to some seven tons of gold, which nearly ruined the kingdom. Thereafter, he spent his life in constant and increasing ill-health as a result of syphilis, and virtually on the run from the Emperor's agents, while the Emperor plundered Italy and even captured the Pope. Nevertheless, François managed to build all sorts of fairytale castles, founded the port of Le Havre, sent the explorer Jacques Cartier to Canada, reformed the judicial system, moderated the religious feuds that were by then breaking out all over his kingdom, founded the Collège de France, and decreed the use of French in all legal documents.

And it was specifically François's truly traumatic imprisonment and release – and not, as I originally imagined, his birth, accession or death – that provided the real match. For, having, during the spring of 1999, duly looked up the planetary positions for that period, I discovered that in August 1525 (Julian) there was indeed a good match with July 1999. The charts below both demonstrate the resulting identical 'Z' pattern extremely clearly (the planets shown in black are those that, significantly, are in the same signs on both charts, while those above the thick line were, of course, unknown to Nostradamus).

So what did this mean? After all, the future period that was pinpointed (*not* the original planetary configuration) did fall more or less within the period covered by Nostradamus's 'seventh month' of July (our 14 July to 13 August). Interestingly, though, the brief period actually pinpointed by the astrological match *didn't* include our 11 August, with its celebrated solar eclipse that was so often linked with this verse at the time.

So who was the original 'great heavenly defraying king'? The Pope at the time, whose court was certainly lavish? Or the Archbishop of Tournon, whose bedside ministrations during his captivity in Madrid apparently helped save

HOROGRAPH FOR: 14 August 1525 TO: 23 August 1525

	Aries	Tauru	Gemin	Cance	Leo	Virgo	Libra	Scorp	Sagit	Capri	Aquar	Pisce
Pluto										☆		
Neptune												☆
Uranus			☆									
Saturn	☆											
Jupiter		★										
Mars								★				
Venus						★						
Mercury					★							
Moon				★	★	★	★	★				
Sun						☆						

Solar noon declination (to nearest degree):   10° N to 7° N

Geographical latitude: 40° N

LOCATION: Madrid
EVENT: 'Restoration to health' by Emperor Charles V of mortally ill King François I

HOROGRAPH FOR: 13 July 1999   TO: 23 July 1999

	Aries	Tauru	Gemin	Cance	Leo	Virgo	Libra	Scorp	Sagit	Capri	Aquar	Pisce
Pluto									☆			
Neptune											☆	
Uranus											☆	
Saturn		☆										
Jupiter		★										
Mars								★				
Venus						★						
Mercury					★							
Moon				★	★	★	★	★				
Sun				☆								

Solar noon declination (to nearest degree):   22° N to 20° N

Relative latitude: 12° N to 13° N   Geographical latitude: 52° N to 53° N

POSSIBLE LOCATION: Amsterdam, Berlin or Warsaw
EVENT: Restoration to power by new German leader of ruler formerly deposed in Italy

François from death, even if they didn't actually restore him to immediate health? Or the Emperor Charles V, who had of course been elected Holy Roman Emperor (and would be crowned as such by the Pope himself), who was acting as François's 'host' at the time, and who agreed to his release? Or even the 'divinely appointed' François himself, who was certainly a spendthrift?

It soon became clear that it was in fact Charles V. He was, after all, by definition 'heaven's king' (King of Germany and Spain as well as Holy Roman Emperor) and was currently spending money on arms and armies as if there were no tomorrow – and he was François's 'host' or jailer to boot. At the same time, though, he was a real bogeyman for the French, so that, in the possible subtext, *deffraieur* could also be hinting at 'frightful' (*d'effraieur*), as well as at the more obvious and literal 'host', even if it didn't actually say it.

The details of what happened at Madrid during the period in question are interesting. King François arrived in his Madrid prison in early August, but by mid-August had fallen gravely ill – severely depressed, anorexic, totally apathetic and feverish with a serious nasal abscess – to the point where the doctors actually gave up on him. On the evening of the 18 August, Charles V visited him in person. They embraced tearfully and protested their mutual friendship. Charles made various promises. But by 22 August the king was in a semi-coma. They gave him the last rites.

Then, suddenly, he recovered – the abscess burst, the fever subsided, the king recalled Charles's tearful protestations . . .

Thus it was that *grand Roy du ciel* (i.e. the Holy Roman Emperor, who had been sanctioned by heaven in the person of the Pope) had apparently 'resuscitated' the *grand Roy d'Angolmois*. And the comparative horoscopy of verse X.72, you will recall, pinpoints 14–23 August 1525 – the exact period involved.

Moreover, as a final piece of the jigsaw, it turns out that François was finally released on 17 March 1526, so suggesting that the word *Mars* in the last line refers not to war, as

71

has so often been supposed in the past (not least by myself), but simply to the month of March.

So, thanks to the application of comparative horoscopy to the historical data unearthed on the basis of the 'Janus hypothesis', this information now provides the context for a much more informed translation than has hitherto been possible, though it also needs to cater for the two possible senses of *deffraieur* – the literal and the merely hinted at. I would therefore suggest:

> *When 1999 is seven months o'er*
> *Shall heaven's great King – albeit a dread host, he –*
> *Restore the King from Angoumois once more,*
> *Ere – after March – he'll reign propitiously.*

The puzzling last line, in other words, is merely Nostradamus's compressed version of:

> *Avant (apres Mars) de regner par bon heur.*

What verse X.72 really seems to be predicting, then, is that at some point between 13 and 23 July 1999 (or shortly thereafter) a ruler who has been imprisoned and/or removed from office (and who has possibly fallen ill) will be restored by a redoubtable and/or spendthrift rival (possibly a powerful politician and/or financial figure) in either Amsterdam, Berlin or Warsaw, and that from March 2000 he will rule with great good fortune.

Now I hesitate to be too dogmatic about this – but at the meeting of European Heads of State held in Berlin in March 1999, Romano Prodi, former Prime Minister of Italy, was selected as the next President of the European Commission (i.e. effectively, Prime Minister of Europe), to replace the disgraced Jacques Santer. His main proposers were Tony Blair, Prime Minister of Britain, and Gerhard Schröder, Chancellor of Germany. Prodi presented his cabinet on 9 July 1999, they first met near Antwerp (on 51° 13' North!) on 17

July, and were duly confirmed in office by the European Parliament on 15 September.

One of Prodi's main sponsors at the meeting in Berlin (note!) the previous March (note again!) was Chancellor Schröder – who, as ruler of Germany and the most powerful man in Europe, of course fulfilled the self- same role as the former Charles V (who was King of Germany among other things), as well as being the main contributor to the European budget, too (*deffraieur*).

Could it be Schröder, then, whom the prediction sees as calling back from the wilderness Romano Prodi who – like François I, as it happens – had previously been removed from power in Italy, but who, from July 1999 (note, yet again!), duly became President of the European Commission? Could it be that, from March 2000 he is destined (if the prediction is both correct and relevant) to start to run his much larger empire with notable success?

The fit between the events of 1525/6 and those of 1999 – as indicated by the comparative horoscopy – certainly seems to have been remarkable. Moreover, if valid, it possibly gives us a powerful hint that comparative horoscopy is the correct method to use when trying to decipher the *Propheties*.

If so, then the above exercise has been extremely useful in refining our approach to Nostradamus's prophecies. On this basis, the ideal method for interpreting any given quatrain would appear to be:

a   After locating the earliest possible edition of the text, work out what the sixteenth century French means (without feeding in any prior ideas as to what event it might be about).

b   If possible, find and verify the ancient event on which it appears originally to have been based.

c   Use (b) to help sort out any obvious ambiguities or misprints in the original text.

d   Refine your version of it accordingly (still without feeding in any ideas as to what the prophecy's fulfilment might be), possibly adding any further refinements (e.g. geographical ones) that any clearly related verses seem to suggest.

e   If the dating of the original event is precise enough, use comparative horoscopy to work out when and at what latitudes the event ought theoretically to be repeated, bearing in mind that there may be – indeed, should be – several. (In the case of X.72, Nostradamus has already done part of this for you!)

f   Strictly on the basis of (a) to (e) above, identify and describe the likely fulfilment (*now* you can associate it with a known or expected event, if you like – *if* there is one that fits in all respects!).

g   Finally, attempt a translation in good English verse.

Learning the lessons

At this point, we come to the end of our brief survey of a few of those Nostradamian predictions that are widely believed to have been fulfilled already. To be sure, there are plenty of others, but very few of them match the best of those that I have quoted for clarity or specificity. That these others are adduced at all often owes much more to almost obsessive interpretational bias and distortion than to their genuine predictive quality. Nor is this the only influence that has been at work.

The first 'complete' edition of the *Centuries*, for example, was not officially published until after the prophet's death, any more than were the *Sixains* – a fact that allowed ample opportunity for other hands to edit Nostradamus's work, or even to add or insert predictions of their own (we have already noted Chavigny's efforts in this direction). Most of the apparent prophecies suspected of having suffered this treatment contain factual errors, however – not, on the whole, what one would expect informed hindsight to produce (unless, of course, the perpetrators were clever enough to include deliberate mistakes to give the *impression* of authenticity). Consequently, the possibility of such interference is not now too important to our investigation, especially as the vast bulk of the prophecies have necessarily been immune from it for some centuries now.

Again, just as we have referred to the possibility that Queen Catherine de Médicis might have acted in full knowledge of the predictions, so others may have done so too. The Bourbon kings, Napoleon Bonaparte and the Adolf Hitler of the 1930s (thanks to the intermediary of Frau Goebbels) are all suspected (*see* Pitt Francis[48]) of having regarded them as a kind of 'omen' and thus of having used them as a guide to their own actions. Deliberate self-fulfilment, in other words, starts to muddy the waters further.

But all this is as nothing compared with the prolonged exercise in wilful misinterpretation that has dogged the predictions ever since they first appeared. Generation after generation of interpreters, endlessly repeating each other's mistakes, have determinedly misread what the verses actually say in their desperate efforts to make them mean what they wanted them to mean. An almost infallible sign of this approach has been the tendency to use the predictions to blow up recent or contemporary events out of all reasonable historical proportion, irrespective of the fact that they in no way gel with what Nostradamus's overriding concerns seem to have been.

That tendency still continues today. To support it, grammatical agreements are ignored, tenses scrambled, whole phrases taken as if they were nothing more than magic rune spreads, and all interpretational level-headedness thrown to the winds.

But to the extent that all this is so, it is all the more incumbent on us not to fall into the same trap ourselves. Giving Nostradamus the benefit of the interpretational doubt (as I have sometimes done above) is one thing: the wholesale distortion of what he clearly says to fit our own preconceptions is quite another. Indeed, as we noted earlier, preconceptions of any kind are a luxury with which we can quite simply not afford to indulge ourselves in the first place. Initially at least, the seer's words have to be taken at face value, *though always in context* – right up to the point where we are faced with some piece of obvious nonsense that leads us to suspect that the printer has misspelt the words in front of him, or even that Nostradamus himself has been playing with words for reasons of concealment or even plain contrariness. Only at this point are we entitled to review the text, experimentally investigating what other word or expression might reasonably underlie the 'sticky patch' in question. And even then we are in honour bound to admit the fact, exposing for all to see precisely what changes or substitutions we have assumed.

And meanwhile we shall need constantly to bear in mind the other lessons that we have learned from the predictions quoted in this chapter. Nostradamus, as we have seen, is not infallible. His clear assumption that past events would repeat themselves again in the future in tune with the movements of the planets (the 'Janus effect') may or may not be correct. He frequently seems to fail to recognise how the detailed parts of his picture relate to each other – indeed, he sometimes appears to get them entirely back to front – though this impression could equally well be an indication that we have got hold of the wrong end of the stick entirely! Nostradamus sometimes makes generalised predictions that could refer to almost anybody, and that are likely to be fulfilled somewhere in the world at almost any time or place. He is possibly oversensitive to any threat to the established order, as well as to matters concerning religion and the betrayal of it. He is sometimes so cryptic that a measure of conjecture needs to be locally applied – always, though, in context, and never as a general principle. He tends to see disasters and catastrophes in terms of biblical eschatology – to which he often assigns a larger-than-life scale that it possibly does not merit. He occasionally names names, though he is also prone to resort to anagrams. Occasionally, too, he specifies exact times, though care needs to be taken in establishing the exact *terminus a quo*. He is almost never capable of final interpretation until after the event – or at least until that event is already plainly in the offing. He seems to be clairaudient as well as clairvoyant, frequently picking up topical expressions and turns of phrase that not only are of no interpretational use to us beforehand, but are actually turned into concrete images capable of bamboozling us afterwards – just as they possibly bamboozled Nostradamus, too. And, finally, he is first and foremost a Frenchman, so that events in and around France always tend to loom especially large in his vision.

Armed with this knowledge, then, we can now proceed to examine some of his apparent predictions for our future with a view, not so much to anticipating in any detail the events involved (even though it may be possible to establish a rough sequence, and thus some sort of generalised interpretation) as to recognising them when they come. It may not be an easy exercise. But at least we can take some comfort from the fact that Nostradamus, unlike many of his would-be interpreters, seems always to have remained true to his vision, resolutely refusing to replace or falsify (at least until after the event!) the words that it dictated. It is almost as though he were aware of the immortal words of the *Rubaiyat of Omar Khayyam*, as later rendered by Fitzgerald with at least as much freedom as I have accorded Nostradamus:

> *The Moving Finger writes; and, having writ*
> *Moves on; nor all thy Piety nor Wit*
> *Shall lure it back to cancel half a Line*
> *Nor all thy Tears wash out a Word of it.*

4

THE INVASION OF
ITALY

At that time, great ships from Turkey having associated with the Italians thanks to the support of powers to the north ... craft built by the former military shall sail in company through Neptune's waves. In the Adriatic there shall be such great conflict that those who were united shall be torn apart, and past and present cities shall be reduced to mere houses (including the former omnipotent Babylon of Europe) on the 45th, 41st, 42nd and 37th degrees of latitude.[a] And at that time and in those countries the power of hell shall throw against the Church of Jesus Christ all the power of the adversaries of his dispensation. This shall be the second Antichrist, who shall persecute the church and its rightful Vicar via the power of world leaders who in their ignorance shall be seduced by tongues sharper than any madman's sword ...

Extracted from the *Letter to Henri King of France the Second*

---

[a] Presumably Turin, Naples, Rome (the European 'Babylon') and Syracuse (Sicily).

Q UITE LITERALLY WITH THE WISDOM of hindsight, we are now in a position to apply our acquired knowledge of Nostradamus and his working methods to the majority of his predictions that have not yet been fulfilled.

I use the phrase 'not yet' advisedly. It is an old and well-worn formula among those who cannot quite bring themselves to believe that their favourite prophet might just possibly be wrong. Who is to say, after all, that Nostradamus might not prove as wrong as anybody? Certainly, Chevignard's evidence cited in my Introduction is not encouraging.[14]

Curiously enough, Nostradamus himself seems to have agreed. 'If I should have worked out the timings wrongly, or should fail to satisfy in any way, may it please Your Most Imperial Majesty to pardon me,' he wrote in his *Letter to Henri King of France the Second*, clearly anticipating his own due ration of abject flops. 'I protest before God and His saints,' he went on, 'that it has not been my intention to write anything that is contrary to true Catholic faith, even though I have applied such astronomical calculations as my learning permits.'

The point is well taken, for we have already seen how many of Nostradamus's more apocalyptic prophecies are inevitably vitiated by his own pre-existing religious beliefs and his urgent need to stand by them publicly.

The upshot is clear. We do not have to assume that all the apparently unfulfilled prophecies will necessarily come to pass at all. Nostradamus's 'Janus' theory may or may not be valid. Even those prophecies that do come true are likely, on the basis of that very theory, to do so only as one event in a series, and then only to the extent that human decisions permit. Moreover, until we have successfully identified the original historical events, to try and say exactly what each prophecy means is more or less to offer hostages to fortune.

Even in the absence of such information, however, we can at least try to observe certain basic principles:

1   Look for predictions that are in some way unexpected or

striking. This at least means that they are unlikely to be of a type that happens somewhere or other in the world at least a hundred times a year.

2 Pinpoint those that refer to particular times or places (whether astrologically or otherwise), or that name names where people are concerned, however symbolically or anagrammatically. Take careful note, too, of those that relate to other quatrains, whether thematically or temporally, since such links can provide vital clues for fitting the jigsaw together.

3 Treat with the greatest suspicion (curiously enough) all those that sit too neatly with received biblical expectation, and avoid like the plague any temptation to treat the rest as if they did.

4 Take the whole exercise with more than a pinch of salt: the infallibility of Nostradamus is not an article of faith.

5 Finally, remember constantly that the initial object of the exercise is not to anticipate events at all – since, under the very terms of the 'Janus hypothesis', the next potential occasion may not come to anything – but merely to gain some idea of what to look out for and how to recognise it when it comes. If it then turns out to be possible to establish a rough sequence, and thus some kind of overall context, a measure of interpretation may start to prove possible, especially where an original historical event can be identified.

The great Muslim invasion

One particular theme which, as you will see, emerges strongly from my analysis below is that of a looming Islamic invasion of Europe. So insistent is this theme that you may feel I have some kind of anti-Islamic obsession which I am determined to impose on the Nostradamian texts, in the light of their obvious vulnerability to such dubious exercises in 'interpretation'.

In fact, the origin of that insistence lies with Nostradamus himself. Nobody who reads his original verses can be in the slightest doubt about it. Not only does the imminence of a Muslim invasion of his homeland permeate the *Propheties*, but it comes up repeatedly in his *Almanachs*, too. Clearly he saw the threat as one of the major ones of his day – and one that, under the terms of the 'Janus hypothesis', was therefore likely to resurface repeatedly in the future, too. Moreover, there were good reasons for this.

At that time, after all, Western Europe was threatened by Islam on almost every side. In the east, the advancing Ottomans had managed to capture Belgrade in 1521 and Rhodes in 1522. By 1529, the year when Nostradamus enrolled at Montpellier for his doctorate course, they were besieging Vienna. Ever since the Middle Ages, moreover, Saracen pirate fleets from North Africa had been ravaging the Mediterranean coasts of Italy and France – which is why many of the ancient churches along this coast are so heavily fortified. In the west, the Moors had been expelled from Spain only some eleven years before Nostradamus's birth – and there was no telling when they might be back.

Inevitably, then, under the terms of the 'Janus hypothesis', these events were bound to resurface in his prophecies, too. The intriguing precedent of the campaigns of Hannibal in classical times, as he invaded Spain from North Africa and moved across the south of France towards Italy, merely added further literary grist to his prophetic mill.

My conclusion that the consequent invasion scenario is particularly relevant to our own times is the result, as you will see, of my attempts to date certain key prophecies. I could consequently be wrong. Nevertheless, events seem to be conspiring to suggest that I may not be. Over the past few decades, as the world's subject peoples have increasingly thrown off the old colonial yoke, world Islam – and particularly its 'militant tendency' – has strengthened enormously. Not only are a whole series of local wars in progress against perceived 'Western' oppression, but calls are widespread for a general *jihad*, or war of liberation, against the West and its decadent values. It lacks only some kind of charismatic, unifying leader to produce what could turn into a very nasty world situation indeed.

One of the reasons for this, curiously, is the fact that the vast majority of Muslims are not warlike people at all, but humble, religious, devoted individuals who put most self-professed Christians to shame. In the face of war, poverty and injustice these are fleeing in increasingly huge numbers to the affluent countries of Western Europe, and especially to those in the south and east (thus, in a sense, themselves justifying Nostradamus's 'invasion' scenario, if in unexpected ways) – where they often encounter discrimination, hatred and oppression instead. Under the very terms of the concept of *jihad*, this then justifies almost any action by the more militant members of their communities to redress the situation and protect those involved, if necessary including even physical violence.

The threat is thus already present, not only in the Muslim homelands themselves, but within the very heart of Europe – and no amount of right-wing pressure to expel the immigrants who are perceived as embodying it can now do anything other than aggravate the situation. Understanding, co-operation, assimilation and mutual respect seem capable of relieving the pressures and defusing the rapidly building tensions, so that, as usual, the operation of the Janus effect will depend almost entirely on human attitudes and decisions.

What follows should thus emphatically not be seen as a call to arms against Islam. On the contrary, it is simply a warning of what *could* befall if we in the West persist with our blinkered delusions of superiority and our refusal to see anybody's point of view but our own, whether in the religious, social or political sphere.

Perhaps we should remember that it was our own ancestors who, as long ago as the infamous medieval (and allegedly 'Christian') Crusades, started this particular ball rolling in the first place. Is it too much to hope, I wonder, that we shall be wise enough this time to avoid the operation of the Janus effect and actually learn from our past mistakes?

Assembling the prophecies

Interpreting and assembling the prophecies thus demands caution, time and patience. There are real dangers in trying to interpret any given quatrain in isolation – and a particularly grave one of imposing on it one's own preconceptions and expectations.

Yet the prophecies need in any case to be grouped into subject areas and mini-sequences if the resulting text is not to prove disordered and obtuse. These mini-sequences lead quite naturally to larger groupings, those groupings to yet larger groupings, and so on until, *mirabile dictu*, one finds that one has arrived at something that looks suspiciously like Nostradamus's original, overall sequence – even if, for purely thematic reasons, a few prophecies may have been included in the sequence that possibly do not belong there. Consequently, even where it is not possible to identify too many of the 'original events', one suddenly has a general context within which to attempt some kind of interpretation – and one that is based on Nostradamus himself rather than on imported preconceptions.

The jigsaw pieces having at last been joined together, the picture on the box at last becomes clear – and so, consequently, does the relationship of each individual piece to it.

Thus it is that I am now able to present the relevant quatrains in what appears to me to be more or less their correct order and (more importantly) their correct sense. We can, in short, begin our survey of our Nostradamian future roughly at the beginning. Moreover, thanks to a great deal of detailed dating-research undertaken since the first edition of this book appeared in 1993, we can also tie the events to a firm scaffolding of actual dates which in turn will help anchor and verify the sequence.

I.51   *Saturn and Jupiter in Aries met:*   **1999 (February)**
           Eternal God, what changes are in train!
           In France and Italy what stirrings yet
           As the slow round brings evil times again!

It is in this verse that we have the first indications that disturbing events are set to affect the Mediterranean shores of Western Europe. The quatrain even contains a clear astrological dating. The last time the conjunction in question occurred was between 13 and 28 February 1999. Whether this is a reference to the increasing influence of Muslim immigrants in southern Europe at that time is not clear. Certainly it has not as yet produced any military invasion.

I.15   *With warlike force Mars threatens us again.*
           Full seventy times he'll spill both blood and tears.
           The church first grows, then is destroyed again.
           So, too, are those who'd rather close their ears.

Meanwhile, in a general quatrain, Nostradamus offers an overview of warlike events that seems to encompass both his times and ours. In the process, it would appear that Christianity, after a period of relative prosperity, will be virtually wiped out, in Europe at least. Atheists, suggests Nostradamus, will be no better off, either. For details of the precise how and where, however, we shall have to await subsequent developments.

V.55   *A mighty Muslim chief shall come to birth*
In country fortunate of Araby.
He'll take Granada, trouble Spanish earth
And conquer the Italians from the sea.

The initial developments are set to stir into motion somewhere in the Middle East or North Africa. In this helpful
summary verse (one of many scattered about his prophecies)
Nostradamus foresees a coming invasion of Europe by a
powerful leader whose forces will overrun both Italy and
Spain. By 'Araby', Nostradamus may mean precisely that, or
he may merely be referring to the whole, vast Muslim area
stretching from North Africa far into central Asia. Precision,
alas, was never the seer's strongest suit.

V.84   *Of parentage obscure and shadowy,*
Born of the gulf and city measureless,
As far as Rouen and Evreux he'd see
That prince's power destroyed that all confess.

Nostradamus goes on to reveal the full extent of the Muslim
leader's disturbing ambitions. Born in a city that seems
remarkably like Cairo (the 'gulf' may well be the
Mediterranean, as in the case of Franco in Chapter 3), but
which could equally well be Alexandria or Istanbul, he is
determined to destroy what looks rather like the Pope's
fiefdom – i.e. European Christendom – not merely in the
south, but all the way to Normandy in northern France.

X.75   *So long awaited, never to return*
To Europe, out of Asia he shall lour –
A robber-Hermes who shall trickster turn
And o'er all eastern potentates shall tower.

Not only is the Eastern leader destined to threaten the world (albeit for the last time) with all the god Hermes' most disquieting characteristics (which, unlike Nostradamus himself, I have actually outlined in line three): he is also described as appearing in what Nostradamus calls 'Asia' – which in the seer's day normally meant what we today call Asia Minor or Turkey, and to which we could reasonably apply the modern term 'the Middle East'. Perhaps the most disquieting feature of this quatrain is the first line, which rather suggests that he is a unique figure who has been known about for centuries. If Nostradamus is right, after all, this begs to mark him out – at last we are forced to face the possibility – as none other than the biblical Antichrist, red in tooth and claw. At this point, though, we should (as ever) be wary of attaching too grand or cosmic a significance to such concepts. Both the Bible and Nostradamus are prone to make what are essentially local events look much bigger than they really are.

X.10   *With murder stained and malefactions vast,*
He'll be the enemy of all men living.
Far worse than any like him in the past,
By sword, fire, water, bloody, unforgiving.

Nostradamus goes on to compare him unfavourably even with all his grim forebears – among whom we could presumably number either Hitler or Stalin, if not both – though in this case it is interesting to note that the seer does indeed admit that he will have *had* forebears, thus confirming our earlier suggestion that the 'Antichrist' concept is not used by Nostradamus in any exclusive sense.

V.54   *From Black Sea's shores and greater Tartary*
            To see fair France a monarch westward goes.
            Alania and Armenia lanced, shall he
            On Istanbul his bloody rod impose.

The seer now goes into greater detail. The dreaded Central or Western Asian warlord ('Tartary' refers to the former Mongol Empire, which covered the area roughly corresponding to the modern Turkestan – i.e. most of Central Asia) will set out on an invasion, first of the Caucasus, then of Turkey, and eventually of Western Europe.

II.29   *Forth from his seat the Oriental goes,*
            Crossing the Apennines fair France to see.
            He'll pierce the sky, traverse the seas and snows
            And strike all with his rod, whoe'er they be.

Though often identified with the late Ayatollah Khomeini of Iran (whose details certainly fit to some extent), this quatrain – in effect, yet another summary verse – is clearly the 'pair' of the stanza just quoted. The invading Middle Eastern leader will apparently have land, sea and *air forces* at his disposal in his quest to invade Europe, overrun Italy and eventually devastate France itself. Brind'Amour[9] suggests a link with Attila the Hun: my own feeling is that the original reference is more likely to be with the expanding Ottoman Empire of Nostradamus's day.

VI.55*   *Diving for sponges, chief in noonday sun*
Suddenly sees the Arab fleet sail past.
Tripolis, Chios, Trebizond o'errun;
The Black Sea city wasted, chief held fast.

The invasion commences. A Muslim fleet suddenly appears in
the Black Sea, apparently taking everybody by surprise, and
not least the Turks. The first that Trabzon's local overlord
knows of the invasion is when he sees it with his own eyes.
'Tripolis' and 'Chios' seem sufficiently 'out of area' to be, in
reality, reworked versions of the Black Sea coastal towns of
Tireboli and Sochi. Printers at the time were notorious for
their garbling of place names with which they were unfamiliar.

V.27   *From out that part of Persia that shall lie*
Nearest the Black Sea, Trebizond he'll take
And Arab blood the Adriatic dye
Full red: Paros and sunny Lesbos quake.

With Trabzon overcome, Muslim naval task-forces are soon
threatening the Greek islands and the waters between Greece
and Italy, where they are destined to run into stiff opposition
(the original French word *Pharos* almost certainly refers not
to Alexandria's former lighthouse-island, but to the island of
Paros in the Cyclades). Nostradamus's use of the word 'Arab'
may at first sight seem rather puzzling. As subsequent
quatrains reveal, however, this is merely one of a number of
alternative names that Nostradamus continually applies to
the coming invaders – partly because (as we shall see) he has
good reason for identifying them as Muslims, and partly
because one wing of the invasion force will eventually swing
westwards via North Africa.

V.86*   By *two capes and three sea-arms* **1998/2011/2032**
            separate,
         The city they from seaward sorely
            fret:
         Its leaders having left it to its fate,
         Stamboul by Persian blue-head is
            beset.

As the Turks hurriedly retreat, the clearly-identified Istanbul
is inevitably the next major prize. Extrapolating astrologically
from the Turkish sack of Constantinople in 1453, my original
calculation for the date of this new siege of the city was 1998,
but happily this failed to occur. The next theoretical dating
works out at either early June 2011 or mid-June 2032 – but,
thanks to what might be described as 'astrological time-lag',
the actual start of the attack may be set to occur some time
after any or all of the three possible dates listed.

I.40*   *False spoutings that shall madness' face disguise*
         In Istanbul shall bring new powers to reign.
         From Egypt a reformer shall arise
         New laws on currency to scrap again.

The eventual fall of Istanbul and the rise of a new regime in
Egypt could together serve as a useful warning to us that
things are about to stir into motion on a wider front.
Brind'Amour[9] refers the verse back to the release of the
crusading King Louis IX (Saint Louis) from Muslim captivity
in Egypt in 1254, and his 1263 edict regulating alloys and
precious metals.

Letter to Henri II*   1999/2011

> ... *the great Empire of the Antichrist shall arise in the Atila,ᵃ and [the forces of] Xerxes shall descend in great and innumerable numbers, such that the manifestation of the Holy Spirit emanating from the 48thᵇ degree of latitude shall spread abroad, persecuting and making war against the kingly one who is the great Vicar of Jesus Christ and against His Church ...*

In plain prose, the seer now finally identifies the coming invasion as none other than the war of the future Antichrist. He will emerge (he suggests) like another Xerxes with his vast hordes from the north-western province of Iran to lead the forces of Islam in a devastating crusade against Western Christendom and the papacy in particular. Extrapolating from the astrology of Xerxes' original campaign, the last likely date for this final, overwhelming attack on European Turkey was January 1999, and the next will be late August and early September 2011.

III.60   *Crowds are condemned to death all over Turkey,*
              E'en to the utmost south-west of the nation.
              Of a young black guilty of doings murky
              He'll shed the blood, as in propitiation.

ᵃ The original edition's *la Atila* is almost certainly a misprint for *la Arda* – i.e. the province of Ardalan in north-western Iran. Printers at the time were, as we have seen, notoriously unreliable when it came to setting unfamiliar place names from manuscript.
ᵇ This, too, seems to be a misprint, since 48° (roughly the latitude of Paris) makes little sense here. Reynaud-Plense[51] more reasonably substitutes '24th degree' (the latitude of Medina in Saudi Arabia, the founding city of Islam), though it is not clear which edition he bases this on.

This verse is undated, but may suggest that in Turkish Anatolia widespread and brutal repression will soon be in full swing. The original text specifically mentions the former south-western regions of Mysia, Lycia and Pamphilia.

VIII.96*   *The sterile, fruitless synagogue shall close,*
          The infidels take all under their sway,
          While Babel's daughter clips the wings of those
          Who, sad and wretched, try to flee away.

Soon, the invasion will reach Israel, which will in due course succumb as its inhabitants flee.

V.96   *At the world's centre rules the mighty rose,*
          For new designs with state blood profligate.
          If truth were told, t'were best one's mouth to close,
          Even if what's to come must needs come late.

The oriental invaders (here symbolised, not for the first time, by the rose) duly enter Palestine, and specifically Jerusalem, traditionally regarded as standing at the world's centre. The verse is presumably based on the historical expansion of the former Ottoman Empire. Within Islam the rose is, among other things, a prime symbol for the blood of Iranian Shi'ite martyrs. Etymologically, the word 'rose' is also cognate with 'Rhodes'. Nostradamus's reaction is to suggest that the less said, the better. Within the occupied lands at least, resistance will not be an issue, still less public unrest. Those aching for change will simply have to wait for their salvation to come from somewhere or someone 'out there'.

Presage 40 *Seven kings in turn death's deadly hand shall
smite,
Hail, tempest, plague and furious desecrators:
The Eastern King shall put the West to flight
And subjugate his former subjugators.*

The theme continues. Seven successive administrations
(presumably of France – compare IV.50, p. 269) will be
plagued by invaders from a part of the orient that was
formerly colonised – or at very least subjugated – by the
West. *Presage* 40 was originally for June 1559, but the tradition of re-applying the *Presages* to events in the more distant
future was started by none other than the seer's own secretary
Chavigny. Under the terms of the 'Janus hypothesis', of
course, he was presumably entitled to. However, there is no
obvious planetary match for June 1559 in the near future –
not that this need be seen as too significant, since it is doubt-
ful whether Nostradamus used comparative horoscopy for his
Almanachs and *Presages* in the first place.

II.39 *A year before war comes to Italy,
French, Germans, Spaniards shall think might is
right.
When falls their infantile republic, see
How right is mostly choked to death by might.*

With large-scale war now in the offing, foreign might seems
destined to overwhelm some kind of administrative commu-
nity recently cobbled together by the three rather over-
confident powers mentioned – 'the schoolhouse republic',
Nostradamus calls it. This naturally begs tentative identification with the present European Union. Evidently, then, the
conflict is likely to involve a good many more countries than

merely France and Italy. (I have to confess, however, that the play on the expression 'might is right' is my invention, not Nostradamus's!)

XII.55*   *Law shall by gloomy counsels be betrayed:*
Traitors' and fleecers' follies shall advise,
The fretful folk be wild and restive made,
And towns and citadels shall peace despise.

In particular, a general breakdown of morale and public standards seems to be indicated, thanks partly to incompetent political leadership. Nostradamus will return to the theme again and again. However, he may never have intended this particular verse to be published. The various 'extra quatrains' first published in 1605 for *Centuries* VII, VIII, XI and XII look suspiciously like discarded drafts that Chavigny had found lying around after his master's death, not least because some of their numbers duplicate the previously published ones.

I.53*   *Behold, alas, a mighty race sore tried*
And Holy Law cast down and undermined!
O'er Christendom shall other laws preside
Once gold and silver they shall newly find.

Thus it is that the newly-financed oriental campaign against the nominally Christian West can resume its onward march. The 'great race' is unidentified, but it could be Israel, France or even Western Europe as a whole. Prévost[49] points out that the original reference is no doubt to the year 1524, a significant one in Cortés's treasure-seeking expedition to Central America.

XII.36   *In Cyprus they the fierce assault prepare*
(Weep now your coming ruin, ere you falter!).
Arabs and Turks the evil deed shall share
'Twixt separate fleets: huge ruin via Gibraltar.

In this further supplementary quatrain the scene is now set for
the ensuing action. Evidently the Eastern power is destined to
make Cyprus its main base for what looks like a mass invasion of Europe, split into a northern and a southern wing –
the latter, swinging through North Africa, being of a particularly brutal and violent kind.

IX.97*   *The naval force in three parts they'll disband,*
The second lack wherewith themselves to feed
As, desperate, they seek their Promised Land.
The first to fight in battle shall succeed.

In fact the split appears to be a three-way one. Nostradamus
seems to indicate that a prime motivation for the invasion will
be understandable Third World envy of Western Europe's
relatively rich lifestyle, much as a variety of modern psychics
also suggest.[33]

III.27   *A Libyan leader in the West ascendant*
Shall make the French against Islam irate,
To literary scholars condescendent
Who into French the Arabic translate.

In an effort to defuse the increasingly threatening situation,
someone who looks remarkably like the present Muammar

al-Gaddafi will attempt to bypass the official interpreters and take upon himself the responsibility for representing Arab intentions to the Western world. Evidently, he merely succeeds in stirring the pot.

Sixain 29*   *Let Griffon now himself prepare*   **1999+**
                To fight the foemen everywhere,
                And let his army strengthened be,
                Or else the Elephant shall him
                Surprise with sudden force and grim.
                Six hundred seven burns the sea.

This warning *Sixain* (surprisingly written in lines of eight syllables instead of the usual ten) seems likewise to refer to 1607 by Nostradamus's 'liturgical count', and thus to the year 1999 – the omission of the initial thousand being perfectly normal practice at the time. Of special note is his use of the term 'Elephant' to refer to the invaders, and of 'Griffon' as a suitably composite symbol for the combined Western allies. The fact that the last line failed to happen in 1999 could possibly suggest that the West providentially took the right measures just in time, as proposed by the first part of the verse.

II.84   *From Naples north as far as Florence falls*
          No drop of rain for six months and nine days.
          An alien tongue across Dalmatia calls
          Ere running on, the land entire to raze.

Nostradamus now starts to give us what appear to be the first details of the route of the mooted invasion. Possibly the first line – which in the original actually specifies Campania, Siena, Florence and Tuscany – is intended to serve as a kind of meteorological warning of things to come. It is after the temporary drought that alien forces will enter Dalmatia on the former Yugoslavian west coast, prior to over-running the whole country. Whether Nostradamus intends this to mean Yugoslavia or Italy is not at this point made clear.

IX.60   *Muslims at war, all clad in headdress black:*
        'Midst bloodshed shall the great Dalmatia quake.
        The mighty Arabs press home their attack:
        When Lisbon helps, though, all their tongues shall
           shake.

No doubt the original reference of this verse is to the Ottoman invasions of the seer's own day. For the future, there seems to be some kind of Western European support for the former Yugoslavian forces as they fight a desperate rearguard action. Evidently, this is enough to cause some agitated discussion among the invaders. The word 'ranes' (from Latin *rana*, 'frog') in the last line poses all kinds of difficulties for the commentators, though. Why, after all, should the *frogs* shake – other than to make it possible for Nostradamus to get up to a favourite trick of his, namely to repeat an idea from the first half of his verse (in this case, that of trembling) in the second half as well? The answer lies in Nostradamus's own *curriculum vitae*. He was, after all, an apothecary (if not a doctor) of long experience. He was thus fully aware that the word's diminutive form *ranula* ('little frog') refers to a 'ranine' cyst – i.e. one on the underside of the tongue. Hence, his word *rane* inevitably means 'strange tongue' in the most literal sense – the same 'strange tongue', presumably, that he has just referred to in II.84 above. Clearly Nostradamus had a healthy, if wry, sense of humour.

II.32   *Milk, blood, strange tongues over Dalmatia,*
Contagion near Balennes, and joined the fight,
Great is the cry throughout Slavonia
When first Ravenna's monster sees the light.

Nostradamus now takes his grim joke one stage further. In line one of this stanza he actually refers to the alien tongues via the word *grenoilles* ('frogs') – so fooling generations of interpreters into assuming that he is predicting something akin to the biblical plagues of Egypt – though no doubt he is quite happy to give that impression too. The rest, however, is no joking matter. True, there do seem to be strange (but by no means unknown) meteorological phenomena along the Yugoslavian coast at the time – unless, of course, they really indicate something much more sinister – but the main point is that war now spreads to the north of the former federation, apparently connected with some kind of 'monster' that first arises in Ravenna, northern Italy. According to both Brind'Amour[9] and Prévost,[49] the historical back-reference is to the celebrated monster that was born in Ravenna in 1512: the infant was androgynous, had no arms, but did have wings, a single foot like that of a bird of prey, a horn on its head and an eye on its knee – to say nothing of a letter 'Y' and a cross on its chest. Such things were always regarded as omens (in fact, this was the original Latin meaning of the word *monstrum*), and Nostradamus typically uses them as indications that the rest of the events predicted in the verse in question are about to happen. 'Balennes' seems to be the classical Trebula Balliensis, which lies in central Italy, near Capua.

IX.30   *On blessed Nicholas' and Pula's shore*
In Kvarner's Gulf shall northern fighters die.
The chief the Muslims' pillage shall deplore.
Cadiz and the Philippian stand by.

As the fighting spreads northwards, the retreating defenders are driven into the sea near the former Yugoslav port of Puli, not far from the Italian border, possibly as a result of being trapped on the Istra peninsula. Spain, and possibly Greece, offer what help they can.

III.75   *Vicenza, Saragossa, Verona, Po –*
Sword-free, yet soaked with blood their countries
    are
When mighty shells shall pestilences sow.
Help's near at hand, yet remedies afar.

The assault continues in Lombardy, while once again the nearby allies fail to intervene. The surprise appearance of *Sarragousse* at the end of the original list of places affected suggests that Nostradamus may have misread his original notes, or indeed that it may be a late replacement, possibly for Saronno, inserted so as to rhyme with *gousse* in line three. Certainly his need to rhyme often interferes with the sense and makes the last word of a line somewhat suspect.

VIII.11   *A people numberless invades Vicenza –*
Though not by force – basilica aglow.
Near to Lugano falls he from Valenza,
While Venice from the sea shall face the foe.

98

Interestingly enough, Nostradamus reveals that the invasion will not always involve fighting. Sometimes the incoming hordes will simply be allowed to enter the towns and cities unopposed. Elsewhere, though, the defence will be fierce. One commander is forced to retreat from Valenza (which lies in the middle of the triangle formed by Turin, Milan and Genoa) into the mountains, where he is duly defeated on the route

The invasion of Italy

north between lakes Maggiore and Como. Meanwhile, in the Adriatic, Venice is still resisting. Prévost[49] detects a back-reference to the accidental burning of Vicenza's basilica and the contemporary military activities of 1502.

III.11*   *Long time aloft the sky shall battle chase,*
           Once at the city's heart shall fall the tree.
           Vermin at large, war, torch applied to face,
           Venice's lord shall then death's victim be.

Resistance eventually collapses, however, under the pressure of prolonged air-attacks – though Prévost[49] refers this verse back merely to the accidental burning of King François's face and the death of Pope Leo X in 1521. The possibility cannot be written off, though, that Nostradamus, having put his chosen historical events into verse, might have seen further prophetic possibilities in the words as they actually turned out, much as his own secretary Chavigny did, and as later commentators have similarly been prone to do. Indeed, as we have already seen in connection with verse I.35 (Chapter 3), we have actual written evidence of his having done so.

II.33   *As by Verona's torrent, rushing on*
          Towards where great Po's deltaic courses end,
          Mighty disaster strikes, so on Garonne
          When force Genoan shall on them descend.

The hordes draw ever nearer. There is to be great loss of life on the river Adige, which flows into the Adriatic just north of the Po. Evidently, the invaders are sweeping in from the north-east and about to spread out over the Plain of

Lombardy. There can thus no longer be any question of the text's referring to the former Ottoman invasion: the back-reference has to be to an earlier invasion entirely, such as that of the ancient Lombards. The text's use of the word *naufrage* ('shipwreck') suggests that there will be great loss of men and materials in the waters of the river Adige itself. Meanwhile, the considerable extent of the expected conflict is starting to become clear: Nostradamus expects virtually the same scenario to be repeated later on around the river Garonne, in south-western France, when forces from the area of Genoa cross that river in turn. This does not necessarily make them Italian, however: as we shall see, Nostradamus constantly names invading armies after the territories they are currently occupying. There can be little doubt, in other words, that it is the self-same Asiatic invasion force, by then in control of north-western Italy, that will eventually be responsible for the later French disaster, too.

II.94   *Great Po for France great woes endures, alas!*
       The mighty Lion at sea no terrors bind.
       A race unnumbered shall the ocean pass.
       A quarter-million no escape shall find.

An immense conflict now ensues on the banks of the river Po, which is seemingly being used as Lombardy's last major line of defence. The invaders are being reinforced all the time by sea in massive numbers. The original 'lion' reference is presumably to Venice, but for our own day it might be interpreted in terms of Britain. If so, then only the British, restricting their participation to naval operations, remain relatively secure.

I.9   *From Orient Afric hearts a passage beat*
To th' Adriatic, Italy to try,
Accompanied by all the Libyan fleet:
Emptied each Maltese church, each isle nearby.

Nostradamus now suggests that the coming Asiatic invasion will have a sea-borne component, too, based somewhere in north Africa. The back-reference is clearly to the Carthaginian Hannibal's assault on ancient Rome, but a more recent one seems to be to the pirate Dragut, commander of the Turkish fleet, who attacked Malta in 1551. Naturally, the Mediterranean islands will be among the first territories to be affected, offering as they do a convenient jumping-off point for further operations against southern Europe. Meanwhile, the enemy's naval activities in the Adriatic are likewise confirmed. From the quotation at the head of this chapter one gains the impression that the Asiatic invaders will have purchased a large number of surplus ships from their northern neighbours Russia and/or the Ukraine, the inheritors of most of the armaments of the former Soviet Union.

VIII.84* *In Sicily Paterno's cry ascends:*
Trieste's Gulf's with armaments replete.
As far as Sicily war soon extends.
Flee, flee the plague of ships, the ghastly fleet!

The mighty task-force duly descends on Sicily, while battle rages throughout the Adriatic.

IV.48*   *On Latin plains so fertile and so wide*
So many flies and locusts shall have bred
That the sun's light shall all but be denied
And, eating all, great pestilence they'll spread.

Generally speaking, Nostradamus's quatrains can be interpreted surprisingly literally. In the present case, however, he
seems to be talking about something a good deal more
disturbing than mere locusts (even though Prévost[49] suggests
that the original event was indeed a huge plague of grasshoppers that descended on the Milan area in 1542): after all, in
V.85 (p. 205) he has them attacking the Swiss as well – whose
land is hardly locust-country at the best of times, even allowing for the fact that in the present case he merely refers to the
insects as *sauterelles* ('grasshoppers'). Possibly the clairaudient Nostradamus has somehow managed to 'hear' the oriental
invaders described as 'swarming like locusts' across the plain
of Lombardy and has then – not for the first time – translated
the expression into an actual, visual image. The last line, similarly, could have resulted from his having 'heard' the
expression 'plagues of locusts': on the other hand, in the light
of the foregoing quatrain it is just possible that this time he
means what he says, and that as the invaders spread out,
ravaging the country's food supplies as they advance, some
kind of disease epidemic will indeed break out in their wake.
However, the much less exciting possibility of *real* locusts or
grasshoppers cannot, of course, be entirely ruled out either.

III.33   *When in the city's heart the wolf shall call*
The enemy shall then be close at hand.
Friends, too, at hand upon the Alpine wall
As alien armies devastate the land.

Here Nostradamus seems to be referring to one of the far

northern Italian cities such as Verona, Milan or Turin. The impression is given that, although Italy's allies are watching from the borders, they will decline to intervene. If the reference to wolves is to be taken literally, it is perhaps worth noting that wolves tend to move into towns in search of food mainly during the winter – a fact which could help date the events in question. The back reference is evidently to one of numerous cases when wolves are recorded as having entered towns in Roman times – but, as usual, if Nostradamus knows the date of his 'original event' and used it as a basis for his calculations, he is not about to tell us! For us to date the event is therefore virtually impossible.

IV.66   *Secret explorers under colours fickle*
Shall be sent forth by seven with shaven pates.
In wells and fountains they shall poison trickle.
Man shall eat man within Genoa's gates.

The shaven-headed overlords are unidentified. Evidently, though, they do not care over-much what measures they use to achieve their nefarious ends, as long as they are effective: Genoa is both poisoned and starved.

Presage 31 *Up stormy Danube Muslim vessels fare.*
At sea, troop-carrying ships off Sicily.
Florence reduced, Siena passed, the pair
Of chiefs whom friendship joined soon dead shall
be.

The invaders are appearing on the horizon in increasing numbers – and not merely on land (both in Italy and further east), but on the sea, too. Nostradamus specifically refers to them, both here and elsewhere, as *Barbares* – a term which means not merely 'uncivilised', but 'Arab' (Barbarie was a traditional name for Arab North Africa by association with the Berbers) and thus (for the Judaeo-Christian Nostradamus at least) 'Muslim', 'infidel' or simply 'heathen'. As we have already started to see, there are good reasons for assuming that 'Muslims' is the correct interpretation. The word *deux* in the last line theoretically means 'two', but Nostradamus also habitually uses it as if it were a version of Latin *dux/duces* ('leaders'). My translation therefore reflects both possibilities.

IX.94* *The weak shall rush alliances to make.*
Treacherous foes shall scale the strongest wall.
Attacked and weakened, Bratislavans quake:
Lübeck and Meissen for the Muslims call.

As the invaders move further up the Danube, there are some voices, from the formerly Communist East Germany and its borders, who actually support them.

V.47 *The mighty Arab ever onward goes,*
Yet is betrayed by Turks behind his back.
Then antique Rhodes confronts him, while worse woes
Follow the stern Hungarian's attack.

The invaders will not have it all their own way, however. Even while the European campaign is in progress, there will be troubles at home. The island of Rhodes will refuse to lie down, while the Hungarians will apparently manage to push the Asiatic forces back – or perhaps at least to restrict them to the area south and west of the Danube.

V.48   *After the setback to their rulership*
Two enemies before their forces fall.
To Hungary comes ship on Afric ship.
By land and sea shall dreadful things befall.

The Asiatics are not about to give up, however, as this direct successor to V.47 reveals. The Hungarian campaign is redoubled – though their 'two enemies' are not specified. Possibly they are Italy and France once again. At the same time there is no question of an Asiatic walk-over.

II.96   *A flaming torch aloft the evening sky*
Near to the head and source of mighty Rhône.
Famine and war: too late relief comes by.
The Persian turns his troops on Macedon.

A further spearhead now thrusts southward from the former Yugoslavia into northern Greece. Perhaps taking the David-and-Goliath situation of the ancient Graeco-Persian wars as his symbolic precedent, Nostradamus here describes the invaders as *la Perse* – thus at the same time living up to his normal practice of naming them after the countries that they are currently occupying. A comet or meteorite over Switzerland marks the event.

V.90*   *Larisa, Corinth and the Cyclades*
With death and plague by traitors are infected,
Along with Sparta and Peloponnese –
Nine months the whole peninsula affected.

The after-effects of war are now taking their usual toll in Greece. Fortunately, Cheetham's celebrated 'false dust' mistranslation of *faux connisse*[11,13] can be safely disregarded.

IX.91*   *Pestilence Corinth and Nicopolis*
Shall sweep, all Macedonia and western Greece –
Thessaly, too, besides Amfipolis –
Unknown in type. All social life shall cease.

In the aftermath of the invasion, most of Greece is infected with some previously unencountered form of disease epidemic. Nicopolis is now known as Preveza. The last sentence is my interpretation of the French *le refus d'Anthoine*, which I take to refer to the fourth-century St Anthony of Thebes' celebrated withdrawal from society.

IX.44   *Flee! Flee Geneva, each and every one!*
Saturn shall pure gold into iron change.
Land of the rose wipes father out and son.
Before th' assault shall signs the sky derange.

As ever, there are warning signs, and consequently there is always an extent to which we are ourselves responsible for what happens to us. As we shall see, Nostradamus never tires of rubbing the point home. At the same time, he refers here to the symbolic 'rose' mentioned in V.96 (page 91), this time making great play of the invaders' pinkness or even redness via the capitalised anagram *RAYPOZ* ('pays rose'). As we shall see later, the colour red will become a standardised feature of his description of them – though to assume on this basis (as many commentators do) that they are therefore necessarily communists is perhaps to jump rather too hastily to conclusions. The word could simply describe their aggressive nature.

I.61* *Hapless and sad shall the republic pine*
     When the new overlord shall ruin it.
     Their mighty horde, by exile made malign,
     Shall force the Swiss their principles to quit.

As the envious invaders continue to devastate Switzerland, the Swiss are at last forced to abandon their age-old principle of neutrality, which dates from the time of François I.

II.100 *Among the isles so dread a tumult roars*
     That nought is heard save murmurs of defiance:
     So great the onslaught of the predators
     That all shall rush to join the grand alliance.

Unless, once again, this is merely a reference to the attempted Ottoman invasions of the fifteenth and sixteenth centuries (which never in fact succeeded in taking over the islands of the western Mediterranean) the picture is of a gathering storm of invasion in the area which will prompt all those concerned to form defensive alliances – and not before time.

II.43   *When into view shall swim the bearded star*   **2001**
         The three great lords shall comrades be
           no more.
         Peace from the sky is shattered, earth a-jar;
         Po, Tiber seethe; snake washed up on the
           shore.

The approach of a comet is accompanied by discord and war, especially in Italy. The original three great *princes*, as the French puts it, seem to have been Mark Antony, Octavian and Lepidus, the warring successors of Julius Caesar, with comet, earthquakes and snakes all reported in the annals – even if, as Brind'Amour[9] points out, the destruction by lightning of Rome's Temple of Peace seems not to have been specifically recorded at the time. Prévost,[49] for his part, prefers to identify historical echoes of the sixteenth-century conflict between Henry VIII, Charles V and François I, with the comet, thunderstorms, earthquake, flooding of the Tiber and washing up of a monster – allegedly half-fish and half-human – on the Ripa Major in Rome in November 1523 all duly reported. On the basis of comparative horoscopy, this might indicate a possible repetition in November/December 2001.

For the future, certainly, later stanzas will suggest that the 'three princes' are the leaders of the three main wings of the oriental invasion, who are now about to fall out and go their separate ways, as though from now on in competition with one another. The *serpent* that is cast up on the shore (the French uses the singular rather than the plural) could then possibly refer back to the 'coiled serpent' of V.25 (page 62) – apparently a symbol for the oriental invader. Whatever it means, some kind of insinuation of newcomers into Italy by unexpected means is apparently hinted at, possibly via Albania (*see* V.46 on page 144).

III.21*   *Where Conca's waters to the Adria race*
There shall appear a fish of fearful look
With fishy tail and yet a human face
That lands itself with neither net nor hook.

More details of the landing seem to follow. The 'fish' –
conceivably an amphibious craft recognisably conned by a
human being – lands at Cattólica, between Rimini and
Ancona on the Adriatic coast. However, the original was
much less technological. As both Brind'Amour[9] and Prévost[49]
report, it was a real sea-monster washed up on the Illyrian
coast in 1523. Its fate was to be stoned to death.

I.29   *When fish aquatic and terrestrial*
Through mighty waves shall land upon the beach
In form horrific, sleek, fantastical,
The seaborne foes the wall shall shortly reach.

Numerous modern commentators have interpreted this verse
in terms of the massive 'D-Day' invasion of Normandy in
1945, in part using inflatables. However, if so, Nostradamus
once again seems to have got one of the details back to front
in describing the liberating invaders as 'foes' when they are
supposed to have been friends – which may well suggest that
the quatrain really refers to some other occasion entirely,
even though the term 'wall' seems oddly reminiscent of the
Germans' term for their massive coastal defences around the
French coast (the 'Atlantic Wall'). The original may well have
been the self-same monster referred to in III.21 above, in
which case line four may not be the result of the other three
lines at all, but merely the event for which they serve as an
'omen'.

II.5   *From out a fish where papers, arms are stowed*
Shall one shall emerge who then shall go to war.
Across the sea he shall his fleet have rowed
At length to appear off the Italian shore.

Possibly this quatrain encourages the 'technological' reading, however. It seems to suggest that at least one submarine is involved in the landing – if not of the invading forces as such, then at least of their high command. In line three, Nostradamus indicates that he does not actually expect the fleet to come in under sail, yet is certainly at a loss to understand how his self-propelled fleet could possibly cross the sea other than under oars. As ever the picture is observed, in other words, through sixteenth-century eyes. However, Brind'Amour, substituting *prison* for *poisson* in line one (such misprints and misreadings of Nostradamus's fairly illegible writing are not unknown!) suggests a simple reference to the release from prison of the Baron de la Garde, Admiral of France's Eastern Fleet and a known friend of Nostradamus. But then even the reading *poison* is not impossible – in which case line one would read more like:

When letter poisoned dagger has bestowed...

Nostradamus, after all, was quite keen on the theme of poison hidden within the folds of letters!

V.62   *Blood falls like rain the very rocks upon:*
Sun rising, Saturn o'er the western lands.
Great evil seen in Rome, war near Orgon,
Ships sunk, and Trento's hills in hostile hands.

Following a dawn assault by sea, this further summary of the

111

more immediately forthcoming events confirms that the eastern invasion is destined to spread first into Italy and then into south-eastern France, where the invaders will soon start to make inroads into the eastern fringes of the Rhône delta. The town of Orgon is an important administrative centre just north of Salon, impressively commanding the Durance pass between the Alpilles and the Lubéron.

VII.6   *Palermo, Sicily and Naples are*
Alike inhabited by heathen force.
Salerno, Corsica, Sardinia –
Death, plague and war (some think) have run their
course.

As already foreshadowed, the Mediterranean islands are soon engulfed at the start of what promises (despite the eternal optimists) to be a long drawn-out struggle. The southern cities are not slow to follow.

VI.10   *Awhile shall all the Christian churches stay*
Commingled with the colours black and white.
Reds, yellows then their flocks shall steal away:
Blood, fire, fear, plague, hunger and water white.

Nostradamus now looks ahead to what is awaiting European Christendom. Prévost[49] traces back the phrase 'black and white' to a diary entry by Louise of Savoy, regent during the imprisonment of François I in Spain, in which she applies these terms to the various breeds of Lutheran 'heretic' who had been troubling the kingdom since 1522. But Nostradamus then goes on to have fun with other colours, too. The 'reds and yellows' (the colours of the duchy of Ferrara, perhaps?) seem to refer to the fact that this was where some of the French Protestants took refuge in 1534. But who knows what future troubles this might also indicate?

VI.20
The holy union shall not long survive.
Of those who change most shall change back again.
In vessels then a hard race shall arrive
When over Rome a new lion comes to reign.

This evident recapitulation of the events surrounding the formation of the Holy League of 1537 between Pope Paul III, Venice and Charles V against the Ottomans[49] seems *à propos* – always assuming that the French *faincte* is a misprint for *ʃaincte*, as sometimes happens. The 'new lion' seems to refer to a new Pope.

X.3
After five years he'll fail his flock to feed.
A fugitive he'll free for Poland's sake.
Of help false rumours here and there shall speed,
Until the pastor shall his see forsake.

This quatrain seems to continue where the previous stanza left off. It seems likely that the term *chef* in the last line refers to the reigning Pope – in which case this verse would confirm very satisfactorily the proposed interpretation of V.92 (*see* Chapter 3). Almost at the end of his new, five-year-term the present pontiff is forced for some reason to relinquish his duties – possibly as a result of the growing eastern influx. Some kind of international difficulties ensue, which are only resolved when he finally leaves Rome.

VI.25   *Mars shall afflict the sacred monarchy:*
         In trouble ruinous great Peter's barque.
         A dark young red shall seize the hierarchy.
         Traitors shall act 'neath rain-clouds dank and
         dark.

The war has its expected dire effects on Rome and its Church. As we have already seen, Nostradamus constantly associates the invaders with the colour red – a possible indication of their aggressive nature. He also repeatedly refers to *bruine* ('drizzle') in connection with the various assaults, in a way which suggests some sinister connotation. The possibility of chemical or even biological attacks can therefore not be ruled out. The word *hierarchie* is one of Nostradamus's favourite words for ruling Church circles, especially in Rome. Its 'proper' meaning (and Nostradamus and his educated contemporaries were very prone to use words with their original Latin meanings) is, after all, 'priestly rule'.

VI.96*   *The city is abandoned to the hordes:*
         Never was mortal tumult closer by.
         Save one offence that clamours to the sky
         What dread disaster moves the town towards!

Thus it is that Rome is destined to be abandoned not merely by its people, but (as we shall see) by the Pope as well. The fact that this verse has an unusual rhyme-scheme probably has no significance other than that Nostradamus found it more convenient at the time.

114

I.11   *The way in which minds, hearts, feet, hands all tend*
Is one in Naples, Leon, Sicily.
Sword, fire and water on Rome's lords descend:
Killed, drowned and dead through addled idiocy.

Throughout the conflict, suggests Nostradamus, it will be the same old story over and over again. In the face of the Asiatic threat, what is likely to pose the chief danger is not the enemy, nor even betrayal and sedition, but the Europeans' own apathy and incompetence. The message, in other words, seems to be that the eventual outcome, far from being predestined, is at least partly in our own hands. Fatalism – unsurprisingly – is merely likely to prove fatal. The word *Leon.* (in one copy of the first edition followed by a dot indicating an abbreviation) probably stands for *Leontini*, now Lentini, between Catania and Syracuse.

Presage 83* *Leaders hold talks while Christendom is shaken:*
By alien hordes the Holy Seat's attacked,
Their advent first as ill, then lethal taken.
From th' East death, plague, famine and evil
pact.

Nostradamus belabours the point further in the telegrammatic style for which the *Presages* (in this case, originally for April 1563) are so notable. Words will be substituted for deeds, lethal threats played down and paper agreements misused to disguise dire political and military crises.

II.41   *Seven days the mighty star burns on its way –*
             A cloudy star, like two suns in the sky.
             The whole night shall the burly watchdog bay
             When the great Pontiff shall his country fly.

Virtually all these details are taken from the account by Julius
Obsequens of events following the assassination of Julius
Caesar in 44 BC[9] – not merely the comet and the *parhelion*
(the appearance of multiple 'mock suns' due to ice-crystals in
the solar halo), but the howling of dogs in front of the resi-
dence of Lepidus, one of the late dictator's immediate
successors. Similar phenomena were reported in France in
1527[49] and in Germany in 1554.[9] However, the expression *el
gros mastin* in line three was also used at the time for
Cerberus, the three-headed canine guardian of the
Underworld, so Nostradamus was clearly not averse to giving
the event's future repetition something of an end-of-the-world
flavour too!

VIII.99   *By power of the three kings temporal*
              The Holy Seat shall elsewhere be removed,
              Where spirit's seat and substance corporal
              May be restored and for its truth approved.

Prévost[49] traces this verse back to the transfer of the Church's
General Council to Trent in 1545, culminating in 1563 with
the affirmation of the 'corporal' presence of Christ in the
Eucharist. In terms of the future, however, it could suggest
that the Pope in power at the time of the oriental invasion
will be forced to leave the Vatican, in his case by an alliance
of three secular leaders. As we shall see later, this seems to
refer to the three heads of what is evidently the Asiatic
confederacy itself.

V.75   *High in the property, rightward some way,*
Upon the square-shaped stone he'll sit and look
Beside the window at around midday,
His mouth clamped shut, holding his twisted crook.

Prévost[49] traces this picture back to the inauguration of the mythical King Numa in around 715 BC, almost at the very start of Roman history, as deliberately recapitulated by the Emperor Charles V both in Bologna in 1529 and on his triumphal entry into Rome in 1536. Yet the phrase *sur la pierre carree* in line two is also, by a possibly unconscious play on words on Nostradamus's part, oddly reminiscent of 'St Peter's Square' – in which case the picture here could be of the Pope at the window of his apartments at the time of his traditional Sunday noon blessing of the pilgrims below. In this case, though, two points are worthy of note. The first is that he is sitting, rather than (as is traditionally the case) standing – which might suggest that he is either ill or a very old man. The other is what Nostradamus actually calls his 'twisted staff' (oddly reminiscent of the present Pope's crucifix-staff, with its curiously distorted upper end): its presence possibly suggests that the Pontiff is about to embark on some pastoral journey. Seen in the present context, then, the image is a moving one. It is of the old man appearing at his window for the last time before going into exile, and casting a final, wordless look on the beloved city over which he has ruled for so long.

IX.99   *The north wind shall the see oblige to quit,*
As red-hot ash and dust blow o'er the walls.
Through rain thereafter (much harm comes from it)
Their last hope lies towards where the frontier calls.

Most commentators suggest that this quatrain refers to Napoleon's retreat from Moscow in 1812. If it applies here, however, it indicates that, as the invaders close in and parts of Rome are already aflame, the Pope and his staff will hastily set out for the French border. As in VI.25 (page 114), the 'rain' may or may not be natural.

X.91*   O Roman clergy, in 1609,   **2001**
          At the year's turn you shall election make:
          Campanian he, who'll grey and black combine.
          Never worse fiend; never more grave mistake!

At this point an acting Pope has to be elected, and Nostradamus seems to devote a whole flurry of predictions to him. Once again, the seer uses his 'ecclesiastical count', apparently based on the Roman Empire's exclusive adoption of Christianity as its state religion in AD 392, to date the crucial election. It will, he suggests, take place at the beginning of 2001. Oddly, none of the lines of the original French rhyme.

VII.23   *The royal sceptre he'll be forced to take,*
          As those before him had engaged to do,
          Since with the ring poor contact they shall make
          When to the palace comes that plundering crew.

At this point, with the Vatican no longer occupied by the reigning pontiff, and the latter not even contactable any more, somebody has to take over the administration of the Church pending the arrival of the invaders. It looks as if the task falls to one of the senior cardinals.

VI.24   *When Mars and Jupiter are in conjunction,*   **2002**
'Neath Cancer ghastly war shall be at hand.
Later a priest anoints with royal unction
A king who brings long peace to all the land.

Here we seem to have the two halves of a quatrain applying to events widely spread in time. Mars and Jupiter are next in conjunction, while the sun is in Cancer, at midsummer 2002. Nobody should be fooled, however, by Nostradamus's use of the phrase *un peu apres* at the start of line three: the projected coronation of a royal saviour-figure is destined to occur (as we shall see) not 'a little after' 2002, but a little after the end of the conflict itself – and that auspicious, if surprising, event still lies an almost unbearably long time away in the future.

II.62   *When Mabus shortly dies, there shall ensue*   **2002**
Of man and beast a laying waste most dread.
Then suddenly shall vengeance heave in view:
Thirst, famine, blood, with comet overhead.

We now come to the curious 'Mabus' episode that has had people quaking in their boots for far too long. 'Mabus', it is widely assumed, must be some kind of Antichrist – especially as the original French's *cent, main* in the last line is clearly a homonym for *sang humain*, 'human blood'. Nevertheless, all that the verse actually says he will do is *die*.

As we have already seen on numerous occasions, most of Nostradamus's prophecies are based on the repetition of past events, in time with the recapitulation of their horoscopes. The fact that the former US ambassador to Saudi Arabia was one *Raymond E Mabus* is interesting, but probably irrelevant, since he had not yet been born in Nostradamus's day. What *is* relevant is the fact that Jan Gossaert de Mabuse, the celebrated Flemish painter, *had* died on 1 October 1532. In that same year, the forces of the Emperor Charles V had finally managed to push back the Ottoman hordes from before the very gates of Vienna – thus 'avenging' their previous 'laying waste of man and beast alike'. In the same year, too, there had been a notable daylight comet – though apparently not Halley's. Clearly, then, these are the events upon which Nostradamus is basing his prediction.

The astrological situation between 14 and 18 September 1532 Julian (it seems to have been Nostradamus's normal practice to take the situation shortly *before* the event, as though trying to pinpoint the 'causes' rather than the event itself) had been as per the upper chart on page 122. The next time the same situation occurs (I have not so far managed to find a match involving Jupiter and Saturn as well – but Nostradamus seems normally to have been quite satisfied with such five-planet matches) is between 18 and 29 October 2002 (Gregorian) – which is when, if we follow Nostradamus's usual logic, the same sequence of events ought therefore to follow, too.

The place of the original Mabuse's death in 1532 was Breda, in Brabant (Netherlands), which lies on latitude 51° 35' North. This means (once again according to what appears to be the normal Nostradamian logic) that the future Mabus should die in late October 2002 between latitudes 42° 35' and 41° 35' North, in a town which similarly is not too far from the sea and preferably lies at the confluence of two rivers. The most similarly sited places look to me to be Valenca or Gerona, in Spain.

Incidentally, the latitude calculation has theoretically to apply to the latitude of the counter-attack against the Muslim invaders, too. In Charles V's case, this took place not at Vienna itself, from which the Ottomans had had to start withdrawing towards the end of 1529 after a failed attack, but some way to the south-east, at Güns in Western Hungary, near modern Szombathely, which lies at 47° 12' North. Applying the above 9–10° southward latitude correction

based on the sun's new declination in 2002, this gives a lati-
tude-band of roughly 39° N to 37° N for the future event –
which corresponds to Sicily and the toe of Italy.

Thus, the prediction would seem to suggest that, following
the death of a prominent painter, a battle will take place in
October 2002 in Sicily or southern Italy, during which the
invading Muslim forces (presumably from North Africa) will
be dramatically pushed back and their invasion stalled for a
while. A comet will mark the event.

VI.57* *He who within the realm*   **2003 (December)**
      was close to rule,
      A Cardinal close to the hierarchy,
      Shall make himself so feared, so hard, so cruel
      When he assumes the sacred monarchy.

Meanwhile, the pontificate falls to one of the senior cardinals
who is destined to show a surprisingly nasty turn of character. Prévost[49] refers this to the installation of Pope Julius II
(*uomo terribile*, as he was called) on 26 November 1503,
following his election on the 1st. If so, the comparative
horoscopy provides an excellent five-planet match for the
latter date (though not a solar one) in early December 2003.

VIII.41* *The Fox shall be elected, keeping mum,*
      Playing the saint, living on barley bread;
      Then suddenly a tyrant he'll become,
      Trampling at will on each distinguished head.

The surprise is all the greater for the fact that no-one seems to
have spotted this side of his character previously.

HOROGRAPH FOR: September 14 1532 TO: September 18 1532

	Aries	Tauru	Gemin	Cance	Leo	Virgo	Libra	Scorp	Sagit	Capri	Aquar	Pisce
Pluto										*		
Neptune												*
Uranus				*								
Saturn				*								
Jupiter								*				
Mars							*					
Venus								*				
Mercury							*					
Moon	*	*										*
Sun							*					

Solar noon declination (to nearest degree): 1ºS to 2ºS

Geographical latitude: 51º 35'N

LOCATION: Breda, Netherlands
EVENT: Death of Jan Gossaert de Mabuse, Flemish painter

HOROGRAPH FOR: October 18, 2002 TO: October 29, 2002

	Aries	Tauru	Gemin	Cance	Leo	Virgo	Libra	Scorp	Sagit	Capri	Aquar	Pisce
Pluto									*			
Neptune											*	
Uranus											*	
Saturn			*									
Jupiter					*							
Mars							*					
Venus								*				
Mercury							*					
Moon	*	*										*
Sun							*					

Solar noon declination (to nearest degree): 10ºS to 12ºS

Relative latitude: 9º to 10ºS Geographical latitude: 41º to 42ºN [±1º]

POSSIBLE LOCATION: Valença de Minho, Portugal - or Gerona, Spain
EVENT: Death of prominent artist followed by repulsion of invaders in southern Italy

VI.30 *By one who feigns deep sanctity to keep*
The see's betrayed to enemy most arch,
E'en on that night when all thought safe to sleep.
Near Brabant, Liège's host is on the march.

Ecclesiastical betrayal from within is likely to prove just as deadly a weapon in the hands of the invaders as actual military aggression. The last line of this verse is interesting. It suggests that some of the northern powers are likely to prove more vigilant than those immediately threatened in the south. Evidently Belgium, foreseeing a more general invasion of Europe, is starting to re-arm.

II.52 *For several nights the earth shall quake amain.*
Springtime shall two successive spasms see.
War shall be waged by doughty champions twain.
Ephesus, Corinth drowned by either sea.

While the ding-dong battle continues in the Mediterranean and Aegean, matters are suddenly complicated by two massive earthquakes which bring enormous tidal waves crashing down upon the coastal cities of Greece and Turkey.

III.3 *Mars, Hermes, silver shall conjunction*   2004
make:
Towards the south a great drought shall ensue.
In central Turkey, Earth is said to shake;
In Ephesus confusion, Corinth too.

Here, Nostradamus widens the picture somewhat. At the

123

same time as the seismic disturbances in the Mediterranean there are further ones in central Asia Minor, as well as droughts in North Africa (or possibly merely in southern France). Hermes was the Greek equivalent of Mercury. With *argent* ('silver') the alchemical equivalent of the moon, the reference seems to be to a conjunction that next occurs in August 2004, rather depending on what Nostradamus understood by a 'conjunction': he often gives the impression that for him it simply means the presence of two or more planets in the same sign of the zodiac.

VIII.16　　*There where great Jason built his famous boat*
　　　　　　So huge a flood shall burst old Ocean's banks
　　　　　　That hearth and homeland out of reach shall float
　　　　　　And waves shall climb broad-based Olympus'
　　　　　　flanks.

Once again, consequently, the great flood already mentioned looms into view, but this time more explicitly. One is tempted to wonder whether the mighty volcano of Santorini has perhaps exploded once more, as it did back in Minoan times to such catastrophic effect. Some commentators, though, link the boat not with the mythical Jason (the original French word is spelt – and capitalised – *HIERON*), but with one of the two ancient Tyrants of Syracuse who were of that name.

I.69　　　*The mighty mountain near a mile in girth*
　　　　　　Shall – after peace, war, hunger – floods beset.
　　　　　　Far they shall roll to countries of the earth,
　　　　　　However old, however mighty yet.

Nostradamus pursues the theme, confirming the present mountain's Olympian identity by giving its girth (a prominent feature to which he also refers in the previous quatrain) as seven Greek *stadia*, or about 1,400 metres.

V.31   *That Attic land, in wisdom first of all,*
Which still remains the flower of the world
The sea shall ruin: its eminence shall fall,
By waves sucked down and to perdition hurled.

Certainly Greece itself will be severely affected. Virtually the whole country – or at least its lower-lying portion – is destined to be laid waste by the sea, and no doubt a good many of its artistic and monumental achievements with it.

V.63   *Too much they'll plead vain enterprise's glory.*
Among th' Italians boats, cold, hunger, water:
Not far from Tiber all the land is gory:
All kinds of plagues shall human beings slaughter.

The tidal waves duly reach Italy, bringing their usual dire effects to add to the existing catalogue of woes.

IX.82*   *With floods and ghastly pestilence abroad,*
The mighty city shall be long beset.
The watchmen killed, the guards put to the sword,
Sudden its fall, but never looted yet.

The last pockets of Roman resistance crumble. However, the invaders apparently show a remarkable degree of respect for property.

X.60   *Weep, Nice, Savona, Monaco, Siena,*
For bloody war your New Year's gift shall be!
In Malta, Pisa, Genoa, Capua, Modena
Fire, earthquake, flood and dire necessity.

Once again the great earthquake is mentioned, as the tide of war sweeps up through Italy and along the coast of France.

I.75*   *Siena's tyrant occupies Savona:*
The fort once gained, by him the fleet's controlled.
The double host from Marches of Ancona
In fright the chief shall doubtfully behold.

At the same time, the invading land-forces, sweeping through Tuscany from their landing-beaches at Ancona, finally make it to the Gulf of Genoa, much to the consternation of the defending commander.

II.86   *A fleet is wrecked near Adriatic sea*
Lifted by earthquake, dropped upon the land.
Egypt, a-quake the Muslims' spread to see,
An envoy sends, surrender in his hand.

The earthquake in the eastern Mediterranean has had a familiar consequence: the resulting tidal wave has carried boats and even large ships inland – in this case what looks suspiciously like an entire invasion fleet, at anchor off the eastern shores of Italy. Meanwhile Nostradamus uses his familiar technique of repeating an idea from the first half of his verse in the second half – here, the notion of 'quaking' – to give us our first direct indication that the invasion is also about to spread across North Africa. The Egyptians, naturally, are not over-inclined to resist. Prévost,[49] however, traces this verse back to the disastrous battle of Preveza of 1538 – which might suggest that it is a *defending* fleet that is wrecked, in this case by enemy action.

IX.31   *The earth shall quake Mortara all about.*
Saint George, Caltagirone half-flooded out.
Drowsy with peace, by war roused up again,
At Easter schisms rend the church in twain.

Further earthquakes occur at Mortara, some thirty miles southwest of Milan, while floods affect Sicily: Prévost[49] traces these events back to 1542, when the steeple of St George's church at Caltagirone was destroyed by an earthquake, war broke out anew between François I and Charles V, and a new French translation of a Protestant tract by Calvin started to tear France apart. Presumably the original text's *Caſſich* would in this case be the printer's faulty rendering of Nostradamus's abbreviation *Caltag.* – though it has to be said that Prévost's version seems less than convincing here, and Cheetham's suggestion[11,13] that the word is instead a version of Greek *Cassiterides* ('tin-islands', and thus Britain) may actually be nearer the mark. As for the future scenario, there is a similar earthquake within the Church itself. Once again, in other words, Nostradamus achieves a kind of echo-effect within his four-line verse: a physical earthquake in one place is reflected in a doctrinal one somewhere else.

I.93*   *Near to the Alps shall earth Italian quake.*
         Lion shall not with Cock too much unite.
         Only for fear shall they alliance make –
         Only the Celts and Spain forbear to fight.

Britain (the Lion?) is none too anxious to support the French (the Cock), but is eventually dragged in out of sheer self-interest.

III.70   *Great Britain – England in another age –*
         Shall be by water flooded to great height.
         The new Italian league such war shall wage
         That they against them shall combine to fight.

Britain is indeed inundated. Sensing the danger to itself if the invasion spreads, it finally agrees to support France in its struggle against the invaders (note that the term 'Great Britain' had not even been invented in Nostradamus's day).

X.66   *Through power American the British head*
         In icy winds shall rack poor Scotland's isle.
         An Antichrist they'll find and leader red
         Who'll draw them all into the fight awhile.

In this quatrain, the context of the last two lines seems clear enough, with the future invaders being associated (neither for the first nor for the last time) with the colour red. It is the first two lines that pose the problem. The original French word *tempiera* is presumably a fairly 'normal' misprint for *templera* – here meaning 'shall place on tenterhooks'. What is amazing is the suggestion by Nostradamus (in the mid-sixteenth century, remember) that newly-colonised America would at some future date actually be able to wield a measure of power in Europe. The last line seems to suggest that not only Britain, but at some stage America, too, is likely, however reluctantly, to become involved in the conflict.

VIII.72   *Upon Perugia's field what huge defeat!*
And all about Ravenna what affray!
The victor's horse the loser's oats shall eat.
Free passage granted on a holiday.

The invaders in southern Italy now move on northwards. As was ever the case, the conquering army commandeers all the local provisions and resources. There is more than a hint, meanwhile, that its success will be due at least as much to the defenders' incompetence and apathy as to its own military efforts. As we have already seen, this theme recurs repeatedly throughout the conflict – an apparent indication on Nostradamus's part that we have it within our own hands to mitigate, if not to prevent, much of what he predicts for us.

VI.36   *Nor good nor ill the battle shall instil*
The limits of Perugia's lands inside.
Pisa rebels: Florence's star bodes ill.
Chief hurt at night shall muddy donkey ride.

The invaders continue to move on towards Pisa and Florence, largely ignoring Perugia itself. The detail in the last line is something that only contemporary light is likely to be able to elucidate.

VII.8   *Flee, Florence! Flee him who from Rome shall*
            come.
            At Fiesole the battle is declared.
            Blood shall be shed, the mighty overcome.
            Nor church nor any sect shall then be spared.

Line one of the original text apparently uses the expression
'the nearest Roman' to refer not to the original inhabitants
of Rome themselves, but to the city's new occupiers. As we
have already noted, Nostradamus uses this technique repeatedly throughout his quatrains. Once in any given city or
country, the invaders are treated as being *of it* (or rather
from it). It seems that Fiesole, near Florence (which
Nostradamus often refers to as 'Flora'), is set to become the
site of a major battle as the tide of invasion continues to
sweep northwards. In the last line, Nostradamus evidently
plays one of his frequent verbal tricks, substituting the word
sexe for *sectes*.

VI.62   *Both Florences are lost too late, too late.*
            'Gainst holy law no act the snake shall try.
            The French stave off the force confederate.
            Martyrs from Monaco to Savona die.

Nostradamus now predicts the late loss of two *fleurs*. Since he
normally uses the word 'Flora' to refer to Florence, it seems
likely that he is referring here not only to this city ('Firenze' in
Italian), but also to Firenzuola, a few miles to the north. Only
circumstances at the time can hope to explain how either
could possibly be lost *too late*, however. Line two seems to
suggest that the invaders will for the time being let the
Vatican be, despite the apparent contradiction between this
and the last line of the foregoing stanza (VII.8): subsequent

130

stanzas may help to explain this. Meanwhile, the French are not only starting to assist the beleaguered Italians, but also conducting an effective rearguard action, though there are now increasing signs of naval and/or amphibious attacks along the Mediterranean coasts of northern Italy and – for the first time – of southern France.

III.19   *Shortly before the change of overlord*
In Lucca blood and milk fall from the sky:
Famine and thirst, great plague and war abhorred
Far, far from where its rightful Prince shall die.

As the war continues to spread northwards, some worrying phenomena put in their appearance – worrying because, if not of natural origin (as the original historical events almost certainly were), they could conceivably indicate some kind of chemical warfare. The chief local administrator is abducted, and eventually dies or is killed while in distant exile.

IX.5*   *As is the third toe to the first shall he*
Seem but a dwarfish lord, yet tyrant who
Pisa and Lucca shall o'ertake, and see
Done what his predecessor failed to do.

Meanwhile, the invading armies have acquired a new local commander who, though diminutive, threatens to be even more ruthlessly successful than his predecessor.

IX.80*   *Resolved to exile those who him shall back,*
He'll make the strongest far abroad to fare –
The chief who'll Pisa crush and Lucca sack.
Grape-picking Muslims shall no wine prepare.

The new overlord has no sympathy even for would-be collaborators, whom he deports, possibly on the grounds that if they can change sides once, they can do it again. Muslim rules on the drinking of alcohol now start to apply in Italy as well.

IV.58   *In human throats shall stick the burning sun.*
On lands Etruscan human blood shall rain.
Water in pail, the chief leads off his son:
To Turkish lands his lady captive ta'en.

This re-evocation of the Turkish pirate Barbarossa's raids on Italy and southern France of 1543 and 1544 – during the first of which, while in search of water, he met and carried off his future wife Doña Maria[49] – seems to indicate the devastation of Tuscany and the direst of consequences for its leaders and inhabitants.

VI.67   *When power is by another hand attained,*
Further from goodness than felicity,
Ruled is the realm by one from brothel stained,
Who'll realms condemn to mighty misery.

The new Asiatic overlord proceeds to impose a vicious regime on Italy, and will subsequently extend his sway to other lands as well. As Prévost[49] points out, this prophecy is taken virtually directly from the prophecy of the Antichrist in the *Livre merveilleux* of 1522, which was a major source of ideas for Nostradamus.

V.61   *Son of the chief who was not at his birth*
        The Apennines subdues. Nor shall he stop:
        With fear he'll fill the Libran lands of earth,
        And fire the mountains up to Cenis' top.

Apparently born out of wedlock, the invading leader pursues his campaign with great vigour over the Apennines as far as the Alpine border with France. This causes great trepidation among 'those of the balance' – i.e. those countries supposed in Nostradamus's day to be governed by Libra. On the basis of Roussat,[53] these appear to be Arabia, Asia Minor and Italy – which suggests that he will be feared just as much at home as abroad.

VIII.9   *While Cock and Eagle fight around Savona,*
         To Hungary the Eastern fleet sails in.
         Troops at Palermo, Naples and Ancona.
         In Rome and Venice calls the dread muezzin.

The symbolic terms 'Cock' and 'Eagle' presumably refer to the French and Italian forces respectively – though the original 'Eagle' is likely to have been that of the Holy Roman Empire. Even while they are still making a last effort at resisting the invaders around Savona, a further incursion is being made up the Danube to the north. In Sicily and southern Italy, the invaders are by now securely ensconced, while new, Islamic regimes are already in place in Rome and Venice –

though in the last line my 'muezzin's call' is admittedly a rather free interpretation of Nostradamus's *par Barb' horrible crie.*

IX.67   *Upon the mountains all about Isère*
Mass five score at Valence's rocky gate
From Châteauneuf, Pierrelatte and Donzère:
There shall Rome's flock the Muslim force await.

As the invaders cross the French frontier for the first time, this quatrain helps us to narrow down the expected route considerably. 'Valence's rocky gate' identifies itself as the gorge of the river Isère, a fact which in turn suggests that the invaders will have crossed the Alps between Turin and Grenoble, in part possibly via the Fréjus tunnel, which lies quite close to Mount Cenis (*see* V.61 on page 133). Once again, meanwhile, Nostradamus refers to them as Muslims – in this case in terms of the word 'crescent'.

VII.7   *After the combat 'twixt the horses light*
Great Islam they shall claim at bay to keep.
Death, shepherd-dressed, shall stalk the hills at
     night:
The clefts flow red in all the chasms deep.

We do not have to take too literally Nostradamus's reference to light horses, which could quite easily refer to a battle between light-armoured vehicles. What certainly seems to occur is a series of night-time commando-type operations that have extremely bloody consequences.

V.15   *The Pope is captured while en route*   **2007?**
         conveyed:
         The outraged, thwarted clerics waste their breath.
         Absent, the next elected's star shall fade:
         His bastard favourite be done to death.

As though to confirm our interpretation, this apparent evocation of the setting up of the 'alternative papacy' in Avignon in June 1379[49] pursues the theme of the Pope's removal and looks ahead to the unpromising prospects of his successor. There is a reasonable horoscopic match for this event in late June 2007, but its validity rather depends on how far we can trust the identification of the original incident itself.

VII.22   *The people from Iraq shall, furious, fall*
          Upon the friends of Spanish Catalonia.
          With games, rites, feasts, none of them wakes at
             all.
          Pope by the Rhône; Rome taken, and Ausonia.

From the papal flight and possible abduction (whether by enemies or supporters) we turn aside for a moment for a brief *résumé* of the broader picture. The invasion has already reached south-eastern Europe: now it is about to spread to the south-west, apparently via the south-eastern part of Spain. (Nostradamus's singling out of the Catalonian trading city of Tarragona in line two seems to spring purely from his need for an appropriate word to rhyme with *Ausone* in the last line, and so I have returned the compliment.) Meanwhile Nostradamus seems to identify the invaders from the east as 'citizens from Mesopotamia' – i.e. Iraq. Since it seems unlikely that Iraq could ever pose such a serious threat on its own, the true significance of the phrase may well be that Iraq has indeed become part of the invading confederacy, as just mooted. The unprepared Italians, intent on the usual 'bread and circuses' that are by now so familiar to the Western world, will already have woken up to find their country ('Ausonia') under the heel of the invaders. The fact that the Pope has apparently fled, finishing up (like his fourteenth-century predecessors) at Avignon is also well-established by now. Line four is a marvellous example of Nostradamus's penchant for telegrammese, especially when pushed for space in the final line of a quatrain.

III.23*　　*O France, if o'er Ligurian sea you sail*
　　　　　　You'll find yourselves by sea and land hemmed in.
　　　　　　Muslims from Adrian Sea shall you assail.
　　　　　　Of horse and ass you'll gnaw the bones and skin.

Evidently recalling the military disasters in Italy of Louis XII, François I and Henri II,[49] Nostradamus now addresses one of a number of periodic warnings to his own beloved country using the familiar *tu*, as is his wont on such occasions. Sensing that the French may be tempted to intervene in Italy to try and keep the invaders at arm's length, he warns them that any such expedition will prove disastrous.

III.24*　　*Such undertaking chaos would portend,*
　　　　　　Great loss of life and loss of funds untold.
　　　　　　Thither your fight on no account extend.
　　　　　　France, take to heart all that I have foretold.

Unusually, the seer extends his argument into the very next quatrain. Clearly he is much concerned about the issue, and intends his words to be taken as a heartfelt warning. We should do well to note the point, as it has obvious implications for the way in which we react to his whole opus.

III.87*   *Stay far from Corsica, you fleet from Gaul,*
No less Sardinia, lest you regret:
Shorn of Greek aid, you'll die right soon withal,
Bloodsoaked and captive, should you scorn my
     threat.

Nostradamus reinforces his warning. Even to set out would be foolhardy. Brind'Amour[9] points out that this verse is clearly based on the abortive attack on Corsica by the Prince of Salerno and a commander called De Termes in 1553, which was almost contemporary with Nostradamus's writing of it.

IV.4   *In vain the prince shall fret while all complain*
Of French and Afric troops that loot and sack.
On land great hordes; ships countless ply the main:
O'er Italy the French are driven back.

Prévost[49] traces this further prophecy back to the battles between France, the Turks and the Holy Roman Empire over Nice and parts of northern Italy between 1536 and 1544.

II.72   *Hard-pressed in Italy is France's might;*
           Great loss and heavy fighting many-sided.
           Flee those from Rome, O France, with all your
               might!
           Ticino's Rubicon is undecided.

As this evident re-evocation of the disastrous battle of Pavia
in 1525 suggests (compare X.72 in Chapter 3), France,
sensing the imminent threat to its own borders, has belatedly
sent an expeditionary force to Italy to help resist the invaders.
In the event, however, it is not up to the task. Forced back
into north-western Italy, it makes its final stand on the river
Ticino near Pavia in order to prevent what promises to be a
kind of crossing of the Rubicon in reverse. For a while at
least, stalemate is achieved.

IV.90   *The walls can neither fighting force regain.*
           Trembling and fear Milan, Pavia sap.
           Hunger, thirst, doubt shall pierce them all amain.
           No bread, no food: of rations not a scrap.

Two different defending armies – possibly the French and
Italian – now find their retreat cut off. One has the impression that the nearby cities have been encircled and possibly
besieged. With their normal supply routes disrupted, they
start to suffer severe famine.

VII.39   *The leader of the fighting force from France*
            Thinking to lose his principal formation,
            Doubts over food and shelter shall advance.
            Through Genoa shall pour the alien nation.

Apparently demoralised, the commander of the last French forces still in Italy starts to invent good reasons for withdrawing as even more invading troops pour ashore at Genoa.

IX.95 *The new-made chief the host leads where he can,*
Almost cut off, towards the river-bank,
Helped by a force of shock-troops from Milan:
Milan's chief blinded, barred in prison dank.

The remaining defenders in northern Italy now straggle towards one of their last defence-lines, probably the river Ticino (*see* II.72, on page 138).

II.15 *Shortly before the king shall meet his end,*
O'er Twins and Ship the comet shall come in.
State funds by land and sea they shall expend;
The lands cut off from Pisa to Turin.

If this verse refers to the fleeing Pope, his exile in France is not likely to last long, for the same comet that marks his flight also presages his death. Nostradamus actually seems to trace its path. It will, he suggests, pass through the constellations of Gemini and Argo (unless what Nostradamus really means is that there will be two popes attempting to rule the 'ship' of the Church at once, as happened once before in connection with the papal flight to France in the fourteenth century). By this time, the invaders will have consolidated their grip on northern Italy (the original text, which I have been forced to summarise somewhat, mentions Asti and Ferrara as well), to the point of turning it into forbidden territory.

X.93   *Much travel shall the new-found vessel know.*
Here, there and everywhere they'll move the see.
To Arles, Beaucaire the hostages shall go,
Near two shafts, newly found, in porphyry.

This quatrain suggests that the crew of the papal 'barque' of 'Peter the Fisherman' – i.e. the Pope and his party – will initially be moved about the Rhône delta rather like hostages, possibly in order to foil any possible kidnap attempt. The whole area is particularly rich in Roman remains.

I.43   *Before the mighty empire changed shall be*
A thing miraculous shall come to light.
The soil removed, a shaft of porphyry
Shifted to stand upon a rocky height.

Nostradamus seems fascinated by the new archaeological discovery, though he fails to explain what is so miraculous about it. Clearly, though, he sees it as presaging a change of regime – possibly, in this case, the demise of the authority of the Roman Church in Europe in favour of that of the invaders.

IX.32   *A tall shaft found, of porphyry the best:*
Imperial documents beneath the base,
Bones Roman, plaited hair to force attest.
At Mitilini ships stir up the place.

Even as the invaders are about to ship further forces to Europe from the Turkish west coast, with a fleet waiting in high anticipation off the isle of Lesbos, the ever-curious

Nostradamus cannot resist delving further into the details of the discovery.

VIII.46 *Three leagues from Rhône shall die Paul main-*
            soleil,
            While leaders flee of Tarascon the strait.
            Of Eagle and French Cock, dread Mars's sway
            Shall then the worst of brothers three instate.

This extraordinarily obtuse quatrain is one of a number that include the intriguing expression *Pol mensolee/mansole/ mansol/mausol* – conceivably the key to identifying the latter-day Pope to whom so many of the predictions seem to refer at around this juncture. It looks suspiciously like one of those geographical puns on which, as we shall see, Nostradamus is so keen. In the case of VIII.16 (page 124), where he impishly disguises the word *fessan* ('broad of bottom') as a classical place name – for St-Paul-de-Mausole ('St Paul-of-the-Mausoleum') is simply the name of a former priory just to the south of his own birthplace of St-Rémy-de-Provence, named after the adjacent Roman arch and mausoleum of Sextus. Yet the whole point about such puns is precisely that they have a double meaning. *Pol*, clearly, is merely a version of 'Paul', but the word following it begs to be interpreted as a version of the French *main-de-soleil*, or rather the Latin *manus solis*. The word *manus* normally means 'hand', but in Virgil particularly its meaning is often extended to include 'work', and particularly 'handiwork'. 'Hand-of-the-sun', then, or 'labour of the sun' – what can Nostradamus possibly be driving at?

In the event, it looks as if it could be something extraordinarily specific – namely the celebrated and often remarkably accurate twelfth-century forecast by the Irish St Malachy of all the popes from his own day until the end of the Vatican.[33] Each is given a Latin tag which in some way describes his pontificate, and the last figure but two is described as *De Labore Solis* ('Something to do with the labour of the sun', which is actually an ancient term for a solar eclipse). Evidently, then, Nostradamus is referring specifically to this figure. Since, however, the papal succession and St Malachy's list have long since been matched up with each other, that individual's identity is widely known, even in the Vatican. *He is none other than the present Pope, John Paul II*, who in his youth, at least, had the grace to fit Malachy's Latin tag by working in the open air with his bare hands, having been assigned to the Polish stone-quarries by the Nazi invaders – and who, moreover, was apparently born at the time of an eclipse. (The last two on Malachy's list, incidentally, are *Gloria Olivae* ['The glory of the olive'] – here apparently seen by Nostradamus as the worst of three monkish candidates – and *Petrus Romanus* ['Peter the Roman' or 'the Roman rock'], during whose reign the Vatican will allegedly be destroyed.)

Therefore, it is widely assumed by commentators that all the 'Pol mansole' quatrains (VIII.46, IV.27, X.29, V.57, VIII.34) necessarily apply to Pope John Paul II, to whom all the grisly events described are therefore likely to happen, probably in the order listed. Possibly this is to over-state the case, however. Prévost,[49] after all, links the 'brothers three' simply with the three main warring religious leaders of Nostradamus's own day.

II.97   *O Roman Pope, beware lest you come near* 2010?
         The city that shall water rivers two!
         When blooms the rose, those who to you are dear
         Nearby shall spit their blood – and so shall you.

The Pope now flees north towards the city of Lyon, watered as it is by the two rivers Saône and Rhône, where he presumably hopes to find safe haven (though the original French actually has the city watering the rivers, rather than the other way around). On the other hand, Avignon, too, is watered by two rivers (the Rhône and the Durance) and there is already a huge medieval papal palace awaiting him there. The 'rose' reference may be to the time of year – though the original reference may well have been to the flowering of the medieval Troubadours and the *Roman de la Rose*. Elsewhere (V.96, page 91) Nostradamus seems to refer to the rose as symbolic of some future regime that he regards with particular unease, probably that of the invaders themselves.

Note, meanwhile, the important suggestion in the first line that it is actually possible for us to *take warning* from Nostradamus's predictions for our future and to act in some measure to defuse them. The principle, as we have already seen, is basic to the whole operation of the 'Janus hypothesis'. Prévost[49] traces the original event back to the coronation of Clement V in Lyon on 14 November 1305, when many spectators were killed by a falling wall. If he is right, comparative horoscopy suggests that the next reasonable horoscopic match is not until mid-December 2010 – in which case both the date and the nature of the event might indicate that the verse is not really applicable at this juncture at all!

VIII.34   *Leo at Lyon shall triumphant be:*
           To Lua, sacrifice on Jura's slope
           Of thousand easterners seven score and three.
           At Lyon falls down dead the slippered Pope.

Coded though its language is, this quatrain could hardly be more specific. True, 'Leo' is not identified: but a papal connection is by no means impossible. Certainly, up in the Jura there will be a bloody battle, presumably with the invaders, as they try to press down into the Rhône valley via

Haute Savoie. Lua was the Roman goddess who expiated blood shed in battle. But for the Pope – whether currently triumphant or imprisoned – it is of little consequence. By accident or design, he dies either at or not far from Lyon (Nostradamus the versifier constantly switches between the two possibilities, mainly because the one – à – gives him one syllable while the other – *près de* – offers him two to play with).

V.46   *When Sabine candidate shall be elected*
The cardinals shall feud and disagree.
Great theses shall against him be erected
And Rome by force Albanian injured be.

This quatrain begs at first sight to be interpreted as applying to a future pope who hails from the north-eastern quarter of Rome. The *Albanois* could be either singular or plural, and could equally well come from Alba or Albens. 'Rome', similarly, could mean either the city, the Roman Church, the Vatican or even the Pope himself. (Nostradamus, clearly, is quite good at hedging his bets!) The present Pope, John Paul II, was certainly injured in office, but by a Turk: moreover, the other details seem not to be a particularly good fit, despite the controversy which has long reigned within the Church over his policy on birth control. Possibly, then, the quatrain indicates the controversial election of a new Pope at a time of great turbulence, during the course of which Rome is assailed from the direction of Albania. The circumstances of the oriental invasion immediately spring to mind once again. But if so, then we need to refer to the various other quatrains on the same subject. Prévost[49] refers this verse back to the Great Western Church Schism of 1378.

X.65   *O mighty Rome, dread ruin comes again*
Not to your walls, but to your living part.
Horrors you'll see from him of harsh-writ name,
Whose sword shall pierce you to the very heart.

Prévost[49] traces this verse back to the devastating sack of Rome by Imperial forces in 1527. The 'harsh-writ name' he identifies as that of Frundsberg, the Imperial general, as written in German Gothic script. Not only were many buildings destroyed in the course of the epoch-making disaster, but the Protestant section of the army happily desecrated the Catholic shrines and their religious symbols, too. For the future, my hunch is that the prophecy probably indicates the beginning of the end of the Papacy as a major religious force, mainly as a result of severe criticism in books and the media – whether political, moral or theological (possibly the 'great theses' mentioned in V. 46).

VIII.19   *The mighty Pope to help, in trouble sore,*
The reds are on the march (or so they say).
His family, o'erwhelmed, are at death's door.
The reddest reds his Redness wipe away.

We now start to see the reason for the disrepute into which the Vatican has fallen. The invaders have evidently allowed one of the cardinals to ascend St Peter's throne as Pope only on condition that their own candidate be elected, and that all effective power be devolved to them. Putting it about that the College of Cardinals itself has asked for their aid, they then march openly into the Vatican. His 'family' is presumably the shocked and oppressed Church. And so it is that one group of 'reds' (the Asiatic aggressors) is about to put paid to another (the cardinals, and this cardinal in particular).

VIII.20   *Of rigged elections rumours false shall flood*
The city through: broken, the pact's unpacted.
Votes bought, the holy chapel stained with blood,
The empire to another is contracted.

This verse makes it clear that something of the kind has indeed happened. But events do not go according to plan. In the Sistine Chapel, consequently, a mixture of bribery and brute force is brought to bear to produce a new result, thus breaking the secret agreement and destroying even the last pretence of legality.

V.49   *Not from old Spain; instead, from ancient France*
Elected o'er the trembling Barque to rule,
Promises to the foe he shall advance
Who in his reign shall prove a plague so cruel.

The original choice of Pope evidently came of Spanish descent. Now, however, it is a French cardinal more sympathetic to the invaders who is substituted – or at least one with ancient French ancestry – and then only after having offered them some pretty scandalous guarantees.

I.83   *The alien race the booty out shall share:*
Angry-eyed Saturn Mars shall then affright,
Latins and Tuscans fearsome slaughter scare,
Greeks too, though they be straitly charged to
fight.

Nostradamus seems to link the next phase of the invasion with an astrological dating – whether merely involving the

146

presence of Saturn in Aries or (as the decidedly ambiguous text actually suggests) an actual conjunction with Mars. For whatever reason, the newly-attacked Greeks fail to keep the incoming hordes at bay. Note how Nostradamus once again takes up an idea (in this case the word 'alien') from the first half of the verse and re-applies it – rather after the style of the Hebrew psalms – in the second half.

VI.38   *The beaten shall the foes of peace behold,*
             Once prostrate Italy lies dead and still.
             The bloody Moor and red shall then make bold
             Fires to ignite, blood in the waves to spill.

Whether or not because of the new allegations against the Church, the leader of the occupying forces now decides – promises or not – to expunge from the face of the earth all trace of the former regime (both secular and ecclesiastical) that he apparently finds so objectionable. Deliberate conflagrations and persecutions result.

V.73   *Sorely the Church of God shall be oppressed,*
            The holy temples looted of their store,
            The naked child by mother but half-dressed,
            Arabs and Poles allied as ne'er before.

As the Church is pillaged, social conditions deteriorate, and widespread social privations are experienced throughout the occupied lands. The rather surprising last line suggests either an alliance between the invasion's furthest southern and northern flanks or (more likely) a 'forced marriage' between the invading Muslims and the followers of the former Pope.

IV.82   *Out of Slavonia the horde draws near:*
         The city's sacked by old Destroyer's ire.
         Desolate shall his Rome to him appear,
         Nor shall he then know how to douse the fire.

Whether Nostradamus is referring at this point to a second wave of invaders from the north-east is not entirely clear. At all events, massed troops duly descend on Rome itself. The 'he' of the last two lines may refer to the last, beleaguered Pope, who is powerless to defend his city. Alternatively, it could refer to the oriental commander who, once having set the invasion in motion, eventually finds that it has acquired an uncontrollable momentum of its own which actually destroys what it was intended to grasp – in this case the power and riches of Rome itself.

III.84   *The Mighty City shall be desolated:*
         Of its inhabitants shall none remain.
         Walls, temples, women, virgins violated;
         By sword, fire, plague and gun they shall be slain.

The results are inevitable, and need no elaboration from me. *La grand cité* is standard Nostradamian for Rome.

VIII.80   *With innocents bleed maids and widowed dames –*
         So many ills the Great Red shall commit.
         The holy icons dipped in candle-flames:
         For fear and dread not one shall move from it.

Nostradamus's description is graphic. He is evidently so pious as to see the violation of religious monuments on much the same level as that of women and children – not a view, I suspect, that would be shared by many nowadays. The origin of the verse almost certainly lies once again in the sack of Rome of 1527.

II.81   *Fire near consumes the city from the sky.*
        Noah's flood shall loom anew ere winter's done.
        Sardinia's coast shall Afric vessels try
        Once from the Scales has passed the autumn sun.

Nostradamus seems to foresee the use of artillery and/or incendiaries during the new attack on Rome – unless he is referring either to huge thunderstorms or to the much more sinister thermal weapon seemingly referred to in later predictions as being deployed in the south-west of France. For whatever reason, a great flood then follows. Nostradamus associates this with that of the Greek Deucalion, thus apparently suggesting that it will in some way originate in Greece: for metrical reasons, I have substituted the biblical one of Noah. Meanwhile, Sardinia's resistance is likely to continue until new attacks descend on it from the African coast, along which the invaders are now about to spread (*see* II.86 and II.30, pages 126 and 163). If the last line's original reference to Phaëton refers to Jupiter, then it may be possible to assign this prediction to a particular year and month: if, as seems more likely, it refers to the sun whose son and *alter ego* Phaëton was in Greek mythology, then it appears to date the events described to late October or early November.

III.6   *The lightning deep within the churches falls.*
             The citizens behind their walls shall shrink;
             Their cattle too, as water laps the walls.
             E'en weak ones take to arms for food and drink.

This quatrain seems to suggest that the aerial attacks will continue until the expected great flood itself puts a stop to them. To this extent, then, the latter could be seen as something of a saving event, for all the resultant shortages of provisions.

II.93   *Death comes apace hard by the Tiber's flow*
             Shortly before the mighty inundation.
             The vessel's captain's taken, sent below:
             Castle and palace in full conflagration.

This prediction is highly reminiscent of the kind of scenario envisaged by a number of other psychics, too.[33] It appears to refer to the end of the Vatican and the death of the last Pope, often dated to not long after the end of the twentieth century. The 'vessel's captain' who is taken captive into the cellars begs identification with the Pontiff himself. Both Castel Sant'Angelo and the Vatican will be set ablaze shortly before – to cap it all – the great flood already referred to descends on the city. But of course the original circumstances described are clearly once again those of the sack of Rome in 1527, with Pope Clement forced to take refuge in the Angelo – a man-made disaster which the flooding Tiber merely made ten times worse.[49]

VI.6   *Near Cancer's claws and the Septentrion   2008(?)*
Of famed Great Bear, the bearded star appears.
To Susa, Siena, Thebes, Eretrion.
Great Rome shall die the night it disappears.

Here Nostradamus once again links the death of a Pope to an expected comet, and casts some light on its likely track. Line three suggests that the comet will be most easily visible in Italy and Greece – unless these are merely the areas where its astrological significance will be most dire. The word that I have rendered as 'Thebes' is in fact 'Boetia': 'Eretrion' is a Nostradamian coinage for 'Eretria' based on the Latin *Eretriensis*, and presumably forced upon him by the need to rhyme with 'Septentrion'. Prévost[49] traces the verse back to the comet of 1533 and the ensuing death in 1534 of Pope Clement VII. If valid, this identification in turn permits the application of comparative horoscopy: according to this, the event next has the potential to occur in late August to early September 2008. However, this hardly squares with the last dating given above. Besides, the idea that the arrival of comets can be calculated astrologically is, of course, pretty nonsensical in the first place, whether or not astrology can be applied to the potential deaths of Popes.

I.52   *Saturn and Mars in Scorpio are met: 2012?*
The mighty lord is murdered in his hall:
To plague the church a monarch new is set
In southern Europe and the north withal.

If this quatrain is relevant at this juncture, the oriental leader is now destined to be murdered on his own premises. The 'new king' is presumably his successor, and his advent spells the doom of the Catholic Church throughout Europe. Saturn and Mars are next in Scorpio in October 2012.

IX.42   *The plague sweeps Barcelona, Monaco,*
Genoa, Venice, Sicily and more;
Yet to Islam the fleet its teeth shall show
And chase them all the way to Tunis' shore.

Whether the 'plague' in line one refers to actual pestilence
or to the incoming swarms of what Nostradamus elsewhere
describes as 'locusts' (i.e. the oriental invaders) is not made
clear. At all events, at some point there seems to be spirited
resistance by sea. Monaco, as we saw above, is among the
places to bear the brunt of the foreign onslaught.

I.37   *Shortly before the setting sun goes down*
Battle shall start, a mighty race unsure.
Defeated, no response from harbour town:
Burial at sea twice over they'll endure.

In the event, however, the outcome is disastrous. The hard-
pressed European navies, possibly expecting reinforcements
from Marseille or Toulon, are disappointed. The admittedly
obscure last line suggests to me that at least one crew will go
down with its ship. Prévost[49] links this verse to the war
against Parma of 1249 and (rather more tenuously) the death
of the Emperor Frederick Barbarossa.

IX.100   *When night o'ertakes the battle on the sea*
Fire shall destroy the occidental fleets.
Red new-bedecked shall then the flagship be.
Wrath to the vanquished: rain the victors greets.

In line with Prévost's suggestion[49] that this verse refers back to the capture of the Spanish fleet on 11 May 1560 by the Turkish pirate Pyali Pasha, the curious detail in line three suggests that the European flagship may be captured and placed under new colours (Pyali actually painted his prizes red!) – the colour red being, as we shall see later, constantly associated by Nostradamus with the invaders – unless, of course, it is merely stained with blood. On the other hand, this verse was almost certainly written *before* 1560 – which renders Prévost's suggestion rather dubious. The original text's 'drizzle' in the last line may not be as innocuous as it sounds: later predictions seem to see such phenomena as noxious in some way, almost as though indicative of chemical or bacteriological warfare. This in turn may even tie in with Nostradamus's frequent references to 'plague' in connection with the fighting.

II.78
The British power beneath th' abysmal flood
With Afric blood and French shall mingled be.
Neptune being late, the Isles shall swim in blood,
E'en secrets told shall harm far less than he.

In line one Nostradamus seems to use 'Neptune' – presumably complete with trident – to refer to a British submarine-force (compare II.59, page 185). As a result of the disastrous sea-battle, the invaders' southern forces are enabled to carry out sea-borne landings from Africa on the Mediterranean islands off the coast of southern France. Nostradamus seems to suggest that the British will leave their intervention until far too late, while further harm will be done on the intelligence front. As ever, the European defeat will owe almost as much to the Europeans themselves as to the enemy. For Prévost,[49] however, this verse is simply a re-evocation of the attacks by the Turkish pirate Dragut on

Malta and Gozo between 1540 and 1551, with 'Neptune' the nickname of the Baron de la Garde, who as Admiral of the Eastern Fleet, was unable to prevent either it or other attacks on Corsica and Sardinia. But then, as we saw earlier, even Nostradamus himself was quite prepared to take his own words in senses other than those originally intended if the context permitted!

VI.90 *Stinking, outrageous, and a rank disgrace:*
Yet after it they'll praise him to the skies –
The chief excused who turned away his face –
Lest Neptune tempted be peace to devise.

The accusations go further. Evidently, the failure of the British to come to the rescue was some sort of deliberate act of policy. Nevertheless the French are not inclined to make too much of it, lest the British use it as an excuse to withdraw from the fray altogether.

III.1 *After the fight and battle under sail*
Great Neptune shall attain his apogee.
Once red, though, shall the foe for fear grow pale
And terror spread across the mighty sea.

Unless, as Brind'Amour[9] suggests, this merely refers back to the Baron de la Garde's successful break-out through the Straits of Gibraltar with twenty-five galleys in 1545, the disastrous outcome of the future battle does the British navy no harm at all. Possibly its new-found confidence has arisen because, as a direct result, it has received authorisation to use the full might of its nuclear weapons in future if necessary.

Certainly this could explain the enemy's corresponding loss of confidence at a time when by rights it should be feeling cock-a-hoop – as well as providing Nostradamus with the chance for a piece of engaging colour-play.

III.88*   *From Barcelona such a mighty host*
           Shall come by sea that all Marseille shall quake:
           All aid cut off by sea, the Isles all lost,
           On land your traitor shall the sea forsake.

At this point, moreover, there is a hint of treachery at home that aids the invaders considerably. Prévost[49] identifies the historical original as Charles de Bourbon, the turncoat Constable of France who in 1524 attacked Provence on behalf of the Emperor Charles V even while the Spanish fleet was on the prowl at sea.

VII.37   *Ten sent by one the captain's life to strip*
          'Midst fleet in mutiny find him alert.
          Murderous chaos reigns: ship attacks ship
          Off Hyères, Lerins: but he is in la Nerthe.

Once again we are at sea among the Mediterranean islands – in this case the Îles de Lerins, off Cannes, and the Îles d'Hyères, off the town of Hyères between Toulon and St-Tropez. In the wake of the naval defeat, there is fighting within the allied fleet itself, conceivably in connection with the British let-down. Possibly it is the British commander who, forewarned, arranges to be safely ashore in la Nerthe, just to the north-west of Marseille.

155

II.40 *Shortly thereafter, not too long delayed,*
Yet greater shall the naval conflict swell.
By land and sea great tumult shall be made,
Violent fires that shall attack as well.

Even now, however, the naval conflict is not at an end. Both naval and shore-based installations seem to be involved in a further battle involving what sound curiously like guided missiles. One wonders whether the British contingent has finally felt moved to deploy its ultimate weapon.

VI.81 *Hearts cold as ice, cruel, black and hard as stone*
Bring tears, wails, cries of fear and screams
  appalling,
Bloodshed, great famine, mercy never shown,
Leman and Genoa's greater isles befalling.

Nevertheless, the Muslim fleets evidently once again win the day. Upon the lands from Switzerland in the north to Corsica and Sardinia in the south, consequently, a regime of almost unprecedented cruelty and terror is about to descend.

II.4 *From Monaco almost to Sicily*
The coast entire shall be of folk bereft.
No city, town nor suburb shall there be
But has not suffered heathen sack and theft.

The results for the French and Italian coastal towns and cities, similarly, are catastrophic. Note, meanwhile, that Nostradamus, in this evident re-evocation of a whole succession of raids on the French Mediterranean coast from the eighth century Saracens right through to the pirate Barbarossa in the sixteenth century, once again uses the term *Barbares*, meaning not so much 'barbarian' as 'Berber', and thus (erroneously) 'Arab'. Possibly, he was also aware of the evident pun on the name '*Barb*arossa'.

IV.68*   *Within the year near Venice they shall meet,*
The leaders of the Afro-Asian host.
'Rhine'-lord and 'Danube' shall each other greet:
In Malta tears; cries on the Ligurian coast.

At this point, there is an important conference between the leaders of the invasion, and specifically those of its northern and eastern wings, possibly to assign areas of responsibility. Already these last two are being referred to as the 'Danube' and 'Rhine' commanders respectively (compare V.68, page 163), in anticipation of their ultimate objectives.

V.29*   *Freedom shall not recovered be, the while*
The proud, black evil villain's in possession.
'Danube' shall Venice's republic rile
When matters naval occupy their session.

The meeting is a fraught one, since all present know that they will have no real liberty of conduct all the while the central overlord remains in over-all control. The results of the ensuing squabbles will, as we shall see, eventually prove fatal to the invaders' cause.

157

IX.61 *Pillaged shall be the shores along the sea:*
Villeneuve assaulted, other towns hit hard.
Messina's deed shall Maltese then decree
A poor reward – to be tight locked and barred.

The theme continues. Nostradamus's *cita nova* could be any
one of the numerous small Villeneuves that litter the south
coast, from Villeneuve-Loubet just south of Cagnes-sur-mer
to Villeneuve-les-Maguelonne just south of Montpellier
(conceivably the most likely candidate). The occupying
regime in Sicily, meanwhile, is proving particularly repressive
to the inhabitants of the Mediterranean islands.

III.10 *Seven times of blood and famine shall occur*
Growing calamities along the ocean strand:
Monaco starved, all taken prisoner,
Their lord encaged, borne off by hostile hand.

The whole Mediterranean coast, in fact, is in for a succession
of hostilities and other disasters. Monaco in particular is
destined to suffer all kinds of horrors.

Presage 125* *Disease and fire the orchards rage about:*
The olive crop does well: much less the grape.
Leaders shall die, less aliens sally out.
Borders at risk; Muslims by sea shall rape.

If this further *Presage* (originally for July 1566) can legiti-
mately be re-applied at this point, the assaults are destined to
mount in intensity as air attacks are mounted further inland,
possibly involving chemical or biological weapons.

158

Presage 11*   *The sight of it shall make the sky to weep.*
Hannibal lays his plans. War-fleets prepare.
St Denis soaks the fleet. Too long you'll keep
Silent, O France. Little you'll know or care.

The noxious weapons are aimed at the defending navies, too – specifically on 9 October. Meanwhile, with the French populace still paying surprisingly little attention, the invaders' war-machine in North Africa (the great Hannibal came from Carthage in what is now Tunisia) is gearing itself up to strike at Europe. This *Presage* was originally for September 1555.

III.13   *Lightnings the treasures in their chest shall melt.*
Both captives shall the other sore assail.
Upon the deck the city's lord is knelt,
When 'neath the waves the mighty fleet sets sail.

This quatrain is very difficult to decode precisely. One has the impression that some kind of high-level kidnapping has been attempted by submarine in the very midst of an aerial bombardment, during which the governor of a city has been either wounded or killed, while VIP prisoners have also been removed. However, this interpretation could well be completely 'over the top': Prévost[49] simply relates the verse to the various omens that accompanied the death of Lorenzo de Medici in 1492 – including two wild animals that tried to devour each other in their cage, the destruction of the dome ('arch') of the church of Santa Riparata by lightning, contemporary economic troubles and the 'submerging' of the Neapolitan fleet at Rapallo in the spring of 1494.

VII.19   *Over the fort at Nice no fight shall rage:*
It shall be overcome by metal red.
Long time its fate shall people's tongues engage:
The citizens shall find it strange and dread.

The weapon in question in line two seems to be more than a mere naval shell. 'Red-hot metal' seems more reminiscent of napalm, and the term is also oddly reminiscent of the sinister Soviet 'red metal' weapons programme of the Cold War.

Presage 29*   *War thunders. Many folk their farmlands quit.*
Borders attacked, terrors and rumours fly.
Chief betrays chief. Spain, Germany admit
The refugees. The Muslim fleet draws nigh.

In this further *Presage* (originally for July 1558), Nostradamus's text acquires the urgency almost of a series of war telegrams as France starts to buckle and fall apart in the face of the onslaught.

III.82   *Fréjus, Antibes, Nice and the rest shall be*
By land and sea despoiled along the shore.
Locusts shall ride the wind by land and sea:
Captives trussed up, raped, killed 'spite laws of
war.

The theme of war continues as the invaders advance into France with the aid of amphibious landings from the Mediterranean. Note how Nostradamus once again describes the invaders in terms of a swarm of grasshoppers – whether because of their vast numbers or because he has 'seen' (but been unable adequately to interpret) whole squadrons of helicopters descending from the sky.

Presage 60* *In filthy weather plague and storms abound:*
Muslims shall deal invasion's fearful shock.
Infinite ills this month shall us surround.
Of the great leaders all save two they'll mock.

As Western leadership fails, the invasion intensifies. This *Presage*, originally for April 1561, serves to remind us of just how convinced Nostradamus was of an imminent Muslim invasion in his own day.

5

THE INVASION OF FRANCE

Then shall come an unprecedented persecution of the church ... And that persecution shall last eleven years or a little less ... Then a united southern leader shall take over who shall persecute the church's clergy even more severely for a further three years ... This leader shall commit unbelievable crimes against the church ... At the same time there shall be so great a pestilence that two-thirds of the people shall be wiped out, such that none shall be able to identify the owners of homes or fields, and grass shall grow knee-high and more in the city streets. The clergy shall be totally abandoned, and military men shall seize all the revenues from the City of the Sun[a] and Malta and the offshore islands of Hyères, and the great chain of the port shall be broken that takes its name from the sea-bull[b] ...

Extracted from the
Letter to Henri King of France the Second

[a] Presumably either Rome (the headquarters of Western Christianity, which was astrologically associated with the sun at the time for no better reason than that it celebrates its Sabbath on a *Sunday*) or Lyon (the Lion – astrological or otherwise – has always been associated with the sun).
[b] Lat. *phoca* = seal; *Phocaea* = Marseille.

II.30   *One who the hellish gods of Hannibal*
Restores to life again shall men affright:
Nothing more dread shall records ere recall
Since befell Rome what comes by Babel's might.

A<small>T THIS POINT A NEW VARIABLE</small> enters the equation. The great Asiatic invasion, as we saw earlier, will not be confined to southern Europe. It will have a southern wing, too, which will have been advancing along the North African coast (Hannibal mounted his own invasion of Rome from Carthage, in what is now Tunisia), from where it will eventually mount its own threat to the southern coastline of Europe. Nostradamus foresees that events in this particular theatre of operations are likely to prove especially horrific. 'Babel' is simply the standard Hebrew word for 'Babylon' (the Bible's Greek equivalent).

V.68   *To drink he comes by Rhine's and Danube's shore:*
The Mighty Camel no remorse shall show.
Quake, you of Rhône; of Loire quake even more.
Yet near the Alps the Cock shall lay him low.

In this further summary-verse, Nostradamus now turns his attention specifically to the new, south-western theatre of operations. The African invader is described in terms of the Arab 'ship of the desert' using Europe as his distant oasis. In naming the Rhine and the Danube (which – no doubt significantly for our 'Janus hypothesis' – formed the former north-eastern border of the Roman Empire), Nostradamus seems to define the eventual limits of his advance, while suggesting (by his references to the Rhône and Loire) that the devastation he causes will tend to become worse the further north he goes. Finally, he foresees his eventual defeat by the

'Cock' – the familiar symbolic bird of France. As previously, however, the beginning and end of the stanza are not necessarily directly connected: that propitious event could still lie many years in the future.

VI.80   *From Fez shall rulership to Europe spread,*
Firing its cities, slashing with the sword.
O'er land and sea, by Asia's Great One led,
Christians, blues, greens fall prey to his vast horde.

The Asiatic invasion's southern, or African wing, will by now evidently have reached Morocco and be threatening south-western Europe with an unusual degree of violence. The 'blues' and 'greens', though, are unlikely to be identifiable – if at all – until nearer the time.

X.48*   *Marching from deepest Spain their banners see!*
From Europe's furthest borders press their steeds.
Troubles they'll have crossing the narrow sea:
Guerilla war their mighty host impedes.

Nostradamus paints a stirring picture of the oncoming hordes (at least in my freeish translation), but predicts various hitches for them along the way – notably, perhaps, at the Straits of Gibraltar and in the Pyrenees.

XII.59   *Accords and pacts broken on every side,*
Friendships by discords horrid are corrupted,
Hatred stirred up, all faith decayed, denied
All hope; Marseille disquieted, disrupted.

According to this supplementary quatrain (which Nostradamus may never have intended to be published), the former agreements apparently made between the Asiatics and Marseille (X.58) are now peremptorily torn up.

XII.56   *Chief against chief and head 'gainst warring head,*
Fury and rage shall reach the furthest border.
Hatred shall reign, dissension rule most dread:
In France great war, great change and great
        disorder.

The prospects are gloomy. The whole of France looks likely to be torn apart. The word *change* is one of Nostradamus's favourite terms for 'upheaval' and even 'overthrow'.

VIII.77   *The Antichrist – three very soon laid low –*
Twenty-seven years his bloody war shall stand.
Dissenters dead, captives to exile go.
Blood, corpses, reddened water pock the land.

As Prévost[49] points out, this verse is clearly based on John Calvin, whom contemporary Catholics did indeed regard as the Antichrist. The twenty-seven years mentioned in the verse are almost certainly a back reference to Calvin's time at Geneva between 1537 and 1564, with the three 'laid low' presumably including Jacques Gruet and Michel Servetus, who was burned alive for heresy there in 1553 – though the near-genocide apparently described in the last line, no doubt based on the French Wars of Religion, was presumably due more to the excesses of his followers than to his own expressed wishes. Hence, while it is certainly possible to compare his twenty-seven years of struggle with those of both Stalin and Hitler, and thus to project an image of a 'universal Antichrist' into the future involving indescribable carnage, the reference is much more likely simply to be to a future religious figure who persecutes his enemies, and whose followers take his pronouncements to unpardonable extremes. It might thus very well fit the leader of the future Islamic invasion as it starts to make serious inroads into France, but would not necessarily paint him as the *biblical* Antichrist.

IX.28   *Confederate ships shall put in at Marseille;*
At Venice, too, to march on Hungary.
From out the Gulf and the Dalmatian Bay
Others rape Sicily and Italy.

France does not have long to wait. But then it is not alone in its extremity. This originally somewhat obtuse and telegrammatic verse serves to summarise a whole range of hostile naval operations that Nostradamus foresees for the early stages of the war.

X.62*   *From Serbia he'll Hungary attack,*
Though Buda's envoy try him to divert:
The Muslim chief, Slavonia at his back,
To Islam would all Hungary convert.

The troops landing at Venice are apparently intended to rein-
force those already advancing northwards from the former
Yugoslavia towards the Danube and the twin cities of Buda
and Pest. This verse is no doubt based on the Ottomans'
similar invasion of the 1520s.

II.24* *Like ravenous beasts they'll cross the rivers all,*
The major fighting towards the Danube's shore.
In iron cage the great man they shall haul,
While infant Rhine the German watches o'er.

The significance of line three is unclear, but lines one and two
clearly refer to the invading hordes' continuing advance on
Hungary. Here as elsewhere (as Nostradamus's own
Almanachs confirm), 'Hister' (printed *Hiſter*) is the former
name of the lower Danube, not – as Frau Goebbels understandably assumed – a slightly mangled reference to Adolf
Hitler. The 'infant Rhine' would seem to refer to its upper
reaches, which lie very close to the *upper* Danube.

X.61* *Komarno, Buda, Sopron and Vienna*
Would Hungary to Muslim forces yield:
Huge violence, arms, and fires as in Gehenna.
The plotters by an old crone are revealed.

As my admittedly rather free translation of this verse reveals,
sedition from within is likely to prove just as damaging as
force from without. The identity of the old woman is not
specified.

II.90*   *A life-death fight, a changing of regimes*
Bring laws more stern than abject servitude.
Hungary shall be full of cries and screams
When for dominion its twin cities feud.

A grim struggle now descends on the twin cities of Buda and
Pest, with the northern defenders on the east bank desperately
fighting off the invaders on the west bank. The 'life-and-death'
theme suggests a possible link with VIII.15 (see page 55).
Leoni[37] sees the precursor of this verse in the Battle of Mohács of
1526, when the Ottomans took Budapest and killed its last king.

III.90   *The mighty Persian Tiger-Satyr shall*
To those at sea a welcome gift award:
A Persian shall come forth as admiral
To seize the land from Marseille's overlord.

At this point there is an interesting link-up between the orientals' main invasion-campaign via Italy and south-eastern
France and what looks like its southern, or African wing. The
invaders' supreme commander in the north – here described
as from the former Hyrcania, which lay in what is now
eastern Iran, bordering the south-eastern coast of the Caspian
Sea – evidently allows the seaborne forces to take Marseille,
rather than his own troops. They are possibly encountering
stiffer resistance than expected as they attempt to advance
into France over the Alps and along the Mediterranean coast.
According to Nostradamus, the sea-borne commander will
hail from Carmania. It is worth bearing in mind, however,
that Prévost[49] traces this verse back simply to the wild
animals that Suleiman the Magnificent (then fighting in
Carmania) sent to his then ally François I in 1533 via the
pirate Barbarossa, then visiting Marseille – which would
suggest a quite different interpretation!

I.28   *Port-de-Bouc's fort a while for craft shall quake*
From Muslim lands then, later, from the west.
Great toll shall both of beasts, men, chattels take.
What deadly strife at Bull's and Scales' behest!

Port-de-Bouc is a fortified port at the entrance to the Étang de Berre, an enormous inland lagoon some twenty miles long and up to ten across lying only a few miles to the north-west of Marseille and south of Salon, and offering immediate access to the great port's hinterland. The twelfth-century tower of the fort has now been transformed into a lighthouse. Apparently, the sea-borne invaders will cannily choose this slightly roundabout invasion route in preference to a frontal attack on Marseille itself. Nostradamus does not reveal whether the initial landings will be successful, but he does suggest that the episode will be repeated at a much later date – the words *longtemps après* could even mean some *years* later, though this seems unlikely – by a similar invasion force from somewhere further west. The first attack will occur in April/May, the second in September/October. The event directly reflects the Muslim pirate raids of 1526–31 and 1534–6.[49]

X.68*   *The fleet before the city shall remain,*
Then leave again ere many days shall pass.
By land shall many citizens be ta'en.
The fleet returns: much looting then, alas!

Once again Nostradamus refers to the interrupted attack. Clearly the fleet's initial appearance offers a dire warning of things to come.

II.37   *Out of the host that shall be sent to take*
Assistance to the fort so sore beset
Famine and plague shall all of them o'ertake
Save only seventy who are murdered yet.

If I have identified the right fort in the right war, it would seem that all attempts at relieving Port-de-Bouc's besieged fort will prove unsuccessful.

I.71   *Thrice is the sea-fort stormed, then taken back*
By Spanish, Arab and Italian thunder.
Marseille, Aix, Arles shall troops from Pisa sack,
While Turin's forces Avignon shall plunder.

As the ding-dong battle for Port-de-Bouc goes on, Nostradamus is not optimistic about the outcome. He even details which foreign forces will, meanwhile, take various of the towns on and around the Rhône delta, here identified in terms of which Italian towns they are currently occupying (as we have already seen, this is a favourite trick of the seer's). Prévost[49] relates the verse to the three captures of Marseille in 735, 1252 and 1423 – the first of these having been at the hands of the Saracens, just as my scenario for the future would require in terms of the 'Janus hypothesis'.

II.25*   *The foreign guard the fortress shall betray*
In hope expectant of some greater pact.
Guard tricked, the fort shall fall amidst the fray:
Loire, Saône, Rhône and Garonne mortally sacked.

Undermined by political chicanery, the allied forces defending Port-de-Bouc eventually fall down on their vital job, so spelling doom for the whole of France.

I.16   *Scythe joined to pool as Archer of the Night*
            Draws near his highest point of exaltation:
            Plague, famine, death by military might –
            The cycle nears its mighty renovation.

This prediction seems to speak of some significant astrological conjunction. After all, Sagittarius is clearly present, and the 'scythe' seems to indicate Saturn – which would then require the *estang* ('pool') to be a misspelling of *estain* ('tin'), a metal alchemically linked with Jupiter (possibly as pronounced by the 'dictating compositor' in his southern French accent). The verse would then be not (as I previously surmised) a description of the invaders entering France via the Étang de Berre, but a direct reflection of Richard Roussat's *Livre de l'état et mutations des temps* of 1549/50,[53] from which Nostradamus took so many of his astrological ideas and even of his actual words:

> *That is why it seems [Roussat writes] that the World will soon finish and come to its final period and conclude it. For once this present aquatic triplicity finishes (of which, calculating from the current year of 1548, we have only ninety-four years left) the triplicity of fire will come. Then Saturn and Jupiter will join each other in the fire sign Sagittarius, which is the most powerful of its triplicity and thus the father of corruption, death, lamentations, sufferings, anguish and perdition. Saturn in this fire-sign will be exalted and raised to its highest degree . . .*

171

This, of course, gives us some idea of the timescale within which Nostradamus expected this particular prediction to come to fruition, as well as of its apocalyptic nature. Fortunately or unfortunately, the conjunction does not next recur until 2162, and even then the two planets are some twenty-nine degrees apart. So unless my original 'geographical' interpretation was valid after all, possibly this particular prediction is more of general interest than of particular relevance at this juncture.

I.18   *Through French discord and negligence shall be*
To Muslim forces free access allowed:
Siena's lands blood-soaked by land and sea,
And ships and boats shall Marseille's harbour
crowd.

At all events, through sheer incompetence the invasion force (a reflection of the Ottoman maritime raiders of Nostradamus's own time, to say nothing of the much earlier Saracen ones) is allowed to break in and occupy Marseille. Nostradamus is not specific about the nature of the French negligence, but there is a distinct suggestion here that events such as this could well be mitigated, if not actually avoided, were the peoples of Western Europe to be more alert and determined to defend themselves. As ever, in other words, the answers lie in our own hands.

III.79   *Law's constant chain, from age to age imparted*
Another order suddenly denies.
The chain of Marseille's harbour shall be parted,
The city taken, foes as thick as flies.

In describing Marseille's takeover by the new Muslim regime, Nostradamus once again resorts to a familiar stylistic trick: rather like the Hebrew psalms that were so familiar to him from his ancestral Jewish family tradition, he takes a theme mentioned in the first half of his verse and re-applies it in the second, albeit in an entirely different sense.

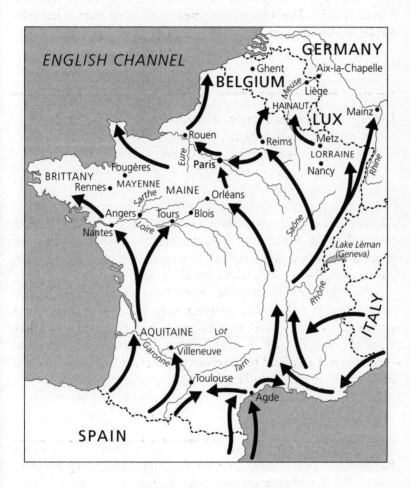

The invasion of France

X.88   *At second watch, mounted and foot alike*
         Shall force an entry, wasting all by sea.
         Within Marseille's defences they shall strike.
         Tears, screams and blood: ne'er worse times shall
             there be.

The details are now graphically spelt out, and need no explanation from me.

I.41   *The town, besieged, by night shall be assailed.*
         Few 'scape: fierce battle rages near the sea.
         Mother exults to find her son bewailed:
         Poison in letters' folds concealed shall be.

This quatrain, too, seems to describe the attack on Marseille. If so, then the last two lines appear to offer both a personal touch and a specific detail whose veracity is only ever likely to be confirmed by those directly concerned. The theme of poisoned letters is a fairly frequent one where Nostradamus is concerned.

VIII.17   *At once the well-to-do put down shall be:*
           By brothers three the world is sorely troubled.
           The foes shall take the city of the sea.
           Famine, fire, blood and plague – all ills redoubled.

Somewhat gleefully echoing the biblical 'He hath put down the mighty from their seat', to say nothing of Virgil's celebrated equivalent phrase *debellare superbos*, Nostradamus seems to foretell the fate of Marseille – and especially of its elite – at the hands of the invaders. Apparently, he confirms

that the latter will constitute an alliance of three 'brothers' –
i.e. leaders, or even powers – conceivably those advancing
along the coast, those invading from the sea and those who
have been advancing from further westwards via North
Africa respectively.

XI.91* *Hewer and Prophet and the third impending*
With plague and new assaults shall vex the
*   borders,*
Aix and the lands around their fury rending.
Then from Marseille come double the disorders.

The assaults press inland. In this supplementary quatrain,
'Hewer' and 'Prophet' seem to be symbolic epithets for two of
the three principal Muslim leaders.

I.72 *Chased and pursued, towards Lyon they shall go:*
Marseille of its inhabitants is bled.
Narbonne, Toulouse by forces from Bordeaux
Outraged. Of captives near a million dead.

As Marseille is invaded, the inevitable happens: the inhabitants flee northwards up the Rhône valley towards Lyon. In
regard to the parallel developments in the south-west,
Nostradamus is possibly using the expression 'from
Bordeaux' as a code version of 'from the seashore' (*du bord
de l'eau*). Nevertheless, it would be unwise to be too definite
about this, as there are hints later of the establishment of
what seem to be particularly brutal puppet regimes in the
areas of Bordeaux and Toulouse.

III.46 *By fixèd stars and signs both bright and clear*
The sky, O Lyon, doth to us foretell
That of your change the time is drawing near,
Whether for ill or yet for good and well.

So portentous and pompous is this quatrain as to tell us virtually nothing at all – except, possibly, that Nostradamus put it together in desperation after a rather fruitless night!

1.8* *How oft, O Lyon, you shall captured be,*
Your laws replaced by alien edicts vain!
Your doom draws near. E'en more you'll bend the
knee
When mighty Venice hunts your blood again.

At all events, in an echo of the long and tragic history of Rome itself, Lyon is now about to suffer at the hands of invaders, this time dispatched from *Hadrie* or Hadria, the ancient equivalent of Venice that gave its name to the Adriatic Sea.

II.85 *By order strict the old, full-bearded man*
At Lyon of French troops is made the head.
The little chief too far pursues his plan.
Arms sound in heaven: th' Italian seas are red.

The southern invasion now achieves what, thanks to the barrier of the Alps, the forces from Italy have so far been unable to manage – a full-scale invasion of the French heartlands. While sea-battles rage off Italy, air-battles seem to be in evidence, too: but then reports of alleged 'celestial battles' date from Roman times.

V.81 *Seven months each night o'er solar city's walls*
The royal bird its portent promulgates.
Midst thunderbolts the eastern bastion falls.
Seven days, no more, and foes are at the gates.

I take the 'solar city' to be Lyon, largely because the lion is traditionally the solar beast par excellence. The 'royal bird' is presumably an eagle, though the possibility cannot be ruled out that it is some kind of aircraft engaged in reconnaissance – or even in propaganda calling upon the city to surrender. At all events, with the southern forces preoccupied with the invasion via Marseille, there is a tremendous clash of arms in the Alps resulting in the final collapse of the eastern defences, too, and within a week the enemy are at the gates. It has to be said, though, that other candidates have been proposed for the 'solar city' – not least Rome, the western capital of the allegedly 'solar' Christian religion that, historically, had of course been sacked by Imperial troops in 1527.[49]

VIII.6 *A blazing light at Lyon seen shall be.*
Malta is quickly taken, blown away.
The Moor Sardinia treats deceitfully.
The Swiss in London feign France to betray.

As Lyon is attacked, developments elsewhere are no more propitious, either. The Mediterranean islands have either been tricked or laid waste by the enemy. Meanwhile, the Swiss seem to be engaged in some kind of double game on the diplomatic front – possibly putting it about that, despite being themselves invaded, they propose to maintain their traditional neutrality, while covertly planning defensive action in France in co-operation with the British.

III.7   *Lightning the fleeing spears strikes from the sky.*
          Of fighting crows the battle shall draw near.
          From earth to heaven goes up the plaintive cry
          When near the wall the combatants appear.

I have placed this quatrain here partly because it seems to fit, and partly because the aerial combat in line two seems to reflect that in the last line of II.85 (page 176) – though Nostradamus could simply be using the word *courbeaux* in the derogatory sense of 'vultures'. Otherwise the details could apply to any beleaguered city, and not merely to the imminent fall of Lyon.

II.83*   *Then Lyon's mighty commerce shall collapse:*
          Most of it into ruins shall revert.
          Marauding soldiers, looting, fill their caps:
          Swabia and Jura both with drizzle girt.

So it is that Lyon falls, while what look like chemical attacks take place in the mountains to the north-east. 'Fill their caps' is my own rhyme-induced invention: the French speaks of a gathering in of grapes.

III.52* *Across Campania rain unending showers.*
Apulia, though, drought most severe shall see.
Though winged and hurt, o'er Cock the Eagle
lours.
Lyon shall place her in extremity.

At a time of contradictory weather in southern Italy, the invaders' forces (the 'Eagle'?) sustain heavy losses while attacking Lyon, and their advance is checked somewhat. Alternatively, the word *Lyon* could stand for Venice, or even Britain.

II.74 *From Sens and from Autun the Rhône they'll reach,*
Then head on out towards the Pyrenees.
The hordes advancing from Ancona's beach
Shall chase them in long files o'er land and seas.

In an effort to hold the line, the French now send reinforcements from further north. Having reached the Rhône, however, they realise that they are too late to help Lyon, and head westwards instead – for reasons that will become clear shortly. They are pursued, however. Meanwhile, line three confirms what we assumed earlier: at least part of the invasion force originally came ashore on the western Italian coast (the Marches of Ancona comprise a long strip of coastline lying opposite Dalmatia, in the former Yugoslavia).

I.54* *Two revolutions of dread Saturn's sphere* **2010–12**
Shall changes bring of age and government,
When in its Libran sign it shall appear
At equinox, there in mid-firmament.

Nostradamus now anticipates a period of severe turbulence lasting the equivalent of two orbits of Saturn – i.e. some fifty-nine years. Saturn is next in Libra from July 2010 to October 2012. Alternatively, he may be referring to the ancient doctrine of planetary ages most recently expounded by Roussat,[53] under the terms of which the next 'Age of Saturn', due in 2242, is destined to be a Golden Age more or less cognate with the long-awaited Kingdom of Heaven on Earth.

V.11   *The solar powers no longer cross the main:*
North Africa shall Venus hold in fee.
Saturn and sun no more with them remain
And Asia Minor greatly changed shall be.

This fascinating summary verse now reminds us of the situation up to this point. In terms of the astrological symbolism of the day so beloved of Nostradamus, the sun, Saturn and Venus stood for Christendom, Jewry and Islam respectively, for no better reason that that their respective Sabbaths were celebrated on *Sun*day, *Satur*day and Friday (*vendredi*, or 'Venus's day' in French). *Affrique* meant North Africa, after the Roman model, and *Asie* was what we now call Asia Minor. In terms of our invasion scenario, then, the Western powers are by now restricted to the European mainland, while Islam is in full control of North Africa and Asia Minor. Line three suggests that all Christians have been either expelled or expunged from North Africa. What is now at stake is what is about to befall them within Europe itself.

VIII.21   *Infidels bringing foul disease along*
At Agde from three small vessels start their rout.
From overseas they'll mass a million strong,
At the third try their beachhead breaking out.

Possibly we now see the reason for the defenders' hasty westward flight. For now, in harmony with the foregoing stanza,
Nostradamus sees further invaders coming ashore in droves
on the long empty quays of the port of Agde on France's
south-western coast. The 'pestilence' mentioned in line one
evidently refers back to the arrival there of the plague from
Marseille in 1347–8.[49] Transferred to the future context,
however, the reference could well be to the 'plague' of
invaders. As often happens in Nostradamus's predictions, an
idea mentioned in the first half of the verse is repeated in the
second, almost as though he were using the one as a kind of
symbol for the other: in the present case, the theme in question is the number three.

III.81   *The great loud-mouth, shameless and just as daring,*
Shall of the army be elected head.
So bold his fight is and so proud his bearing,
The beachhead bursts. The city faints with dread.

Thus it is, at all events, that the invaders break out of their
beachhead and start to fan out over town and country under
a bombastic new leader.

IV.56   *When once the Rabid-Tongue has won the battle*
          The spirit's tempted tranquil rest to seek.
          All through the bloody war he'll crow and prattle
          Enough to roast flesh, bones and tongue (in-cheek!).

He is evidently a leader who never stops boasting about his achievements both past and proposed. Nostradamus is far from impressed, but glad of the opportunity to play his usual repetition trick with the word 'tongue'.

III.20   *Through all the country of Guadalquivir,*
          From Ebro to Granada far away,
          Muslims the Christians from the lands shall clear:
          Of Cordoba shall one the land betray.

Meanwhile, the Muslims are busy re-occupying the Spanish lands from which they were driven out only a few years before Nostradamus's birth. In a re-run of the Moorish invasions of Spain of the eighth century, or even of Hannibal's of the third century BC, the European defenders are expelled from most of the south-eastern half of the country, with Cordoba in particular succumbing as the result of an individual act of treachery.

VIII.26* *Cannon shall be revealed at Barcelona*
          On ruined land half-poking from the dirt.
          The lord who hot and cold blows wants Pamplona,
          Montserrat's abbey thick with drizzle girt.

As a rather uncertain commander heads towards the Pyrenees, chemical warfare is in evidence across Barcelona's

182

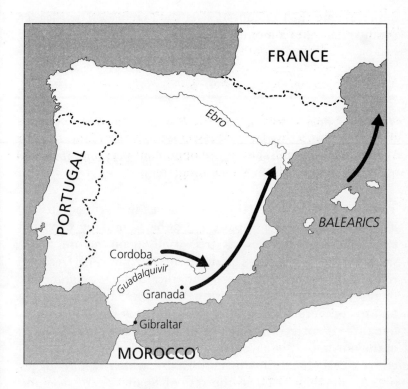

The invasion of Spain

hinterland, while more conventional artillery is dug in around the city itself.

VI.88   *A mighty kingdom desolate shall remain.*
Near to the Ebro they shall all assemble.
In Pyrenees he'll consolation gain
When in the month of May the earth shall tremble.

Most of Spain is accordingly laid waste, and the invading hordes then muster in the valley of the Ebro, prior to attempt-

183

ing to extend their conquests over the Pyrenees. Their leader, meanwhile, takes a mountain holiday a few miles to the east.

VIII.51 *Peace-offerings the Turkish chief shall make*
Once Cordoba resumes its captured state:
Long journey past, Pamplonan rest he'll take.
Prey captured crossing by Gibraltar's strait.

This extremely obtuse quatrain once again refers to the invaders' campaign in Spain. Cordoba is initially captured, but somehow manages to free itself again before finally succumbing, possibly as a result of the piece of treachery referred to earlier. At this point, the invaders' commander (here described as 'the Byzantine') sues for a truce to allow him to recuperate his force's strength. If my interpretation of line three is correct, he then travels to the region of Pamplona in the north-east, in harmony with the foregoing stanza, in an effort to recuperate his own as well – which would suggest once again that much of the rest of Spain is already under foreign control. The 'prey' in line four is not identified, but seems to be some important would-be escapee.

III.68 *Leaderless folk roam Spain and Italy,*
While dead and dying mainland Greece shall flood,
Their laws betrayed by crass stupidity
And every crossroads swimming with their blood.

Nostradamus paints a sickening picture of the consequences of the conflict as it continues to spread through a Europe that is positively swimming with refugees. At the same time, he once again presses home his point that the Europeans are themselves largely to blame. More wisdom rather earlier could yet help to avert much of what he predicts.

III.62 *By Duero (closed the great Tyrrhenian Sea)*
Through the high Pyrenees a path he'll seek.
The shortest route and crossing noted, he
On Carcassonne his stratagems shall wreak.

With maritime difficulties now apparently preventing a further sea-invasion from Italy, the invasion force in Spain is described as taking a route from the River Duero, in northern Spain, across the Pyrenees and thence into south-western France.

II.59 *Supported is the French fleet by the hand* **2013(?)**
Of Neptune and his warriors' tridents tall.
To feed the horde Provence lays waste its land.
War at Narbonne, with missiles large and small.

It is commonly assumed by British commentators that 'Neptune' refers, here as elsewhere, to Britain. Prévost[49] points out, though, that the back reference is almost certainly to the Baron de la Garde who, in April 1543, authorised the Turkish fleet to attack Nice on behalf of France: François I then emptied Toulon of its citizens to accommodate his new allies from the East until the spring of 1544. The wide historical date-spread naturally makes any application of comparative horoscopy difficult, but Saturn will next be in Scorpio and Mars in Virgo, as on that former occasion, in October 2013.

Should the British reference be valid for the future, though, it is intriguing to note that Nostradamus specifically describes its sailors, who have still not given up the fight, as wielding *tridents*. Possibly this somewhat alarming development represents the arrival, rather late in the day, of better-equipped British reinforcements in an attempt to disrupt the invasion from the south-west. The reference to Narbonne will be taken up again in subsequent stanzas.

IV.70* *The mighty Pyrenees quite close about*
Shall one his army 'gainst the Eagle throw.
Blood shall be shed, the forces all wiped out,
Their chief pursued and chased as far as Pau.

This verse is probably based on an earlier encounter between French and Spanish forces fighting on behalf of the Emperor Charles V. For the future, however, it looks like a catastrophic reverse for the defenders at the hands of the Muslim invaders.

IV.94 *Two brothers out of Spain shall harried be,*
The elder vanquished in the Pyrenees.
From Agde, Narbonne, Béziers; from Germany,
Rhône and Leman infected: bloody the seas.

Written in Nostradamus's best telegrammatic style, this prediction reveals specifically that the main invasion will have both a south-western and an eastern wing. The former will, as indicated above, come in not only via Spain, but also via the port of Agde in south-western France, the latter via southern Germany and western Switzerland into the Rhône valley.

186

I.5   *Harried they'll be as fight leads on to fight:*
The country districts shall be most oppressed.
City and town put up a better fight.
Carcassonne and Narbonne put to the test.

It is not clear from the text which of the invaders' two south-western spearheads will be involved here, though IV.94 suggests that it will probably be the sea-borne one.

Sixain 27 *Out of the west shall fire burn in the sky:*
Out of the south, too, eastwards running by.
For lack of food shall worms die in the earth.
A third time shall the warlike Mars return.
With eerie light the carbuncles shall burn:
An age of carbuncles – and then great dearth.

Here Nostradamus (if, indeed, he was the author of the *Sixains*) sets the scene for continuing developments in the south-west of France. Some extraordinary celestial phenomenon will bring fire from the sky and widespread famine, while strange, luminous fires will burn all over the landscape. While his letter to the then Governor of Provence of 1554 describes what is evidently a meteorite in just such terms, quite possibly the invaders are destined to get hold of some ghastly new aerial weapon whose effects will sear the very landscape and blight it for a very long time to come. The 'carbuncles' – originally mythical, self-luminous jewels – seem curiously reminiscent of modern laser-technology, though of course it would be unwise to draw any definite inferences. Commentators hitherto have been extraordinarily keen to use line four as an excuse to jump on the Third World War bandwagon, but nothing so grandiose is suggested. Certainly it will be the third time since 1900 that France will have experienced war on its home territory, but the stanza could equally well mean that the Asiatic invasion will have three main military phases, of which the 'fire in the sky' one moving in from the south-west will merely be the last. It could even suggest nothing more general than a triple exchange of missiles. The final dearth, or famine, seems to be the direct result: evidently the attack burns up all the crops.

II.3 *Like sun the heat shall sear the shining sea:*
The Black Sea's living fish shall all but boil.
When Rhodes and Genoa half-starved shall be
The local folk to cut them up shall toil.

This simple quatrain – which Prévost[49] relates to an old Greek legend that fishes that jumped out of their frying pans at the time of the Ottomans' sack of Constantinople would not be finally cooked until the city was liberated again – needs little explaining. Picking up on line two of the foregoing stanza, it suggests that the 'fire from the sky' phenomenon will even be felt as far east as the Black Sea. Whether this once again indicates an exchange of thermal missiles between East and West, or merely that the orientals will have first tested their new fire-weapon in their own home area, is by no means clear – especially as the second line's *Negrepont* was also the medieval name for the Greek island of Euboea, now Evia. The self-same scenario is re-echoed in V.98.

V.100 *The firebrand shall be burnt by his own fire,*
Carcassonne and Comminges, Foix, Auch, Mazères
Burnt from the sky: away the old grandsire
The troops from western Germany shall bear.

Evidently, the enemy, as yet inexperienced in its use on the battlefield, deploys his new fire-weapon much too near his own lines to start with – unless, of course, Nostradamus is merely using the words *boutefeu* and *feu* in a figurative sense. Nevertheless, the attack is devastatingly effective. One old leader, however, manages to escape, thanks to the intervention of troops from Hessen, Saxony and Thuringia – which at least suggests that the Germans, anticipating an eventual threat to their own country, are starting to involve themselves on the Mediterranean front, as well as defending their own southern borders against the Asiatic forces advancing through Switzerland.

II.6   *Of ne'er-seen scourge shall fall the double stroke*
Each city deep within and at its portal.
Famine and plague within, expelled their folk,
Calling for help upon great God immortal.

Nostradamus does not give the names of the two cities concerned. Past commentators have been keen to identify them with Hiroshima and Nagasaki. In the present context the most likely targets, however, are Carcassonne and Narbonne. The unprecedented scourges may be the new fire-weapon already described, but (as line three suggests) could as easily be some kind of bacteriological weapon. Brind'Amour[9] reminds us that removing the plague victims' bodies from the town had been part of Nostradamus's plague policy at Aix-en-Provence in 1546.

III.85   *Taken the town shall be by ruse and fraud,*
Through one young beau who shall deluded be:
Midst fighting by the Robine, near the Aude,
He and all his die for their treachery.

Nostradamus does not state which of the two towns
mentioned is involved here. However, since the attack in
question is met by an effective counter-attack beside the
Robine – nowadays a canal that joins the River Aude near
Narbonne – the latter seems the more likely. For a brief
moment, then, the advance of the invaders is stemmed. The
leader who dies is possibly one of the two 'brothers from
Spain' mentioned above.

IX.64   *The latter Philip vaults the Pyrenees:*
No armed resistance shall Narbonne present.
Such schemes he'll hatch by land and on the seas
The chief shall know not where to pitch his tent.

Literally in the light of the new fire-weapon, Narbonne finally
capitulates to the second wave of invaders advancing via
Spain. We do not have to take too seriously Nostradamus's
apparently Hellenic term *Aemathion* ('Macedonian') in the
first line. Current research tends to the view that this is a
reference to the contemporary Philip II of Spain, son of the
Emperor Charles V, by way of Philip II of Macedon, father of
Alexander the Great (Nostradamus even makes this particular
substitution in his annual *Almanachs*). It may even be that the
seer is using the term to suggest that he will be a 'reincarnation' of Alexander the Great himself. As we have already
seen, Nostradamus endlessly rings the changes on his names
for the invaders, often using their current habitat as a kind of
pseudonym. At all events, this particular leader seems espe-

cially powerful and his influence especially wide-ranging. We shall meet him again later, too.

IX.63   *Wailing and tears and screams shall rend the air*
Near to Narbonne, in Foix and at Bayonne.
What dread calamities, what changes, ere
Mars round his track shall many times have gone!

Catastrophe now follows for the people living in the south-west. Since Mars takes nearly two years to revolve about the sun, Nostradamus seems to envisage that the conflict is likely to last a good many years – not less than six, say, though possibly not much longer than ten or so. If Nostradamus seems particularly sensitive to coming events in the south-west and south-east of France, this is of course only to be expected: the area around the Rhône delta was, after all, where he was born, grew up and first went to university, while it was in the south-west that he spent much of his early professional life.

IX.73   *Blue-turbaned chief in Foix himself*   **2013/2024**
shall find.
E'er Saturn's back he'll no more rule the land.
White-turbaned chief wipes Turkey from his mind.
Sun, Mars and Mercury near Aquarius stand.

With the aid of an astrological dating that depends to a large extent on just what Nostradamus means by the word *pres* in line four (as we saw earlier, he tends on occasions to use it in place of *dans*, depending on how many syllables are available in the line), Nostradamus suggests that the invaders' occupation of the south-west will last less than the orbital period of the ill-omened planet Saturn – i.e. some twenty-nine-and-a-half years. Assuming that he means 'in Aquarius', the astrological conditions described apply between 20 January and 3 February 2013 and 14 and 19 February 2024, though there are 'near' matches in January 2015 and in the spring of 2022 as well. The two chiefs seem to be the local commanders of the two opposing sides: in his 1566 *Almanach*, the blue turbans and white turbans are simply members of opposing Islamic sects. Brind'Amour[9] refers the verse back to the quarrels between Persia and the Ottomans of 1534.

II.2   *Blue-head shall white-head harm in such degree*
As France's good to both shall e'er amount.
Hanged shall the Great One from the yard-arm be
Once the King of his captives gives account.

In this oddly convoluted quatrain, Nostradamus adds a few further details to the struggle between them – though which of them (if either) is the Great One and which the King is something that it will doubtless take contemporary eyes to figure out. The 'captives' seem to be prisoners taken from the 'Great One' by the 'King'.

III.92   *As the world's final age draws near apace*
Saturn comes slow his influence to wreak.
Empire shall be transferred to th' eastern race;
Narbonne's bright eye plucked out by goshawk's
*   beak.*

Here Nostradamus seems to suggest that the invasion of France from the south-west will serve as advance warning of the approach of the eventual millennium. He sees it, in other words, as a 'sign of the times', or as one of the inevitable birth-pangs of the millennium, however remote in time. But then the same could be said about most of his predictions for our future. In the present case, he foresees eventual victory for the invaders, whom he calls *Brodes* – a double-edged term which is both a derogatory Old French expression for 'unworthy dark-skinned people' and the Provençal for the former Allobroges, an Alpine (and thus 'eastern') tribe vanquished in classical times by Fabius Maximus in the area of the River Isère (as Nostradamus's own son, César, points out in his *History of Provence*). As ever, in other words, Nostradamus invests the incoming invaders with the name of the territory they have just conquered. Narbonne appears to have been made by the defenders into some kind of regional headquarters: the 'eye' does not have to be anything so specific as a radar-installation – in fact, on the evidence of his covering letter to King Henri II, Nostradamus may well be using the term simply to refer to the town's *ruler*. Prévost[49] refers the verse back to the fall of the Roman Empire and – appropriately – the arrival of the Arabs in Narbonne.

VI.56 *The dreaded hostile army from Narbonne*
Shall daunt those in the west. Emptied shall be
Perpignan by the blinding of Narbonne.
Then Barcelona shall attack by sea.

With Narbonne taken, the invaders will start to run riot in the south-west. Once again, Nostradamus refers to the 'blinding' of Narbonne. The precise role of Barcelona is unclear, but it seems to have been turned by the invaders into some kind of primary attack-base. Prévost[49] refers this prediction back to events from 1503.

VI.64   *They shall not hold to what they shall agree.*
            All who accept them shall be duped at will
            By pact and truce. Fighting by land and sea,
            Till Barcelona seize the fleet by skill.

Indeed, forces from Barcelona now manage to capture what is left of the French fleet, using any kind of treachery to achieve their ends. Possibly they surprise it at its moorings.

VIII.22   *Coursan, Narbonne's revolt use all your wit*
             To warn; for Perpignan betrayed shall be.
             The city red will not put up with it.
             High-flying, grey, beflagged, your killer see.

There now seem to be revolts in three of the captured towns. In the spirit of V.96 (page 91), Nostradamus goes out of his way to discourage this, even – in an extraordinary last line – apparently describing the missile (unless it is merely a flag!) that is likely to be launched against them in retaliation.

I.73   *Negligent France on five fronts to assail*
           Shall Persia, Tunis, Algiers urge from distance.
           Leon, Seville and Barcelona fail
           To keep the fleet, at Venice's insistence.

While the Asiatics' supreme command continues to direct the overall campaign from the Middle East, its theatre commanders become increasingly prone to squabbling among themselves. The occupying regime in Italy is jealous of Barcelona's recent naval success, and demands its share of the spoils. Meanwhile, the 'five fronts' mentioned in line one serve as helpful confirmation of our analysis thus far: France has been attacked along the Riviera coast, across the Alps, across the Pyrenees and, from the sea, via the ports of Marseille and Agde. Interestingly enough, no separate invasion from the north-east seems to be indicated.

IX.52   *Peace shall approach from one side, war the other.*
         Ne'er did such persecution e'er advance.
         Blood on the ground: moan, parents, sister, brother!
         What goes for one shall go for all of France.

Thus it is that France is, as it were, squeezed between two sets of forces – on the one hand those in the east and south-east, who are by now tending to settle down into some kind of peaceful occupation of the land, and on the other those in the south-west, who are ever more brutally on the warpath. The last line suggests that it is the latter who will now spread throughout the whole of France.

VI.98   *Woe to the Languedocians, terror-racked,*
         Their mighty town stained with contagion rank!
         By Muslims Christian churches shall be sacked,
         Their rivers red with blood from bank to bank.

The terror duly starts to spread out northwards and westwards. Since the original French text specifically mentions *two* rivers, the city begs to be identified as Toulouse (which lies at the confluence of the Canal du Midi and the river Garonne), thus suggesting a continuing emphasis on the south-west. Meanwhile, the invaders, no doubt heartened and strengthened by their new aerial weapon, are endeavouring to push across the various rivers which the defenders from the north have hitherto been using as defence lines.

XII.71   *Rivers and streams may slow the evil tide,*
But anger's ancient flame will not be checked.
Through France as fast as rumour it shall ride:
House, manor, church and palace shall be wrecked.

Whether or not he intended this supplementary verse (no doubt based on the religious wars of his own day) to be published, the seer seems to confirm both the defensive strategy and its relative lack of success.

I.31*   *The wars in France shall untold years endure*
Beyond the orbit of the lord of Spain,
And yet the three lords' triumph is unsure:
Cock, Eagle, Moon, Lion, Sun shall fight again.

Nevertheless, the ultimate victory of the Muslims' triple confederacy over France, Italy (or the USA), Britain and the other 'solar powers' of northern Europe who are opposed to the Muslim crescent is by no means a foregone conclusion. The back reference of line two seems to be to the Emperor Charles V, part of whose motto (*Plus ultra*) is reflected in the word *outre* at the beginning of the line.

IV.43 *The noise of war is heard aloft the skies,*
Made by the foes of all the priestly caste,
Their aim of holy edicts the demise.
Lightning and fatal war the faithful blast.

A particular aim of the south-western invaders will be the destruction of the Christian Church and all that pertains to it. Reports of 'celestial battles' had, as Brind'Amour[9] points out, long been regarded as of evil omen.

VI.9 *In holy churches scandals shall be done*
That shall be counted honours fit for praising.
Of one for whom gold medals shall be done
The end shall come 'midst torments most amazing.

Indeed, the anti-religious campaign will be pursued with almost sadistic relish.

I.96 *He who was charged with putting to the torch*
Churches and sects shall change upon a whim.
The stones more than the people he shall scorch,
By beauteous speech sense being restored to him.

At least one of the leading invaders is not totally deaf to pleading, though. The Asiatic equivalent of Henry VIII's Thomas Cromwell is persuaded to restrict his destructive activities ('burning' is merely my own selection from them) to the religious buildings, rather than immolating the people within them too. Both Brind'Amour[9] and Prévost,[49] though, relate this verse to a description by the first-century Roman poet Lucan of a

Gallic painting in which the tongue of the Gallic Ogmion (the equivalent of the Greek Hercules, and much referred to by Nostradamus) is attached by little chains to the ears of his listeners to indicate his almost magical power of speech – an image taken up again for the celebrations for the entry of the young Henri II into Paris in June 1549.

I.46   *Near Auch, Lectoure, Mirande, with scarce a pause*
            Three nights shall mighty fire from heaven rain –
            Stupendous and miraculous the cause –
            Then shortly earth shall quake with might and
            main.

This prediction clearly applies mainly to the Département of Gers in south-western France. Whether the earthquake (natural or otherwise) is likely to be a purely local one, however, is not entirely clear. The 'stupendous and miraculous' cause of the aerial fire once again suggests some human agency at work, whether military, scientific or technological. The most obvious candidate, clearly, is the African invasion force, as it continues to spread into south-western France from Spain. Prévost[49] finds plenty of historical antecedents for the events described. Unfortunately, however, most of them took place in the 1560s, and thus probably too late for the verse in question!

IX.51   *Faithful resisters shall the reds assail*
            By fire, iron, water, rope shall peace expire.
            About to die the plotters, who shall fail –
            Save one, a world destroyer uniquely dire.

Nevertheless, widespread resistance continues, albeit now driven underground. It fails, however.

VIII.2   *At Condom, Auch and all*   2017/2019/2021
        around Mirande
        Fire do I see that from the sky shall fall.
        Sun, Mars in Leo: lightning at Marmande
        With hail: then falls Garonne's defensive wall.

This seems to be a further elaboration of I.46 (page 198). This time an astrological timing is added. Mars and the sun are in Leo in the summers of 2017, 2019 and 2021, but not thereafter for some time. Once again, the towns targeted are all in or near the Département of Gers in the south-west, and the Asian invaders may well thus have a hand in the phenomena mentioned. The strange detail concerning a wall falling in the Garonne area may refer to the final collapse of the local French defences: apparently the defenders will indeed have attempted to turn the river or one of its tributaries into a major defence-line, as suggested in XII.71 (page 196).

II.91   *At sunrise shall a mighty fire appear,*
        Its roar and glare towards the north extending:
        Within the circle death and screams they'll hear,
        Famine and death the flames of war attending.

Once again the 'fire from the sky' phenomenon all too easily presses the 'nuclear attack' button in the minds of a good many commentators, as the foreign assault extends steadily northwards. The 'circle', however, seems well enough defined to suggest something much more surgical and precise. Once again, in other words, what is involved could be something more akin to the laser – though all such conjectures are of course extremely risky. After all, Prévost[49] merely sees this as a re-evocation of a comet – though in this case one that was at least a year too late for the verse in question! Brind'Amour[9] rather more convincingly adduces the celestial omen of 91 BC reported by Julius Obsequens that allegedly portended the subsequent civil war of the Roman Republic.

VI.97 *Latitude forty-five, the sky shall burn:*
To greater Villeneuve shall the fire draw nigh.
For a long moment flames shall chase and churn
When with the North conclusions they shall try.

Yet again, Nostradamus returns to the horrific phenomenon of fire from the sky. This time he suggests that it has now moved north to the area of the forty-fifth parallel, as well as specifying that an unnamed *grand cité neufve* will be a main target of it. Commentators apparently anxious to scare the public with a picture of worldwide nuclear devastation as a result of a Third World War are only too prone to ensure that the 'new city' (thus, in all probability, a town with 'new' in its title) *is* named. It is, they suggest, Geneva, New York, Naples (from Greek *Neapolis*, 'New City'), even the determinedly un-'new' Paris. Needless to say, Geneva is close to the forty-sixth, not the forty-fifth parallel, while neither New York nor Paris is anywhere near either.

The various Villanuevas in Spain lie even further away. The Villeneuve just north-west of Avignon is a better candidate, but on the wrong parallel (the forty-fourth) – and clearly Nostradamus lived close enough to it to know what he was talking about. Villanova d'Asti, just south of Turin, is on the right latitude, but geographically more likely to be subject to an east-west battle than a north-south one. Naples is suitably

200

named, but much too far to the south. Villeneuve-sur-Lot in south-western France, on the other hand, fits the case perfectly. It is well within the forty-fifth degree (lying on about $44\frac{1}{2}°$ north) and just north of the Garonne. True, it is not particularly 'great', but it is a good deal bigger than Villanova d'Asti: moreover, Nostradamus does tend to fling the word *grand* around rather liberally, more or less as a form of poetic padding – in fact, there are remarkably few quatrains without at least one example of it. Evidently the town is a focal point for the battle between the invaders from the south and the defending northerners, or *Normans*, as Nostradamus archly calls them here.

VI.34　　*Of flying fire th' ingenious machine*
　　　　　The great beleaguered captain sore shall bruise.
　　　　　Within, there shall be such sedition seen
　　　　　That those it touches every hope shall lose.

Although this prediction is not specific as to time or place, it does appear to fit in at this point. The celestial fire, it seems, is indeed of human origin, though the consequent loss of morale among the defenders will prove at least as damaging as the ghastly weapon itself.

I.87　　*Earth-shaking fires from the world's centre roar:*
　　　　　About Villeneuve the earth shall be a-quiver.
　　　　　Two leaders long shall wage a fruitless war,
　　　　　Till Arethusa reddens a new river.

The battle continues around Villeneuve, with neither side gaining the upper hand (*faire la guerre aux rochers* is simply a

201

French idiom meaning 'to struggle fruitlessly'). However, with the aid of their fire weapon – apparently directed in some way *from the Middle East*, unless it is simply a reference to the Greek subterranean earthquake god Poseidon – the invaders eventually succeed in pressing northwards across the river Lot whose waters, like those of the Garonne before it, are now reddened with the defenders' blood. Arethusa, one of the Hesperides, or daughters of Night, was also the goddess of natural springs. Once again, meanwhile, Nostradamus takes an idea from the first half of the verse (the 'new' of 'New City', i.e. Villeneuve) and re-applies it in the second.

III.12   *By Ebro, Tagus, Tiber, Rhône and Po*
            And by Geneva's and Arezzo's lakes
            From Bordeaux and Toulouse shall leaders go
            Captive, drowned, killed, as war its booty takes.

The war in south-western France has now become the main theatre of operations. The captured leaders of the cities on the Garonne are taken prisoner and transported as 'human booty' to Portugal, Spain, south-eastern France, Italy or Switzerland, where they are shamefully treated.

IV.47   *Once the fierce Moor his bloody hand has tried*
            And the whole land to fire, sword, bow has put,
            The people shall be shocked and terrified
            To see their leaders hanged by neck and foot.

Others are publicly hanged as an example. The specific weapons in line two do not have to be taken too literally: they were merely the standard weapons of Nostradamus's day, just as automatic rifles and machine-guns are of ours.

IV.76   *Those at Agen by those from Perigord*
          Are harried all the way to flowing Rhône.
          The foolishness of Gascons and Bigorre
          The church betrays ere yet the sermon's done.

Thus it is that the invaders from Africa (albeit continually
harassed by European forces from further north) start to break
out of the south-west, first occupying the whole of France's
Mediterranean littoral as far as the Rhône, where their Asiatic
counterparts seem to have come to a halt some time previously.
It is difficult to decode the last two lines, though, other than to
suggest that they indicate a quick campaign.

V.98   *At forty-eight degrees of latitude*
          As Cancer ends shall come a drought so dire
          That fish-filled sea, rivers and lakes are stewed,
          Béarn, Bigorre seared from the sky with fire.

The fire scenario continues, this time stretching as far north as
the river Loire at Orléans. Possibly the defenders have made the
river into their fall-back defence line as the invaders now press
further northwards. To the south, in the Pyrenean foothills, the
environmental effects are already horrific. Nostradamus seems
to date this new development to the end of July.

IV.46   *Your good defences being your crowning virtue,*
          Beware, O Tours, your imminent demise.
          London through Nantes and Rennes shall not
              desert you.
          Do not go out when rain drifts from the skies.

Further down the Loire valley, Tours is also attacked but, being protected on all sides except the east by the rivers Loire and Cher, has a good chance of resisting the assault. Apparently, the city of Rennes, to the north-west, is serving as the defenders' area-headquarters, while Nantes has its own forces in the field. The British, too, sensing the increasing threat to their own shores, are at last starting to play a more active role in the fighting. Line four, however, hints at a rather sinister development: evidently the attackers, in their frustration, will once more resort locally to something that looks remarkably like chemical or bacteriological warfare.

VI.44   *By night near Nantes a rainbow shall be seen.*
Maritime arts raise rain out of thin air.
Fleet sunk off Araby: monster obscene
In Saxony is born from sow and bear.

One of Nostradamus's more fantastic quatrains, this one is no doubt just as rationally explicable as all the others. Some kind of worrying technological wizardry is deployed by the enemy navy as the invaders attempt to cross the Loire. The same noxious 'rain' seems to be referred to as in the last stanza. The 'monster' in the last line is no doubt simply another of Nostradamus's typical 'timing omens'.

IV.74   *From Lake Leman, from rivers Eure and Sarthe,*
All meet to face the threat from Aquitaine.
Germans in droves, and more Swiss, shall take part,
Yet shall be beaten, as shall those from Maine.

The signs are that even the more northerly defensive line is destined to fall. All the defenders except the Swiss, after all, appear to come from north of the Loire.

V.85 *Among the Swabians and the Swiss shall they*
Against the swarms prepare themselves to fight.
Ships' shrouds shall locusts and mosquitoes stay,
Geneva's weaknesses exposed to light.

Clearly, neither naval activities nor locusts fit south-east Germany or Switzerland particularly well. Since the foregoing stanza describes the Swiss as fighting alongside their allies in northern France – presumably to defend the Loire defence line – the action would appear to be taking place in the area of St-Nazaire, which lies on the northern shore of its estuary. Evidently, though, they will not prove very effective. As for the 'locusts and mosquitoes' to which the original line three refers, it seems once again as though Nostradamus has adopted the image as a code word for the swarming invaders (or possibly for their helicopters), along much the same lines as are suggested in IV.48, page 103.

II.64 *Genevans shall for thirst and hunger cower*
When once their last and brightest hope recedes.
At near collapse shall be Cévennian power:
To put in at the port no fleet succeeds.

Once again the mention of fleets and ports suggests that the Swiss are fighting well outside their own homeland. As previously, then, the River Loire suggests itself. Troops from the Cévennes, in the south of France, are also evidently making what is virtually their last stand there. Indeed, the geography suggests that the two armies will be responsible for defending the river's lower reaches. The impression is strong that they are expecting to be supplied via Nantes, but that the invaders' blockade of the port has reduced them virtually to impotence.

I.20   *Tours, Blois, Reims, Angers shall a change intense*
Like Orléans and Nantes soon overtake:
About them foreigners shall pitch their tents.
Missiles at Rennes: both land and sea shall quake.

So it is that the northern defence line falls, like the southern one before it, and the whole of northern France is opened up to the swarming invaders. Rennes, as a regional defence head-quarters, comes in for special treatment, and both there and near St Nazaire massive bombardments ensue involving what the sixteenth-century Nostradamus can inevitably only call 'darts' or 'arrows'.

X.7   *When mighty war at Nancy he prepares,*
'New Philip' says, 'I am the conqueror, I.'
Or drunk or sober, Britain's full of cares.
Metz shall not long continue to defy.

The Asiatics' eastern flank is likewise rapidly pressing north-wards via Nancy and Metz. It is headed by the same powerful 'reincarnation' of Philip II of Macedon – and latterly of Spain, too – whom we have encountered on several occasions before, described by Nostradamus as *l'Aemathien*, or 'the Macedonian'. Seeing the tide of invasion sweeping towards the English Channel, the British are naturally starting to become alarmed: neither reason nor drink is able to make things look much rosier for them.

IX.19 *Amidst the leafy forest of Mayenne,*
With sun in Leo, lightning shall descend.
The mighty bastard of the lord of Maine
That day a weapon shall at Fougères rend.

The summer sees alien forces pressing into north-western France, too, and nearing the borders of Brittany – while still deploying their aerial fire-weapon. Still the defenders are hard-pressed and one of their commanders killed (whatever his family pedigree).

I.26* *In daylight broad a bolt shall fell the lord –*
So does this humble messenger predict.
As long foretold, too, night sees war abhorred
London, Reims, Tuscany with plague afflict.

By now London and Reims are starting to suffer bombardment – as possibly anticipated by *Sixain* 54, already quoted in Chapter 3. As in Italy, the attacks seem to have a worrying chemical or biological component.

III.18 *After long rain of milk upon the ground*
Shall Reims be touched by lightning from the sky.
What bloody conflict shall the place surround!
Fathers, nor sons, nor kings dare venture nigh.

At Reims, meanwhile, something more sinister seems to be in play – what looks remarkably like a renewed outbreak of chemical or bacteriological warfare. No wonder the actual fighting takes place exclusively *outside* the city, and that nobody dares venture near.

V.30   *About the mighty city there shall roam*
Troops billeted in every town and farm
To strike at Paris on behalf of Rome.
There on the bridge great ravages, great harm.

With Paris now surrounded on three sides, it inevitably becomes the invaders' next target. Possibly they regard it almost as their ultimate prize. The French, naturally, are determined to resist to the utmost, and the bridges over the Seine are liable to see heavy fighting, especially if some of the defenders attempt a symbolic last-ditch stand at the city's heart on the Île de la Cité.

IX.56   *Past Goussonville is Houdan's force diverted,*
Leaving its standard to the Scythian host.
At once, more than a thousand are converted,
Lest chiefs be chained to pillar and to post.

With the army in full retreat past Paris, the oppressed French people (such as still remain, that is) are forced to swear instant allegiance to Islam: both Goussonville and Houdan lie just to the west of the city.

V.43   *The ruin of the priesthood's next in line*
Throughout Provence, Spain, Italy and France.
In Germany, Cologne beside the Rhine
Harassed to death as Mainz's hordes advance.

As the campaign continues, the invaders make a new attempt to wipe out organised Christianity throughout the occupied lands. Apart from Provence, the French text specifically mentions Naples, Sicily, Sées and Pons – symbolic respectively of mainland Italy, island Italy, France and Spain. At the same time, their eastern flank continues to move northwards from Mainz along the west bank of the Rhine in an echo of former wars with the Holy Roman Empire, apparently without at this stage crossing it and making inroads into the heart of Germany.

VIII.98*   *The blood of churchmen shall be freely shed:*
Long time shall pass ere it shall cease to flow.
As though 'twere water see it flowing red!
Woe, ruin, grief the priests shall undergo.

As Nostradamus points out in his covering letter to the King, too, the persecution of the Church is destined to be of unprecedented severity.

IV.19   *To Rouen troops from Italy lay siege,*
By land and sea all access having barred.
Of Hainaut, Flanders, Ghent and of Liège
Like drunken men they'll waste the borders hard.

As the central front moves northwards to Rouen, the assault's right flank presses on towards the Belgian frontier. There is just a hint in the last line, though, that the advance may not persist very far beyond this point, especially in the rather more easily defended terrain of the Ardennes. The back reference appears to be to the sixteenth-century wars between France and the Holy Roman Empire to the East.

IX.45*   *His lust and greed ne'er satisfied one whit,*
       The False One's sway shall spread unceasingly.
       Worst of all tyrants, far shall run his writ,
       Subverting Piedmont, Paris, Picardy.

Nevertheless, the invaders are by now in control of most of
Italy and France.

I.89*   *From Lérida they'll come to the Moselle,*
       Slaughtering all the folk of Loire and Seine,
       Sea-going ships at hand with full-pressed sail.
       How much blood shall be spilt by those from Spain!

With Arab troops from eastern Spain on the rampage
throughout northern France, supported by a naval task force
in the Channel, the fighting finally approaches the German
border near Metz. Once again the back reference is no doubt
to the sixteenth-century wars between France and the Holy
Roman Empire.

IV.86   *When in Aquarius sun with Saturn makes*   2021
       Conjunction, shall the mighty king and great
       Received, anointed be at Reims and Aix:
       War won, the innocents he'll immolate.

The ritual coronation of the invading warlord in the prime
royal sanctuaries of the ancient Frankish and French kings
marks the summit of his achievements in Europe. It was at
Reims that no less than six French kings were crowned during
the Middle Ages and – even more significantly – Aix-la-

Chapelle or Aachen is where the former emperor
Charlemagne was both crowned and buried. The sun and
Saturn are next in Aquarius together in January and February
2021, with their closest approach on 24 January.

X.50*　　*Saturn plus three within Aquarius*　　　　**2021**
　　　　　The Meuse and Luxembourg by day shall hail,
　　　　　Flooding Lorraine, cities and strongholds various,
　　　　　Mountains and plains. Bucketfuls of betrayal!

Whether Nostradamus is here referring to literal inundations
or merely to the floods of invaders is not entirely clear.
Possibly he means both. Certainly he is determined to have
fun with the symbolism of Aquarius, the celestial water-
carrier, at this point. Saturn is next in three degrees of
Aquarius from 13 to 21 January 2021. Alternatively, it and
three other bodies (Jupiter, Venus and Mercury) are next in
Aquarius in the company of the sun ('by day') from 2 to 18
February in the same year: the moon joins them from 11 to
12 February. No similar conditions apply for some thirty
years thereafter. Prévost[49] suggests fairly convincingly that
the original events took place in 1523, and that the original
betrayal was the defection of the Constable of Bourbon to the
Empire prior to attacking Provence on its behalf.

X.51*　　*The lower portion of the fair Lorraine*
　　　　　Shall be united with Low Germany,
　　　　　While Picards, Normans, Swiss and those of Maine
　　　　　All sore beset, united too shall be.

Thus it is that, as Nostradamus wryly puts it, virtually all of
France is now united – but only by dint of being occupied. In

the north-east, only a small part of Lorraine manages to escape the invaders' clutches by uniting itself with Germany. And so, Nostradamus's beloved echo-effect reigns again – as, of course, does the 'Janus hypothesis' in respect of France's former wars against the Empire.

IX.50*   *The False One, at the zenith of his reign,*
       Shall of the fair Lorraine o'ertake a part,
       The pale red heritor of his domain,
       For fear of the Barbarians sick at heart.

However, the Asiatic overlord's days are numbered. His youthful successor is destined to be a good deal less aggressive and self-confident, and possibly less politically committed, too.

I.4*   *O'er all the world a mighty king there'll be*
       Whose reign – and peace – shall not endure too long.
       Then shall St Peter's Barque be lost at sea,
       Having been steered towards ruin and towards
           wrong.

No doubt this verse originally applied to the Roman Emperor Charles V who ruled over one of the largest empires ever seen, both in the Old and New Worlds. But possibly it applies to the new European overlord and the virtual collapse of the Roman Catholic Church in mainland Europe as well.

V.13   *The lord from Rome in furious anger black*
Shall send his Arab horde Belgium to rape:
But just as furious they shall chase them back
From Hungary to stern Gibraltar's cape.

At last, light starts to show at the end of the long tunnel of death and destruction. Eventually, the defending forces are destined to stage a break-out from Belgium which will end in the reversal of all the invaders' successes and their ultimate expulsion from Europe.

III.49   *O France, what changes lie in wait for you!*
To foreign lands your government shall pass.
You shall be ruled by laws and customs new.
Rouen and Chartres shall hurt you sore, alas!

That, however, is for the future. The darkness has to be lived through first. Virtually the whole of France, after all, has fallen into the hands of the invaders, who have promptly imposed on it an entirely new system of government. Under the terms of it, the country is no longer run from Paris – possibly because the city is no longer available to exercise that function. Instead, regional centres such as Rouen and Chartres take over all administration. Indeed, in these two cases, the occupation regimes turn out to be of a truly repressive and brutal kind.

VII.34   *In grief the land of France shall mope and pine,*
Light-heartedness be foolishness decreed.
No bread, salt, water, beer, medicine nor wine:
Their leaders captive: hunger, cold and need.

Abject deprivation and misery result. War and occupation
have their customary results all over France.

IX.55   *After dread war that westward is prepared*   **2022**
Contagion comes with but a year's demur.
Blood, fire. Nor old nor young nor beast is spared.
In France, Mars, Mercury and Jupiter.

Since France was associated with Aries in Nostradamus's day,
the final line – evidently an astrological one – suggests that a
three-planet conjunction in that sign will mark the widespread epidemic predicted (sometimes associated by
commentators with the 'Spanish 'flu' epidemic of 1918):
Jupiter and Mars are both in Aries at midsummer 2022 – but
Mercury 'misses' by a whole sign. However, this could be
explained by the fact that the orbit of the fast-moving and
difficult-to-observe planet Mercury was not well calculated at
the time, so that in his horoscopes Nostradamus does sometimes have it in the wrong sign.

VI.43   *Long time unpeopled shall the country lie*
That's watered by the rivers Marne and Seine.
Tempted the armies England are to try:
Folly to think to beat them back again!

The invaders having now moved north into Normandy and left it desolate, England lies open before them. Nostradamus warns its defenders (*les gardes*) against assuming that they can push back the Asiatic hordes once they have been allowed to land. Taking their lesson from the earlier saga of Italian and French apathy and incompetence, the British would be well advised to use their air- and sea-power to fight off the attackers well before they come ashore, perhaps taking urgent steps in the meantime to seek powerful allies from abroad, much as they did in the Second World War. In some respects, meanwhile, *Sixain 54*, below, seems potentially more applicable to this situation than to the Second World War to which it is generally applied. Both England and Flanders, in other words, could now be subject to a long period of aerial bombardment. Nevertheless, Nostradamus's historical precedent for much of his invasion scenario may lie in the long-distant past, with the Roman invasion of Gaul under Julius Caesar, as described in his *Gallic War* – while this verse, as is often the case, could equally well be taken to refer to the reverse scenario, i.e. *English* attacks on *France*, possibly going right back to the Hundred Years' War.

Sixain 54   *Six hundred, fifteen, twenty, Lady dies.*   2007–12+
        Thereafter soon a long rain from the skies
        Of fire and iron shall hurt those countries sore.
        Flanders is of their number, England yet:
        Long shall they by their neighbours be beset
        Until to them constrained to take the war.

As its 'ecclesiastical' dating reveals, this verse applies not to the so-called Blitz of the Second World War, but to events in the twenty-first century. The death of the 'Great Lady' evidently refers to the defeat of France at the hands of the southern invaders whose course we have been following throughout this chapter. And now, as the years roll by, the attacker's eyes will increasingly be turned towards England and the Low Countries.

V.71   *With the great rage of one who waits the tide,*
With such great rage the whole host seethes and
hums.
Loaded on boats seventeen commanders ride:
Too late along the Rhône the message comes.

Unless this stanza refers to earlier invasion attempts, such as those of Napoleon or Hitler (which, of course, in view of the *Propheties*' essentially cyclic nature it could very well do), it seems that the Asiatics in northern France will indeed prepare an invasion fleet, only awaiting the order to attack the English south coast. Unfortunately for them, this is too slow to arrive from the south, and the vital moment is missed.

II.68   *Throughout the North their efforts shall be great,*
Upon the sea the door be open wide.
The island power shall all re-integrate.
London shall quake when first the fleet's espied.

In consequence, the British defenders and their allies are given both a salutary shock and a golden opportunity to rally and consolidate their forces.

III.71　　*Those in the Isles besieged shall by and by*
Build up their strength against the foreign foe.
Abroad, the beaten peoples starve and die,
And famine worse than ever they shall know.

This quatrain – equally reminiscent in some ways of the
Second World War – suggests that a pattern similar to that
particular one will now be followed, and history will consequently repeat itself, as Nostradamus himself was always
convinced that it does. Once again, in fact, Britain seems to
be destined to serve as the eventual jumping-off point for
some kind of massive counter-attack.

Sixain 50*　　*Before or after straight shall England lie,*
Through Wolf laid low, prostrate and fit to die.
Then shall the fire against the water rise.
Relit, it shall increase its strength and power
And human hearts shall superhuman tower.
Of food not much; of weapons vast supplies.

In his *Sixains*, meanwhile, Nostradamus starts to present us
with a whole new cast of symbolic beasts. To the Asiatic
invaders he applies the terms 'the Elephant' (compare *Sixain*
29, page 95) and 'the Wolf' – possibly the invasion's African
and Asiatic components respectively. The Northern
Europeans (as we shall see shortly) he calls 'the Leech' and
'the Doctor' – presumably in token of an eventual mission by
two of the major northern powers to draw the blood of the
invaders and to heal Europe's wounds respectively. He also
calls them 'the Griffon' – apparently a symbol for the
composite nature of their alliance. In light of this verse, then,
as well as of *Sixain* 30, below, there seems to be hope for the
patient yet, provided that the old fires of national pride and

martial ardour can now be kindled anew, especially as Nostradamus seems to regard fire – and specifically the burning of olive-branches – as a treatment for epilepsy's *grand mal*, the so-called falling sickness.

Sixain 45*   *A blow of steel shall all the world amaze*
Dealt by the Crocodile in curious ways
To a great kinsman of the Leech-to-be:
And soon thereafter, as in ambuscade,
Shall yet another 'gainst the Wolf be laid:
And of such deeds the outcome we shall see.

Once again, Nostradamus reiterates in symbolic terms his combined message of disaster and hope for the future Europe. The 'Crocodile', as elsewhere in the *Propheties*, presumably represents forces from Africa.

Sixain 30* *Shortly the Doctor of the Sickness Falling*
And the Great Leech (of lesser rank and calling)
Shall burn the olive branch throughout the south.
Rushing both here and there with might and main
From the free world such flames shall light again,
There'll be no further foaming at the mouth.

And so Nostradamus sees signs of hope. A new war of liberation is about to ensue, and a fallen Europe is destined at last to be revived.

6

THE GREAT RETURN

The Holy Sepulchre, so long revered, shall long remain exposed ... to sun, moon, sky and stars. The sacred place shall be turned into a stable for livestock small and large, and put to other profane uses ... The tongues of the Latin nations shall be mingled with Arabic and North African forms of speech (but) ... the said reign of the Antichrist shall not last ... The third northern leader shall raise a greater army than any of his predecessors to restore everybody to their original estate ... A new incursion shall be made from the sea-coasts by those who ever since the Muslim occupation have been anxious to act as liberators ... All the oriental leaders shall be driven away, overthrown and reduced to nothing, not entirely by the strength of the Northern leaders ... but by the three members of the secret confederacy itself who shall attempt to trap, ambush and kill one another ... The great Vicar of the church shall be restored to his former state, now desolate and totally abandoned following its destruction by the pagans and the rejection and burning of Old and New Testaments alike ... Then shall two Northern leaders overcome the orientals, and such shall be the noise and tumult of their campaign that all the East shall quake at the name of these two northern brothers who are nevertheless not brothers ... Afterwards the

French Ogmion[a] shall pass the Mountain of Jove,[b] accompanied by so great a number as to permit distant powers to impose on the Empire its own, greater law ... For then the oriental overlord shall be vanquished, mostly under pressure from those from the North and West, who shall kill him, defeat him and put all the rest to flight ...

Extracted from the
Letter to Henri King of France the Second

THUS IT IS THAT, IF NOSTRADAMUS is to be believed, the mighty pendulum of war is destined finally to reach its furthest extent in Europe. As is ever the case with pendulums, all that can now possibly follow is a mighty reverse swing, for it is in the nature of reality as we know it that neither good nor evil can ever lord it for ever over the other. The one, indeed, depends for its very life upon the other, and so events always tend towards some kind of uneasy equilibrium. Whether this state of affairs might eventually change is, of course, entirely dependent on whether we ourselves can learn to change our consciousness, our very way of knowing. Nostradamus and those with similar views might well associate that ultimate human achievement with the coming of the millennium. But between that event and the current crisis there is, it seems, a very great deal still to happen.

---

[a] *Ogmios* was the eloquent ancient Gallic version of Hercules.
[b] Either the Capitol Hill in Rome, ancient seat of government and site of the temple of Jupiter Capitolinus, or the Mons Jovis in Barcelona.

VI.12   *Against the Empire armies he shall raise:*
        Loyal to the Vatican the prince shall be.
        Belgium and England (Spain can only gaze)
        Prepare to fight both France and Italy.

The detailed scenario – clearly based by Nostradamus on the contemporary wars between France and the Empire – now continues. France's ruler in exile, a keen Catholic, starts to co-ordinate the armed build-up that must necessarily precede any attempt to win back the conquered lands.

Sixain 58*   *The Leech shall soon thereafter die –*
        A goodly sign for us, say I,
        And for the growth of France again.
        Allied shall then be either land,
        Two mighty kingdoms hand-in-hand,
        And France in power shall o'er them reign.

Reverting for a moment to lines of eight syllables, Nostradamus reveals that at around this juncture the 'Leech' – possibly the British supremo – will die, whereupon France will take over the leadership of the Grand Alliance.

II.1   *From out the British Isles towards Aquitaine*
        Of English troops great movements there shall be:
        Dreadful the lands are made by icy rain.
        On Lunar port fall great assaults by sea.

Thus it is that we come to the great turning-point of the Asiatic conflict as, rather as in the Second World War, the defenders at last return in force to Western Europe, many of them using Britain as a base. True, *Port Selyn* (i.e. 'lunar port') in line four is not easy to identify: in Nostradamus the term *Selyn* usually simply refers to the lunar crescent of Islam. In the seer's day, links were still strong between England and partly Protestant Aquitaine.

V.34 *From out the heart of England's farthest west*
Where of the British Isles the chief's residing
A fleet invades Gironde at Blois's behest
Dread fire, not wine or salt, in barrels hiding.

The first invasion target, however, is France's west coast, and specifically the protected waters of the Gironde estuary. 'Blois' seems to refer to the prospective French leader who, as we shall see in due course, seems to have royal blood, which he traces back to that city.

II.61 *Hail, England, in Gironde and Rochelle's port!*
Hail Trojan blood! War at Port de la Flèche:
Beyond the river, ladders scale the fort.
Flashes of fire, great slaughter in the breach.

The invasion fleet arrives, and the British assault on the western coast commences. The initial target is indeed La Rochelle and the vast, protected estuary of the Gironde to the south of it. The 'Trojan blood' refers to the tradition, much espoused by Ronsard and Nostradamus, that the kings of France were descended via the Merovingians from Priam of Troy – though here the term could possibly refer to the French in general.

The liberation of France

VI.60*   *The Prince who from abroad to France comes back*
           By his interpreters is roundly fleeced;
           Troops that shall Rouen and Rochelle attack
           At Blaye deceived by Breton monk and priest.

Despite an initial failure of intelligence – associated by
Prévost[49] with historical events from 1547/8 – the landings in
the Gironde estuary duly take place at the port of Blaye.

III.83   *The long-haired warriors of Celtic Gaul*
Accompanied by troops from overseas
In Aquitaine take captive one and all,
Subjecting them to all their own decrees.

In this evocation of the ancient invasions of the Vandals and Visigoths, Nostradamus seems to confirm the participation of French forces in the attack.

III.9   *Bordeaux, Rouen and la Rochelle shall fight*
To hold the lands that border on the sea.
But English, Bretons, Flemings shall unite
And force them to the river Loire to flee.

Despite determined resistance by the occupiers of western and northern France, the liberation forces succeed in pushing them back at least as far as the Loire. Indeed, the last line of the French text specifically mentions the town of Roanne which, though on the Loire, is actually only a few miles to the north-west of Lyon. It is interesting to note that Nostradamus lists the liberators as coming from England, Brittany and the Low Countries – a fairly clear indication that all three lands have somehow managed to escape the worst of the Asiatic invasion.

IX.38   *English attacks on la Rochelle and Blaye*
The latter-day King Philip soon outflank.
The Gaul awaits, to Agen very high,
Then helps Narbonne, deceived by falsehoods rank.

After confirming that the British forces have landed not only at la Rochelle, but also at Blaye, deep within the Gironde estuary, this verse once again refers to the enemy overlord as the *Aemathien*, and thus as a 'reincarnation' of Philip of Macedon and/or Philip II of Spain. In the south-west, meanwhile, a commander who looks suspiciously like some kind of powerful resistance leader is waiting to join up with the liberators, prior to freeing Narbonne, which is half-inclined to side with the retreating Asiatic invaders.

IX.85   *They'll pass Guyenne, the Languedoc and Rhône,*
Thanks to Agen, Marmande and la Réole.
Defences lowered, Marseille's lord takes his throne.
Battles shall rage near St-Paul-de-Mausole.

The victorious invasion forces now sweep westwards across the south of France, fighting a number of set-piece battles along the way at places such as those named in the second line. Marseille is recaptured, and a campaign is fought close to St-Paul-de-Mausole, just south of Nostradamus's birthplace of St-Rémy.

IX.58   *On the left bank at Vitry-le-François*
They shall keep watch o'er France's red ones three:
All reds are killed, no blacks, though, murdered are.
By Bretons they shall all enheartened be.

In the north-east, meanwhile, the counter-invasion via Flanders continues. Three of the fleeing Asiatic overlords are captured and lynched. Historically, Vitry-le-François, on the River Marne, had been rebuilt in 1545, after being destroyed by Charles V's forces.

225

V.70   *Of regions Libran some at very least*
With mighty war the mountains they'll assail.
Captives of all religions throughout the East
From land to land each dawn they shall bewail.

In due course, the liberating forces will also start to expel the
invaders from the uplands of Central Europe, presumably
approaching Italy via southern Germany, eastern France and
Switzerland. Roussat[53] seems to identify the 'Libran regions'
as Arabia, Asia Minor and Italy, but Prévost[49] suggests a
further back reference to the Turkish sack of Constantinople
in 1453, in part using Scythian troops.

II.50   *When those from Hainaut, Brussels and from Ghent*
Their siege of Langres duly laid shall see,
Behind their lines shall lands by wars be rent:
The ancient wound worse than the foe shall be.

Military success is not all, however. The unaccustomed
luxury of peace and freedom always brings its own problems.
Behind the north-eastern front, what sound suspiciously like
ethnic or religious squabbles break out – or possibly revenge-
killings – if anything, even more hateful than what has gone
before. Brind'Amour[9] identifies the 'ancient wound' as the
plague. The first line makes it clear, meanwhile, that the
Belgians, too, will be deeply involved in the great counter-
attack.

VIII.10   *From Lausanne shall a mighty stench arise*
        Whose origin no-one alive shall know.
        Expelled the foreigners 'neath fiery skies:
        The aliens they at last shall overthrow.

The country around Lake Geneva, Switzerland, is among the next territories to be liberated, despite the invaders' apparent continued use of their airborne fire-weapon.

VIII.73   *An Arab soldier shall assail the lord*
        Almost to death, yet without reason due.
        Ambitious mother is the cause abhorred.
        That day both plotter and regime shall rue.

This verse seems to describe some kind of attempted palace coup on the invader's side.

II.47   *The mighty foe, long-wailed, of poison dies,*
        His generals overcome by numbers vast.
        Stones from the skies or deeply hidden spies
        He vainly blames, as death comes on at last.

Eventually, it seems, the oriental leader is 'helped' to die, as his cause goes from bad to worse and, in customary human fashion, he seeks to lay the blame on everything and everybody but himself.

X.32*   *All feel constrained to seek almighty power;*
                One above all, though, shall to it attain.
                But not for long his star aloft shall tower:
                Two years by sea his power he'll maintain.

Naturally, there follows a scramble for power in the Asiatic camp, but the late supremo's successor is not destined to last long. The detail seems to be taken from the prophecy by the Abbot of Cambrai, which Nostradamus had probably found in the popular prophetic anthology entitled the *Livre merveilleux* of 1522.[49]

VIII.52*   *In Avignon shall reign the Blésois king:*
                From Amboise first his host the Indre ascends.
                A claw from Poitiers maims his sacred wing.
                Before Bonny [his army makes amends.]

Amid hints that a leader from the former French royal haunt of Blois will eventually set up his headquarters in Avignon, Nostradamus, meanwhile, outlines the route of the chequered central campaign in an unfinished quatrain that I have tentatively completed for him.

IX.93   *Far from the fort the foes are driven back:*
                Tanks shall a wall defensive constitute.
                Above, the crumbling walls of Bourges shall crack
                When Hercules 'New Philip' shall confute.

This quatrain describes a great victory at Bourges: in other words, the counter-attack has now reached a point well south of Orléans and the River Loire. Nostradamus describes the use of *chariots*: the equivalent word *chars* nowadays means 'tanks'. Line four's *Haemathion*, or Macedonian , seems to be the same enemy leader who originally invaded France via the Pyrenees (*see* IX.64, page 190) and a re-evocation (as previously) of Philip II of Macedon, father of Alexander the Great, *as well as* of Philip II of Spain. 'Hercules' is worth watching. As following quatrains will reveal, he is a strong man who will eventually loom especially large not merely in the campaign itself, but in subsequent French history.

V.80*   *Ogmion shall the might of Islam face:*
Routed shall be the pagan dispensation.
The Muslims' mighty league away he'll chase,
Yet foe and free prolong their confrontation.

This verse is a case in point. Referring to him by his Gallic name of 'Ogmion', it summarises his apparently decisive role in the campaign. Despite his destined success in expelling the invaders, however, he will not succeed in prosecuting the war to its ultimate conclusion.

VIII.60   *The first in France, the first in Italy,*
That noble house shall wondrous things attain
For England – Paris, too – by land and sea.
Violent monster, though, shall lose Lorraine.

Already, in fact, it looks as though Nostradamus is referring to 'Hercules' almost as if he were destined to be a member of a dynasty of conquerors. There are hints of future successes stretching far down into the Mediterranean. There is, though, to be some kind of violent setback on the eastern front. Further details of this may follow.

V.51   *Romanians, English, Poles and Czechs alike*
         A new alliance shall together knot
         To pass Gibraltar's narrow strait and strike
         Both Spain and Italy with fiendish plot.

At the same time, a western strategy is devised to attack the invaders in the Mediterranean via what Churchill once called 'the soft under belly of Europe'. This is clearly by way of a surprise attack. It is particularly interesting, meanwhile, to note the involvement of the peoples of Eastern Europe. This suggests that they will never have been overrun by the orientals in the first place – a fact which in turn confirms that the latter's attack will have taken an almost exclusively southern route.

VII.10   *A mighty force from France and all the north*
         By land and sea past stern Gibraltar's cape
         For Maine's great lord shall valiantly go forth –
         Their leader's task Majorca's isle to rape.

This stanza (whose lines I have been forced for poetic reasons to recast completely) offers more details of the projected western sea-borne strategy. In the first place, it is organised by a doughty commander from the area of Maine in France – possibly the same 'Hercules' as mentioned in IX.93, page 228. The aim is apparently to turn the Balearics (or 'Barcelona's isle', as Nostradamus puts it) into a staging-post and possible marshalling area for large-scale landings in the Mediterranean.

III.78   *The Scottish chief, with six from Germany*
            By Eastern seamen shall be captive led:
            Crossing Iberia via Gibraltar, he
            Shall come in fear before Iran's new head.

At this juncture, there is an unhelpful development. Somehow one of the British commanders manages to get himself captured at sea, along with six German colleagues. Well may the prisoner quake in his boots!

X.87   *Near Nice the mighty chief shall shoreward ride*
            To stab to death the far-flung empire's heart.
            At Antibes he shall lay his broom aside.
            At sea all pillage shall at last depart.

The Mediterranean task-force comes ashore on the French Riviera. His task of sweeping the invaders from the seas finally accomplished, the European commander sets up his initial headquarters on the coast at Antibes.

X.23   *Th' ungrateful people shall be argued with:*
            The force shall seize Antibes, make it its fee.
            'Board ship shall Monaco complain forthwith,
            While Fréjus shall be taken from the sea.

Curiously enough, not everybody welcomes the liberation, however. Some people have evidently profited from the long occupation.

V.76   *In open land he his encampment makes,*
      Nor will in any city have his base –
      Carpentras, Cavaillon, Vaucluse or Aix:
      Where'er he goes he'll leave no single trace.

The task-force commander now starts to play a cat-and-mouse game all across Provence. Always on the move, he starts to harry the enemy from every side.

III.99   *From Vernègues' fields and Alleins' pastures green*
      To Lubéron's mount not far from the Durance,
      Bitter on both sides though the fight has been,
      Iraq at last shall lose its hold on France.

Nostradamus foresees that, following a bitter struggle around his own home-area in the Rhône delta, the tide will at last start to turn in favour of the European defenders. Once again he associates the occupying invaders with the biblical – if not also the geographical – Babylon.

I.32   *Transferred shall be the Empire's power entire*
      To a small spot which soon shall grow apace –
      A tiny spot within a tiny shire –
      And at its heart his sceptre he shall place.

Once the south-eastern corner of France is secured, 'Hercules' (if he it is) transfers control of all the liberating forces – and seemingly of France itself, too – to some hitherto relatively unimportant centre somewhere in that area.

III.93   *In Avignon the lord of France entire*
Shall come to rest, Paris being desolate,
While Tricastin fends off the Afric ire.
Lyon shall at the change bewail its fate.

The riddle is solved. Paris having been virtually destroyed earlier in the campaign, Avignon becomes the new French capital. Possibly the former papal palace is turned into the new centre of administration. Evidently, Lyon had hoped to win the honour, and is disappointed. Meanwhile, hostilities are still continuing in the mountains to the east – Tricastin being the area now occupied by the *départements* of Drôme and Vaucluse.

IV.21   *Most difficult the change is bound to be,*
Yet town and country both from it shall gain.
High-placed, wise-hearted (banned the bungler!), he
Shall change their state by land and watery main.

There are hints in this verse, meanwhile, that 'Hercules' will in some way be a cut above his fellows, as well as being the cunning tactician that we have already supposed him to be. The French *lui habile* in line three is, seemingly, a misprint for *l'inhabile*.

VIII.38   *In Avignon Blois's king shall set his throne,*
Once more a ruler o'er a single land.
Up to four residences by the Rhône
He'll have, in Nola yet another planned.

Nostradamus seems to suggest that 'Hercules' has some ancestral connection with Blois, on the River Loire, former alternative capital of the French kings. It is a similar role, indeed, that Avignon too has now started to play as alternative capital of the whole of France. Evidently, 'Hercules' himself is starting to show a certain regal resplendence and even extravagance. The mention of Nola, near Naples, suggests that his power is about to extend far into Italy as well.

VIII.4 *In Monaco the French Cock is received.*
The cardinal of France then to him comes.
By Ogmion the Romans are deceived.
Weaker the Eagle, stronger the Cock becomes.

The impression is strengthened. Apparently, a plot is being hatched between the Church and 'Hercules' – here represented by the traditional French cockerel – to hoodwink the occupying regime in Italy.

IX.6 *Unnumbered English occupiers bestow*
On fair Guyenne the name 'Anglaquitaine';
From Languedoc to honey-bee'd Bordeaux
Dubbed Ahenobarbus' Occitan domain.

British troops are now moving in huge numbers into depopulated western France, while leaving the area to the south of the Garonne to a local French commander to whom Nostradamus repeatedly assigns the name 'Ahenobarbus'. This is a historical reference not to the Emperor Nero, whose name it certainly was, but to his earlier namesake Lucius

Domitius Ahenobarbus (d. 48 BC). This prominent Roman politician and general is best remembered for his passionate opposition to the rise of Julius Caesar and his clique. It was after the Senate had appointed Ahenobarbus to replace Caesar as commander in Gaul that Caesar carried out his celebrated crossing of the Rubicon and marched on Rome itself. Captured after confronting him in Italy, Ahenobarbus was released, but immediately raised a new revolt in Marseille, only to be killed in battle. By referring to the new southern governor as 'Ahenobarbus', Nostradamus thus tells us a great deal about him. His prime aim in life is to free his fiefdom from an overweening conqueror and dictator – in this case the Asiatic one, presumably – while his main power-base lies in Provence, and probably in Marseille. Hence the word *Occitan* – a local word, popular among regional separatists, that refers to anything pertaining to the Languedoc, and especially to Provence and its language.

XII.24 *The mighty succour coming from Guyenne*
Near Poitiers shall its furthest limit find.
Lyon shall yield to Montleul and Vienne
And plundered be by folk of every kind.

In the west, the British invasion of western France has its clear limits. In the south-east, Lyon is finally taken by a pincer-movement mounted from Montleul (just to the north-east) and Vienne (in the Rhône valley to the south).

IX.69   *On Bully's mountain and l'Arbresle's high top*
The proud ones of Grenoble shall be in hiding.
At Vienne, beyond Lyon, hail shall not stop,
Of locusts in the land no third abiding.

Evidently, a kind of resistance *maquis* has been operating in the mountains north-west of Lyon throughout the occupation. For obvious reasons, Nostradamus is at pains to disguise the site of their hideout, ostensibly indicating in his original verse some unspecified hilltop near Bresle and Bailleul in northern France (though, no doubt thanks to the printer's usual vagueness about place names, the text actually gives *Bailly*, which is in the Paris area). The 'hail' in line three may, of course, refer to a continuing hail of bullets and projectiles, rather than to their natural equivalent. By this stage of the campaign, meanwhile, less than a third of the original Asiatic occupiers (to whom Nostradamus once again refers by the name of 'grasshoppers') still remain in France.

Sixain 46*   *The Great Supplier shall put them all*   2026
       to flight –
    The Leech the Wolf (or hear they me aright) –
    When Mars shall in the Ram conjoinèd be
    With Saturn, and dread Saturn with the moon.
    Then, with the sun aloft at blazing noon,
    The nadir of your fortunes you shall see.

Thus it is that France (recognisable by the fact that she is, as usual, addressed in the familiar second person) can start to climb back out of her pit of war and destruction thanks to support from overseas, her fortunes having finally hit rock bottom. The 'Supplier' or 'Provider' – another new symbolic character in the drama – could conceivably be the USA. The astrology is quite specific: the triple near-conjunction next occurs on 16 April 2026. The invaders, in other words, are finally put to flight – as perhaps already anticipated in VIII.77, page 165 – just twenty-seven years after 1999.

IV.12   *The greater army routed, put to flight,*
Hardly much further shall the hunt advance.
Their host unhosted, and reduced their might,
They shall be chased completely out of France.

So it is that France is finally freed of the invaders, and the liberating forces earn themselves a short period of well-earned rest.

V.42*   *Mars once ascended to his apogee,*
The East retreats from France at his behest,
'Spite fear that's spread by those in Lombardy
To those of Eagle who 'neath Scales do rest.

Thoughts of pursuing the war into occupied Italy (apparently, along with Arabia and the Middle East, one of the 'Libran lands') can now start to enter the liberators' minds, as this evident echo of former wars between France and the Holy Roman Empire attests.

VII.4   *Langres' great general is at Dole beset –*
Colleagues from Autun and Lyon he'll boast –
Geneva, Augsburg, Mirandela set
To cross the Alps against Ancona's host.

The coalition continues to build up its strength. Despite a local setback at Dole, in the foothills of the Alps, a coalition of Swiss, Germans and Portuguese is only awaiting the signal to cross into Italy and chase the invaders all the way back to their original beachhead on the Adriatic shores of Italy.

VII.31   *Ten thousand come from Languedoc, Guyenne*
Once more across the Alps to trace their track.
Towards Brindisi Savoyards shall then
March on: but Bresse, Aquino, chase them back.

It is not all plain sailing, however.

II.65   *The northern powers sow great calamity*
In Italy and round Milan o'ergoing.
The church aflame, plague and captivity.
In Archer Mercury, and Saturn mowing.

War sows its inevitable seeds of destruction and disaster in *Hesperie* (a poetic term used either for Italy or for Spain), and especially around Milan. The last line appears to offer us an astronomical dating, but it merely describes the time of harvest – though the image of Death wielding his scythe is no doubt appropriate, too.

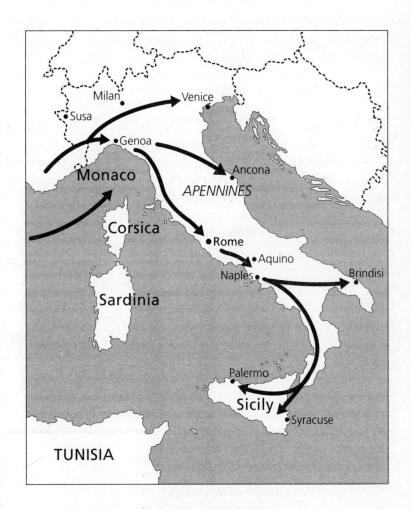

The liberation of Italy

I.6*   *Ravenna's eye shall be removed, plucked out,*
When wings shall shortly fail its speeding feet.
French forces shall Turin, Vercelli rout,
Leaders from Bresse restore them to their seat.

The enemy's fleeing leader (the 'eye' of Ravenna) is taken out, while the north-western cities are first reduced, then re-established under new administrations.

IV.23 *The warriors of the task-force maritime*
Shall burn magnesium, sulphur, pitch and lime:
The long repose of place without concern –
With fire shall Hercules Genoa burn.

Unless this incident applies to some other scenario entirely, the commander of the Mediterranean task-force (here confirmed as being the self-same 'Hercules' referred to earlier) now springs into action once more. As though attempting to emulate the oriental forces' original 'fire from the sky', he proceeds to attack a port that may conceivably be Genoa with some kind of incendiary weapon – which Nostradamus describes chemically in terms of 'Greek fire', the original 'secret weapon' used by both Greeks and Byzantines.

V.35 *The stone lies heavy on the stomach thin*
Of the free city of the crescent sea.
Through misty rain the British fleet sails in
To seize a prince: its lord at war shall be.

As elsewhere, however, the 'misty rain' suggests that the Genoan occupying forces will attempt to fend off the attacking fleet with chemical or biological weapons.

IV.37   *In bounds the French shall pass the mountains o'er,*
Milan's own heartland soon to occupy.
The mighty host shall reach its furthest shore.
From Genoa, Monaco the red ships fly.

Ashore, the fight is meanwhile continued over the Alps and
into northern Italy. Line one may foreshadow the use of para-
troops. Looking ahead, Nostradamus foresees the success of
this campaign too. So, apparently, do the Asiatics, who are
hurriedly starting to pull their forces out by sea.

VI.79   *Near the Ticino, warriors from the Seine,*
From Loire, Tain and Gironde, Sâone and Garonne
Beyond the Alps a bridgehead soon shall gain.
Fight joined and Po secured, their wave rolls on.

Once the River Ticino has been successfully crossed, the plain
of Lombardy lies open before the liberating forces.

II.26   *Because the city shall a favour show*
To the great lord who'll later lose the fight,
Ticino shall o'ercome the fleeing Po,
Hacked to death, bleeding, drowned or set alight.

The rout is complete, compounded by what appears some
kind of internal bickering on the Asiatic side – though it has
to be said that line three could be applied (as is so often the
case with Nostradamus) in the opposite direction, too!

241

VI.3   *When new-come Celt the river shall assay,*
Throughout the Empire discord great shall move.
With Church's help the youthful prince that day
Of peace the crown and sceptre shall remove.

As 'Hercules' – or possibly a younger kinsman – pursues his campaign into Italy, there is news of unrest behind the enemy lines.

Presage 39* *When, scorning marriage vows and wedding*
    night,
    The Reds and Shaven Heads are all but fled,
    The youthful King restored, his soul alight,
    Ogmion shall to Neptune turn his head.

Meanwhile, 'Hercules' is keen to call in support from the British.

VI.16   *What from the youthful Hawk is taken back*
By northern troops from France and Picardy
The Benedictines of the Forest Black
Shall make the hostelry of Lombardy.

This quatrain – based on the exploits of the Emperor Frederick Barbarossa in Italy[49] – is rather obscure, but it seems to suggest that one of the strongholds of the Arab governor of northern Italy will be turned over to the Church for use by the Benedictine order, possibly as a refugee centre.

V.22   *Before the lord of Rome gives up the ghost*
        Squadrons near Parma spring an ambush there.
        Terror is great among the alien host.
        Then the two reds a common table share.

There follows what could conceivably be a massive tank
battle that causes further panic among the enemy defending
the southern borders of the plain of Lombardy. As a result of
it, possibly, the enemy commander of the region is forced to
move his headquarters to his superior's quarters at Rome.

VIII.7 *Milan, Vercelli each the news proclaims:*
        Pavia is where the reckoning they'll call.
        Floods in Siena, Florentine blood and flames.
        As May comes in how shall the Mighty fall!

With other conflicts continuing further south, there is a huge
and possibly disastrous battle at Pavia that could go either
way – since this prophecy is a direct reflection of the battle of
Pavia of 1525, which was disastrous for the French.

IV.36   *Once more the games in France they shall re-found*
        Once the campaign around Milan is won.
        On western mountains chiefs are gagged and bound:
        Romans and Spaniards quake with fear and run.

In France, meanwhile, mass entertainments of classical type
are re-introduced – unless it is the more modern form of
Olympic Games. In the Pyrenees, however, the south-western
conflict is not over yet. The 'Romans' and 'Spaniards' are

presumably the still-fleeing remnants of the Asiatic invasion force.

III.43   *Beware, you men of Tarn, Garonne and Lot!*
Trace not beyond the Apennines your ways.
Near Rome, Ancona to your graves you'll go.
Black Curly-Beard your cenotaph shall raise.

The fight will not be easy, however. The allies are likely to suffer heavy losses as they attempt to storm both coastal flanks of central Italy. As we shall see, 'Black Curly-Beard' looks like Nostradamus's way of describing the enemy supreme commander.

III.32   *Vast killing-fields for those from Aquitaine*
Not far from Tuscany await their dead
When war not far from Germany shall reign
And over all the Mantuan lands shall spread.

Nostradamus rubs the point home. Even as the allies head south-eastwards across the plain of Lombardy towards the Adriatic coast, stiff resistance is likely to be encountered and heavy losses sustained. The warning in III.43, above, therefore applies: those who do not wish to risk life and limb should make every effort to stay well clear.

III.39* *Three months shall see the seven allied together*
To subjugate the mountains Apennine,
But cowardice Italian and bad weather
Shall suddenly their campaign undermine.

Nostradamus goes on to specify the causes of the disaster that will befall the campaign. I have chosen to take Nostradamus's *mis* in line one as a misprint for *mois* ('months').

III.38 *Both armies French and alien forces vast*
Beyond the mountains casualties record.
Six months from thence, ere harvest shall be past,
Their leaders shall strike up a grand accord.

As ever with Nostradamus, however, there is always a light at the end of the tunnel, unbearably dark though it may seem at the time. Only six months after the murderous spring offensive in northern and central Italy, the allies will be negotiating the remaining Asiatic invaders' surrender.

V.50 *The year when brothers French shall be*   2028?
   of age,
One of them Italy shall hold as fief:
Hills quake: free road to Rome he shall engage,
Plotting to march against Armenia's chief.

Thus it is that 'Hercules' can advance into central Italy virtually unopposed. Meanwhile, it would seem (as hinted earlier) that he has a younger brother who has just come of age. Possibly we shall hear more of him later.

Sixain 4* *Of globe and lily's born a monarch great*
Sooner or later bound for high estate
(Saturn in Libra in high exaltation,
Fair Venus' house's influence wearing thin),
Of female looks, but male beneath the skin,
For blessed Bourbon line's continuation.

Indeed, as this verse and others reveal (*see* IV.14, V.74, V.39 and V.41), he is actually of French royal blood, and destined eventually to achieve supreme power. The astrology is more of a personal assessment than a dating, but since Saturn is next in Libra from July 2010 to October 2012, this would date his birth to the same period – in which case the foregoing verse (V.50) would seem to be dated to around 2028–30.

IV.69* *The mighty city's full of refugees,*
Of dead and dying citizens in flight.
With Parma Aquileians then agree
To guide the troops in, staying out of sight.

The liberators of Parma now attack Rome itself with the help of guides either from l'Aquila, which lies to the north-east, or from Aquileia, a classical city (now reduced to a village) near Venice.

IV.98 *Th' Albanians into Rome shall straightway fare:*
Because of Langres the people are decked out.
Those in control no living soul shall spare.
Fire, smallpox, blood, crop-failures, widespread
    drought.

Anticipating an allied victory not unlike the earlier one at Langres, the citizens of Rome openly celebrate the fact. The occupying forces rush in post-haste to suppress the celebrations. One has the feeling, though, that their morale and authority are steadily weakening, or the demonstration would not have occurred in the first place.

IX.2   *Hear now the voice proclaim from Roman hill:*
         'Away! Forsake the land while it is riven!
         The wrath shall pass: the reds their life-blood spill,
         From Prato, Rimini and Rome all driven.'

As the beleaguered inhabitants of Italy are warned in quasi-biblical terms to keep their heads down, the liberating armies press on towards Rome, eventually expelling the occupation-forces from the whole country. Possibly the original last line's *Columna* refers to the contemporary Colonna family, who were held virtually to embody Rome itself at the time.

Presage 30* *'Spite rumours vain, the losers shall be tied,*
            The shorn-heads ta'en, th' Omnipotent installed,
            Two Reds laid low, four others crucified:
            By rain the mighty Monarch may be stalled.

Despite bad weather or chemical/biological attacks, the liberators complete their mopping-up operations with more than a little brutality.

II.16 *Naples, Palermo, Sicilian Syracuse*
New powers shall rule, new lightnings scorch the sky;
For now 'tis London, Ghent, Brussels and Suze
Shall triumph keep, once the great slaughter's by.

So it is that the liberation forces eventually clear the invaders out of the whole of Italy and Sicily, albeit only after further massive bombardments. Once again, in other words, Western Europe is free, with the possible exception of the Iberian peninsula. The enigmatic *Suses* is probably Susa in north-western Italy.

III.63* *The Roman power is cast down in the mire,*
Of its great neighbour following in the wake,
While hidden hate and civil feuds conspire
The stupid fools somewhat aback to take.

With the collapse of the Asiatic power-base in Rome, all kinds of internal power squabbles start to resurface in Italy, once again giving pause for thought to anybody harbouring fanciful ideas of a blissful, problem-free 'new era'.

VI.42* *To Ogmion the kingdom shall revert*
Of the Great Muslim, who'll defeated be:
O'er Italy his power he'll exert,
Ruling with most expedient subtlety.

Hercules, it seems, is also a slick political operator in his new, Gallic incarnation.

IX.33   *From Rome to Denmark Hercules shall reign,*
Surnamed the leader of tripartite Gaul.
Venice and Italy shall quake again:
Renowned he'll be as high king over all.

The acquired stature of 'Hercules' is becoming ever more
apparent. In this anticipatory stanza, Nostradamus is starting
to treat him not merely as a conquering hero, but almost as
royalty itself. Certainly the area he controls is immense. The
term 'tripartite Gaul' is a reference to the celebrated first
sentence of Julius Caesar's *Gallic War*, which divided Gaul
(present-day France and Belgium) into three parts.

X.80   *When o'er the realm the great King comes to reign,*
By force of arms the gates of bronze are seen
Opened to be by King and chief again.
Port ruined, shipping sunk, yet day serene.

This highly symbolic event – which Nostradamus celebrates
in a first line that is a virtual tongue-twister – is a source of
great contentment to 'Hercules' and his leading aide, for all
the chaos and destruction reigning around him.

X.27   *For him that's fifth and mighty Hercules,*
The church by act of war they'll open wide:
Never such strife 'twixt eagle, sword and keys:
Ascanus, Clement, Julius step aside.

This verse, similarly, seems to foresee a determined attempt to
re-open St Peter's in Rome by force of arms on behalf of

'Hercules'. Evidently, though, this causes great controversy between the church on the one hand (the 'keys' seem to be the papal ones of St Peter) and the military and state on the other. The last line seems to suggest that the papacy is offered to three different candidates (I have reversed their order for metrical reasons), all of whom decline. In the rather strange first line, meanwhile, Nostradamus almost appears to be referring not only to 'Hercules', but also to another (possibly the 'aide' of the foregoing stanza) whom he seems to see as one of a line of French kings – specifically the fifth, possibly of a particular name. If so, no doubt we shall hear more of him later. The prediction is based in virtually every detail on Charles V's notorious sack of Rome in 1527.

VI.78   *To vaunt o'er lunar power the victory*
            The folk of Rome the Eagle high shall raise.
            Pavia, Milan and Genoa shall agree,
            And later shall themselves the great king praise.

Prévost[49] points out that this verse exactly reflects the celebrations that were staged in 1536, shortly before the Emperor Charles V embarked on his triumphant expedition to retake Tunis from the Turkish pirate Barbarossa.

IX.84   *The King shall of the bulls reveal the slaughter*
            Once he has traced its source and its producer.
            The lead-and-marble tomb's revealed by water
            Of a great Roman, masked with dread Medusa.

Meanwhile, natural events are unearthing secrets from the past. Prévost[49] traces this prediction back to the visit by the young Charles IX to Arles and St-Rémy-de-Provence in 1564, in which Nostradamus himself was personally involved.

VI.66 *When they shall come to found the sect anew*
The bones of the great Roman shall be found.
Clad all in marble springs the tomb to view
When earth in April quakes, half-underground.

The theme continues. The attempt to re-found the Vatican regime in Rome is marked by the discovery – following a local earthquake – of what many commentators assume to be the tomb of St Peter. The Medusan symbolism of the foregoing stanza, however, would tend to suggest a Roman noble or emperor instead.

V.7* *The bones of the Triumvir shall be found*
While seeking buried treasure undiscovered,
Nor shall they leave in peace those close around:
With other lead-and-marble vaults uncovered.

Sure enough, the body turns out to be that of a former joint ruler of Rome. The back reference is to the claimed discovery in 1519, and re-excavation in 1521, of the alleged tomb of the Triumvir (and later Emperor) Augustus.[49] Nostradamus is always fascinated by classical archaeological discoveries, just as one might expect of any true Renaissance man.

VI.50*   *From out the pit the ancient bones they'll raise.*
Stepmother cruel shall incest perpetrate.
The new regime shall seek renown and praise,
But Mars shall be the star that rules its fate.

Whatever line two means, armed conflict seems likely to dog the new regime's remaining years.

VIII.66*   *When on the tomb the script 'D.M.' is found,*
And ancient vault by light of torches seen,
The rule of Ulpian leader shall resound,
The chief wrapped in the colours with his queen.

Possibly this verse refers to a second tomb: 'D.M.' was a standard Roman burial inscription meaning 'In(to) the hands of Pluto' (god of the underworld). Indeed, virtually all the Roman tombstones unearthed at Glanum, just south of Nostradamus's birthplace of St-Rémy (now displayed in the town's Musée des Alpilles) bear it prominently – which was presumably where he got the idea from in the first place. Furthermore, it was in due course to form part of Nostradamus's own epitaph – 'D. O. M.'– in this case signifying *Dei (Omnipotentis) Manibus* ('In(to) the hands of God'). In the case of this particular verse, the newly discovered deceased is unidentified, though he sounds remarkably like the Emperor Marcus Ulpius Traianus (or Trajan), whose ashes are supposed to have been interred in the base of his celebrated column in Rome.

III.65   *One day the mighty Roman's tomb is found:*
The next, elected Pope, he'll tread the palace.
The Senate, though, the choice shall straight
*   confound.*
Poisoned he'll be – and by the sacred chalice.

The attempt to re-establish the Vatican continues to arouse violent controversy. A new Pope is elected the day after the momentous discovery, but is then promptly poisoned, apparently at the instigation of the new Italian parliament. The back reference has to be either to the death of Pope Leo X in 1521[49] or to similar alleged papal poisonings in 1517 or 1534.[9] Clearly, there will be enormous popular opposition to any attempt to return to the former ecclesiastical regime, almost as if it is being blamed for much of the catastrophe that has recently befallen Europe.

III.40   *The mighty theatre shall rise up again,*
The dice be thrown, the nets be cast about.
The first to toll the bell shall feel the strain,
Worn out by bows so long ago cut out.

As previously mooted, 'Hercules' now attempts to resurrect the ancient Roman regime of 'bread and circuses'. Prévost[49] relates this to events during the long stay of Charles IX at Arles during the winter floods of 1564. The ancient entertainments prove all too much for the first participants, however: as Nostradamus points out via a metaphor much more familiar to his own age than to ours, old bows are hard to stretch – the ancient practices, in other words, will demand physical skills that have long since been lost and need to be slowly redeveloped.

X.79   *Old roads with new embellishments they'll fit:*
Through gates of ancient Memphis they shall go,
As Gallic Hercules' mercurial writ
Earth, sea and all the lands shall trembling know.

In other ways, too, 'Hercules' is much drawn to resurrecting
the classical past. Much effort is devoted to restoring the
ancient Roman roads and streets to their former glory. I take
the strange word *somentrée* at the end of line two to be a
misprint for *son entrée*.

II.71   *Those long-exiled to Sicily shall sail*
To save from hunger alien victims thin.
At daybreak shall the French to show still fail.
Yet life goes on – for now the King joins in.

There now seems to be a sudden compassionate initiative by
Italian anti-war groups to bring succour to the alien settlers in
Sicily, who have been long-neglected by their own Asiatic
overlords. After their recent experiences, the French are naturally reluctant to join in, despite apparent assurances of
support. However, much to everybody's surprise, 'Hercules'
decides to commit himself to the action on his own responsibility.

VII.33*   *Fraud shall deprive the kingdom of its strength,*
The fleet blockaded, agents everywhere.
Two false companions shall combine at length
To re-awaken sleeping hatreds there.

There are signs, however, that the new regime will become increasingly corrupt as well as racked by plots and disputes, one of which could well-nigh tear it apart.

IV.95   *Once placed in power, not long shall rule the pair.*
             After three years seven months at war they'll be,
             Till both the vassal lands revolt declare.
             The junior wins the war in Brittany.

This quatrain is extremely vague. It seems to suggest, though, that the two joint commanders of the allied forces will now fall out with each other in the most dramatic way. The squabble (possibly military) will spread all across liberated Europe.

V.23   *The rivals twain together shall unite*   **2028(?)**
            Once most themselves to Martial war have given.
            Afric's great lord shall tremble in his fright,
            Till the duumvirate by sea is riven.

The 'duumvirate' seems to refer to the same two commanders, whose quarrel eventually extends as far as the Mediterranean itself. No wonder the pressure is taken off the oriental leader for a while. However, Prévost,[49] who refers the short-lived alliance back to the brief period of accord between François I and Charles V from 1538 to 1541, prefers to see line two as a reference to the multiple conjunction in Cancer of Mars, Jupiter, Venus and Mercury that occurred in the summer of 1539. There is no such conjunction in the future time-frame under consideration. Nevertheless, in April 2028 Mars, Saturn, Mercury and the sun will all be in

Taurus, while at midsummer of the same year Mars, Venus, Mercury, the moon and the sun will all be in Gemini.

VI.58   *Between the now far-distanced monarchs twain,*
When by the Sun the Moon's light dimmed shall be,
Great rivalry and indignation reign
Now that Siena and the Isles are free.

Thus it is that the discord whose rumblings have already been felt across newly-liberated Europe finally breaks out into the open. No sooner does it become possible for everybody to relax a little than the two commanders use the opportunity to pick a quarrel. Possibly they are 'Hercules' himself and his aide and would-be successor. For Prévost,[49] this is a back reference to the renewed hostilities between Charles V and Henri II of France in 1551, which was marked by a solar eclipse in Virgo.

VI.95   *A slanderer the younger shall attack*
When warlike deeds and great o'er all shall reign.
Not much of it the elder one shall back,
But soon the kingdom shall be torn in twain.

Whether this quatrain applies to the quarrel in question is difficult to tell. If it does, though, the 'elder' could be 'Hercules', the 'younger' his prospective successor. In that case the dispute now seems likely to tear the whole regime apart.

II.34   *Th' insensate fury of an angry fight*
       Sees mess-companions draw their flashing arms.
       Injured and split, offended at some slight,
       Their stiff-necked feud fair France severely harms.

The quarrel – whether based on a specific one such as that involving the Borgias of 1497[49] or merely on the general contemporary problem of duelling[9] – is clearly a deeply personal one, having no necessary connection with matters military at all. Yet its ramifications are destined to prove immensely far-reaching.

V.64   *To calm the greater number of their peers*
       They'll countermand advice by sea and land:
       Geneva, Nice shall loom as autumn nears
       O'er fields and towns: against their chief they'll
          band.

The details are extremely confused. Indeed, such squabbles are an area that Nostradamus frequently tends to get back to front, even when he is not entirely ambiguous about them. But it does rather seem that the two main protagonists will at some stage be pressurised by their colleagues to stop their more aggressive actions, even if only temporarily. The urgency of some kind of settlement is underlined as local garrisons start to take sides.

VI.7   *Norway, Romania and the British Isles*
             Shall by the pair of brothers troubled be.
             Rome's mighty chief, of French blood, forced the
                 whiles
             To seek with troops in woods security.

This stanza fills in the picture slightly more. To judge by the
countries listed in the first line, the two 'brothers' seem to
have dire effects on the European allies to the north and east.
Once again, though, the suggestion seems to be that their feud
will extend right down into the Mediterranean. Eventually
the great 'Hercules' is forced to flee, and his armies with him.

V.45   *The mighty Empire shall be desolated,*
             Power transferred to Ardennes' forests cool.
             The bastards by their elder separated,
             Hawk-nosed Ahenobarbus then shall rule.

For a while, at least, the effects are devastating. The new
continental regime is disrupted, its leader ('Hercules', presumably) forced to seek refuge near the Franco-Belgian border.
Eventually, however, a senior commander intervenes to put a
stop to the quarrel. 'Ahenobarbus' now assumes full
command. Unless Nostradamus is so disgusted with the two
protagonists as to use the word 'bastards' to refer to *them*,
the meaning of line three is unclear.

II.38   *Many are they who shall be damned outright*
When reconciled shall be the leaders twain,
But one of them shall soon be in such plight
That their alliance scarce stands up again.

Nevertheless, the quarrel will have had its severe effects on all those involved – and not least on the two feuding leaders themselves. One of them is no longer in a fit state to permit any real resumption of their former friendly relationship – or possibly some further misfortune befalls him. We are reminded once again of the ever-fluctuating quarrels between François I and the Emperor Charles V.

VI.71*   *When of the King they'll come to take their leave,*
Even before he's given up the ghost,
He who shall have least cause to mourn and grieve
Shall sell the Christian crown to who bids most.

Evidently, it is 'Hercules' who is now at death's door. The scene is reminiscent of the deathbed of Charles V at the monastery of Yuste in Spain.[49] His would-be successors seem to be out for all that they can get – though I can make little of Nostradamus's last line. There are signs that all hope will be given up for him some time before he actually dies.

VIII.5   *At Bornel and Breteuil lamps, candles burn.* **2038(?)**
He shall appear in church ornate and shining.
To see that light shall all the region turn
When in his coffin Cock is seen reclining.

These details are a re-run of those of the funeral of François I in 1547.[49] Interestingly, the only reasonable horoscopic match for this in or around the timeframe under consideration is a four-planet match during the first week of April 2038. In the light of this, subsequent quatrains will suggest that the future leader's death will indeed be a lingering one, since his successor will have taken over well before it finally occurs.

V.21   *Upon the Roman monarch's death, to those*
            Whom he throughout his reign has helped and aided
            'Mid burning fires th' ill-gotten booty goes.
            For death, though, shall the honest be paraded.

The deceased, it would seem, is indeed 'Hercules', but it now turns out that his regime has been a pretty corrupt one, such that on his death his cronies blatantly attempt to take everything for themselves. Possibly, indeed, it was this corruption that lay at the basis of the deadly quarrel in the first place.

IV.14   *The first king's sudden death at first appears*
            All things to change. Another comes to power
            Sooner or later, though of tender years,
            Who o'er both land and sea shall fearful lour.

However, a successor soon steps into his shoes. As X.26 (page 262), possibly suggests, he seems not to be the late opponent of 'Hercules', but another leader entirely. Nostradamus suggests that, though young, he was bound to reach the top sooner or later – or possibly this expression indicates that, as already suggested, he may as easily take over before his predecessor's death as after it. He promises to be just as doughty a military leader, too.

V.74   *From Trojan blood of France a heart shall grow*
That is Germanic, lofty power attaining.
Far from the land he'll chase the Arab foe,
The church's former eminence regaining.

Nostradamus goes further. His blood is to be *Troyen* – in other words he will be descended, as both Ronsard and Nostradamus alleged the French kings to be, from Priam of Troy. At the same time, he will also be in some way German. The impression is considerable, then, that Nostradamus expects him to become nothing less than a virtual reincarnation of Charlemagne himself. His destiny, meanwhile, is finally to rid France of its invaders and to restore the Church to its former glory.

V.39   *Born from the true stock of the fleur-de-lys,*
His ancient blood the stuff of many hands,
Then set in place as heir to Italy,
His crest blooms with the flower of Florence' lands.

Quite apart from having French and German antecedents, indeed, he now goes on to inherit Italy from 'Hercules' as well.

V.41   *Shade-born where light is dim and sunbeams few,*
'Midst power and riches he'll the sceptre hold.
From th' ancient source he shall his line renew,
Replacing th' age of bronze with one of gold.

His prospects, in fact, seem to be little less than fabulous. From obscurity he is destined to rocket to something approaching world pre-eminence. The details are borrowed from the optimistic mythology that surrounded the thirteenth-century Emperor Frederick Barbarossa during his lifetime.[49]

X.26   *Succeeding, he'll his brother-in-law requite:*
In vengeance' name to power he shall advance.
For all obstructions he'll his death indict.
Long shall Great Britain loyal stay to France.

Not only is the new leader actually related to 'Hercules', but he will use his strong feelings about his death as a kind of motivation and excuse for imposing his own stamp on events.

IX.41   *Avignon Chyren seizes for his own.*
From Rome come letters sweet and sour together,
By envoys from Canino to him shown:
Carpentras seized by black of reddish feather.

At this point, we are introduced by name to the new leader. Nostradamus repeatedly gives his name as *Chyren* – which everybody from his own secretary onwards has assumed to be an anagram for *Henryc*, or Henricus ('Henry'). There is a hint that he may previously have been on the administrative staff at Avignon, and therefore well-placed to take over control on the death of 'Hercules'. If the latter had set up his headquarters in Rome before his death in the far north-east (he is, after all, described in VI.7 as the 'Roman chief') this might account for the bitter complaints from that city, especially in the light of the endemic corruption referred to previously. Meanwhile, there seems to be a local revolt against the new regime at Carpentras, on the Rhône delta.

Sixain 15* *The new-elected Captain of the Barque*
Long time shall see the torch's brilliant spark
That serves to light the whole of this domain;
What time the armies 'neath his flag shall fight
Alongside those of Bourbon leader bright.
From east to west his memory shall remain.

It seems to be at around this juncture that a new Pope is at last appointed who is universally agreed to be worthy to rule over the new Church, and under whose banner Henry's forces will happily fight.

VIII.54 *Beneath the cover of a marriage pact*
The lunar Chyren does a noble deed.
Thereby Arras, St Quentin he'll exact.
Spain shall provide more butchery indeed.

But Henry is not merely a soldier. Clearly, too, he is a master diplomat, as adept at using words and promises to gain his ends as military might. In this he will imitate his namesake Henri II (whose emblem included the moon) after the disastrous battle of St Quentin of 1557, which was eventually to lead to no less than two diplomatic marriages – and his own death in a celebratory tournament (*see* I.35 in Chapter 3).

IV.3   *From Bourges and Arras easterners shall flood.*
Of Gascons more shall fight upon their feet.
Those from the Rhône in Spain shall spill much
    blood
Near to Sagunto's lofty mountain seat.

Thus it is that the last pocket of Asiatic resistance collapses. In due course, Henry's forces, advancing along Spain's Mediterranean coastal pass, are destined to win a great victory in the shadow of the mountains near Sagunto.

IX.92   *Wishing to enter Villeneuve shall the king*
Approach, the enemy to conquer and subdue.
A captive freed says many a false thing.
The king remains outside, at distance due.

Once again we encounter Nostradamus's *cité neufve*, which we formerly identified as Villeneuve-sur-Lot. Evidently the new south-western campaign has now begun. With enemies on every side, Henry still has to tread carefully.

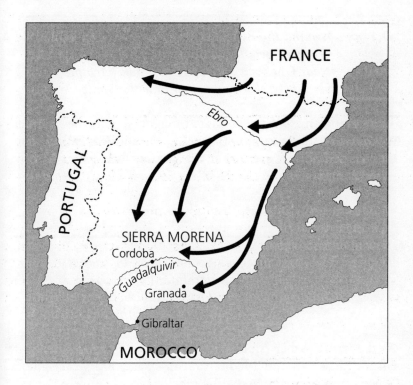

The liberation of Spain

X.11   *The last-born with his multitude shall press*
Beneath Jonchères and through its perilous gate,
Then o'er the Pyrenees, quite baggageless,
From Perpignan, the general to await.

This further stage in the campaign is difficult to decode, but it seems as though Henry will lead troops from the Limoges area south-westwards, with a view to crossing one of the Pyrenean passes into Spain.

265

VI.1   *Around the Pyrenees a concourse great*
Of foreigners the king shall come to aid.
Near Garonne and Mas d'Agenais's temple gate
Shall fearful Roman chief in water wade.

The campaign continues. The 'foreigners' may be English occupation troops from Guyenne. Little can be gleaned from the last two lines, except that the weather is to be extremely wet at the time.

II.17   *The vestal virgin's precinct shall be sought*
Not far from Elne and lofty Pyrenees.
The Great One in a trunk is thither brought.
North wind: the vines shall rot, the rivers freeze.

As the bad weather continues, a further strange development ensues closer to the Mediterranean coast, near Perpignan. What seems to be the body of a rebel leader is delivered to the site of some ancient Roman ruins. Alternatively, as X.2 below suggests, perhaps it is one of Henry's generals who thereby arrives in the area secretly.

V.59   *Too long at Nîmes the English chief shall stay.*
To help, Ahenobarbus heads for Spain.
Several shall die through war that starts that day
When o'er Artois a meteor shower shall rain.

At some stage the English commander from Guyenne visits 'Ahenobarbus' in Provence, possibly to enlist his aid in the Spanish campaign. While he is away, things in the south-west suddenly get out of control, and he and 'Ahenobarbus' hurriedly travel to the front. Prévost[49] links this verse with diplomatic events at Nîmes during the royal visit of 1564. Curiously enough, there *was* a meteorite shower over Artois during the nineteenth century, however, I have been unable to verify the fascinating suggestion that the beer 'Stella Artois' was named after it!

X.95   *Down into Spain the mighty King shall sweep:*
Such ill he'll do the Crescent down to beat!
He'll clip the wings of those who Friday keep.
By land and sea the south he shall defeat.

Thus it is that Henry eventually succeeds in pushing the Muslim forces – 'those who Friday keep' – out of Spain and back into Africa.

II.69   *The King of France upon the Celtic right,*
Seeing how much at odds those Powers shall be,
In all three parts of Gaul shall press his might
Against the dead hand of the Hierarchy.

At this point, Henry (if Henry it is) decides to take advantage of the growing factionalism among the enemy high command, while resisting the machinations of the newly-restored Church (the 'Hierarchy').

Sixain 56* *When the Provider joins the Griffon's side,*
The Elephant shall everywhere abide,
Its ruin near, and dread Mars roaring still.
Griffon shall wonders work near Holy Land,
Great banners fluttering over sea and sand,
Once brothers twain on Church have worked
their will.

As Henry and his allies (the 'Griffon') now contemplate pursuing the enemy back to the Middle East, they receive financial and/or logistical support from overseas. As noted earlier, the 'Provider' could conceivably be the USA.

Sixain 39* *On monster worse than any other one*
The Great Provider glowers like the sun
Ascending towards its zenith at midday.
In routing Elephant and Wolf at last
He'll triumph more than any monarch past:
Let never worse this Prince befall, I pray!

Nostradamus foresees total victory for the American leader (if he it is), likening him to the sun itself. As we saw earlier, 'Elephant' and 'Wolf' seem to be code words for the Asiatic invaders' southern and northern wings respectively.

I.50 *From trigon watery he'll take his birth,*
And from that one where Thursday is made feast:
His fame, praise, rule and power shall spread on
earth,
By land and sea storming the farthest East.

This verse pursues the theme further. Born under one of the three water signs (Cancer, Scorpio or Pisces), the American leader is destined to triumph against the orientals. Whether or not Nostradamus realised it at the time, America's future annual Thanksgiving festival would indeed eventually fall on a Thursday – the last Thursday in November.

IV.50 *Autumn shall see the West's full power deployed,*
Dominion wielding over land and sky:
Yet none shall see the Asian power destroyed
Till seven in turn have held the Hierarchy.

Nostradamus now gives us some kind of timescale for the whole invasion and counter invasion. It will, he suggests, take six changes of papal regime before the whole of Europe is free.

IV.5* *Christians at peace, and Holy writ fulfilled,*
Both France and Spain under one king united.
But doom's at hand, fierce combat, many killed,
No heart so brave as not be affrighted.

However, there is much fighting yet to be done, even if not in Western Europe itself.

VIII.4a *Many shall be desirous to confer*
And beg the warlords their attacks to cease.
In no wise shall the lords to them defer.
Alas for all, unless God sends us peace!

269

Relatively weak by the standards of the 'regular' *Centuries*, this is one of the late additions to Century VIII. It suggests that the peoples in the East who are still under foreign occupation will beg the West not to mount its looming attack – but in vain.

VIII.2a   *To speak of peace there shall come many a one,*
Be they great lords or puissant royalty;
But not so readily shall it be won
Unless they yield their total sovereignty.

Apparently, the alien regime joins in the pleas, sending high representatives of its own, but the West demands nothing less than unconditional surrender.

V.19*   *Backed first with gold and then with bronze, the*
King
Shall break the truce: to war the youth shall go.
Through chief regretted people suffering:
With Muslim blood the earth again shall flow.

Nevertheless, Henry is determined to pursue his destiny further, once he has amassed sufficient funds and armaments.

X.86   *Like griffon shall the king from Europe speed,*
Accompanied by all those from the North.
Of reds and whites great numbers he shall lead
'Gainst Babylon's great ruler boldly forth.

The great expedition against the Eastern powers finally sets out. The curious, composite image of the 'griffon' could conceivably refer to the traditional lion body of Britain allied to the equally traditional eagle of Italy, of Germany, of Poland, of former Imperial France – even, perhaps, of the United States of America. The 'reds' and 'whites' are more difficult to identify: the reference could be either political or racial, or even of some other kind entirely.

III.47*   *The aged leader hounded out from power*
            Seeks from the Easterners a helping hand.
            For fear of Christian might his flag he'll lower.
            To Lesbos he shall flee o'er sea and land.

The local Muslim commander now flees for his life before the Western onslaught.

VIII.81*   *Desolate shall their empire new become,*
            Changed by the power that far to northward lies.
            From Sicily a mighty change shall come
            To trouble mighty Philip's enterprise.

Possibly from the port of Syracuse, Henry now sets out to attack the invaders in the Balkans. On the other hand, the *enprise à Philip tributaire* of the last line could apply not to Philip of Macedon so much as to the new incarnation of Philip II of Spain.

I.74   *Rested, on Western Greece they'll set their sights*
        Deliverance next to Antioch they'll bring.
        The king with black, curled beard for th' Empire
            fights.
        But him shall roast the copper-bearded king.

Nostradamus even refers to the future Henry quite literally in
terms of the former crusading Emperor Frederick Barbarossa
('Red Beard'). After a pause for recuperation and re-supply, a
massive European counter-attack is directed through the
former Epirus – i.e. Albania and western Greece – towards
the Middle East. The site of ancient Antioch is nowadays
occupied by the Turkish town of Antakya, some fifty miles
west of Aleppo in Syria.

Présage 129* *The fearsome foe to Thrace shall then retire,*
            With cries, screams, ruin and pillage in his
                wake;
            O'er sea and land rule silence, faiths expire,
            The godly routed, Christendom a-quake.

The Muslims withdraw steadily eastwards, leaving ruin and
desolation behind them.

IX.75   *Far overseas in Arta and in Thrace*
        The French shall to a sick race aid assign
        Who in Provence have long since left their trace
        And of their laws and customs many a sign.

HOROGRAPH FOR: 21 May 1535					TO: 24 May 1535						
	Aries	Tauru	Gemin	Cance	Leo	Virgo	Libra	Scorp	Sagit	Capri	Aquar	Pisce
Pluto											★	
Neptune	★											
Uranus				★								
Saturn					★							
Jupiter												☆
Mars	☆											
Venus			★									
Mercury		★										
Moon											☆	☆
Sun			★									

Solar noon declination (to nearest degree):	22°N
	Geographical latitude: 36° 47' N

LOCATION: Tunis, North Africa
EVENT: Victorious raid on pirate Barbarossa II by Emperor Charles V

HOROGRAPH FOR: 21 May 2036					TO: 11 June 2036						
	Aries	Tauru	Gemin	Cance	Leo	Virgo	Libra	Scorp	Sagit	Capri	Aquar	Pisce
Pluto											★	
Neptune	★											
Uranus				★								
Saturn					★							
Jupiter			☆									
Mars				☆								
Venus			★									
Mercury		★										
Moon	☆	☆	☆	☆	☆	☆	☆	☆	☆	☆		
Sun			★									

Solar noon declination (to nearest degree):	20°N to 23°N
Relative latitude: 2°S to 1°N	Geographical latitude: 34°47'N to 37°47'N (±1°)

POSSIBLE LOCATION: From Bejaia, Tunis and Algiers, via the Cyclades, to Antakya and Tarsus
EVENT: Counter-invasion of Islamic Middle Eastern heartlands by Henri V of France

273

In what Nostradamus sees as a kind of cultural reciprocation, France meanwhile brings aid and succour to Greece, the very nation that at one time settled and civilised ancient Provence itself, and which is still suffering the after-effects of the earlier earthquakes and catastrophic floods (*see* V.31, page 125).

V.78   *Not long allied the duo shall remain*   2036
In thirteen years against the Arab lord
On either side such losses they'll sustain,
That one the cassock of the church shall bless.

This stanza throws some interesting light on the timescale involved. As Prévost[49] reveals, the verse refers back to the thirteen-year alliance, from 1534 to 1547, between the Holy Roman Emperor Charles V and Pope Paul III against the continual devastating attacks by the pirate Barbarossa's Turkish fleet. When, in 1535, the Emperor decided to launch a huge attack against Tunis, his expedition was indeed formally blessed by the Pope on its departure. Some such alliance between Henry and the Church is thus expected on this future occasion, too. As the charts on page 273 show, the comparative horoscopy for the campaign thus dates it quite firmly for 2036.

II.22   *Seaward from Europe sails th' amazing*   2036
force:
The Northern fleet its battle-line deploys.
Near isle submerged it sets a common course.
The great world's centre yields to stronger voice.

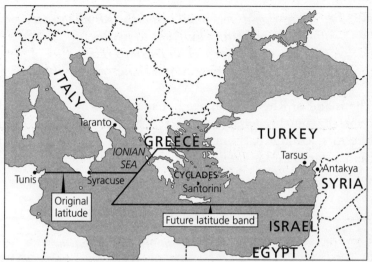

*Henry V's attack on the Middle East, as determined by the
comparative horoscopy*

Evidently the land campaign is to be accompanied by a huge sea-
borne expedition as well, and the eventual result is destined to be
a change of regime in the Middle East, and specifically in
Jerusalem, traditionally the centre of the world. The 'submerged
island' is not identified, but the collapsed volcano of Santorini
seems a good candidate.

VI.85 *By forces French shall mighty Tarsus be* **2036**
Destroyed, all Muslims captured, led away –
Helped by the mighty Portuguese at sea –
When summer starts, on blessed Urban's day.

The invasion of Turkey continues, with further landings at
Tarsus, only a few miles to the north-west of ancient Antioch.
St Urban's Day (25 May) falls slap within the time-scale
defined by both charts on page 273.

IV.39   *For urgent help shall plead the Rhodian race,*
         By its inheritors long left to waste.
         The Arab empire shall its steps retrace.
         The Westerners shall put things right in haste.

The island of Rhodes is in need of special attention, its inhabitants having been badly neglected by the occupiers, rather like their counterparts in Sicily (*see* II.71, page 254). Urgent humanitarian aid is provided by the incoming Europeans.

VI.21   *Once the north hemisphere as one unites*
         The East shall be affrighted and dismayed.
         A new Pope chosen, Church restored to rights,
         Byzantium, Rhodes with Arab blood are sprayed.

Even as European Christianity is steadily getting back on its feet again, the attack is pressed home in the Middle East.

II.70   *The heavenly dart across the sky shall go.*
         Death in mid-sentence everywhere is sown.
         Blasted the tree, a haughty race laid low,
         Alarums, omens, efforts to atone.

This verse seems to show how, though what appears at first sight to be some kind of missile is in fact more likely to be a comet.[9] Nevertheless, the events that accompany it are devastating, totally shaking the orientals' confidence.

VIII.83*   *The biggest fleet that ever Zara knew*
Near Istanbul its deadly business plies.
Great losses to the foe; to friends but few.
A third, though, plunders both – and great his prize.

At the same time, a massive naval attack is mounted on northern Turkey from Zara (modern Zadar), on the Dalmatian coast of the former Yugoslavia. The third party who ultimately profits from it all is unidentified.

IX.43   *Ready to land, the Christian ships approach,*
While Arabs watch with dark, suspicious eyes.
On every side marauding ships encroach,
Ten chosen ones attacking by surprise.

More European ships now come ashore. Quite what Nostradamus means by his emphasis on their Christian nature, though, we shall possibly see in the next stanza.

VII.36   *God's Word at Istanbul shall come ashore*
With seven red shaven-heads, each one a chief.
Against their Graces Trabzon's fifteen score
Shall make two laws: first horror, then belief.

Incredibly, what now apparently follows is the arrival in the former Byzantium of a delegation of missionary cardinals, intent on converting the defeated Muslims to Christianity, as it were, by the sword – unless, of course, line three really means that they are themselves converted Asiatics. Understandably, the local inhabitants' first reaction is one of sheer horror. The missionaries are anathemised by the parliament currently meeting further east in Trabzon, whither it has fled from the European invaders. Yet, possibly in the light of the latter's newly acquired status as victors, the delegation actually starts to make converts.

Sixain 34*   *Princes and lords make war upon each other,*
Cousin 'gainst cousin, brother against his
  brother –
Till Bourbon makes an end of Araby.
The friendly rulers of Jerusalem
Shall by the awful crimes performed on them
To ruin be condemned and penury.

Meanwhile Israel, too, is liberated by Henry's forces, though by now the whole country is in total ruin and economic collapse.

II.79   *By skill he of the curly beard and black*
The race both cruel and proud soon subjugates.
Chyren the Great from far away brings back
All those still penned by Muslim prison gates.

Henry, having pursued the invaders abroad, now subdues them in their heartlands. However, Nostradamus's description of him now seems to be borrowed from that of his Muslim enemy! Possibly the seer is confused on the matter – for consistency was never his strong suit. At all events, this prediction is clearly based on Charles V's triumphant return from Tunis in 1535.[32]

III.97   *A new law in a new land shall hold sway*
          Over by Syria, Palestine, Judea.
          Dominion Arabic shall melt away
          Ere Phoebus shall complete his long career.

On the basis of the system of ages that, for Nostradamus, had most recently been mooted by Roussat,[53] the 'age of the sun' that started in 1887 will finish in 2242. This, then, comfortably covers both the founding of modern Israel in 1947 and its future re-establishment in around 2036, as foreshadowed by this verse on the basis of the nearly contemporary *Prophetie de Cambrai*.

II.60   *Conspiracy collapses in the East.*
          Jordan, Rhône, Loire and Tagus changed shall be.
          When lust for riches shall at last have ceased,
          Fleet scattered, bodies float on bloody sea.

Thus it is that the Eastern alliance collapses, almost of its own accord, under continued pressure from the West. From the Middle East to Portugal (Nostradamus is particularly prone to refer to peoples by the names of their rivers) things are transformed. The invaders, having at last slaked their understandable thirst for the West's riches, either settle down or return home, leaving their military machine in ruins, and especially their naval wing. Here, in other words, Nostradamus seems to be describing the final petering out of the great Asiatic invasion-cum-migration: certainly, little more is heard of it from now on. Other seers[33] refer at this point to a great mingling of the races, just as Nostradamus himself, in his *Letter to Henri King of France the Second*, refers to a mingling of tongues (*see* the headquote to this chapter).

V.52   *A king there'll be who'll turn things upside down,*
Placing the exiles high in men's esteem.
The pure and chaste, once used in blood to drown,
Long time shall flourish under such regime.

Unless it refers to a much later millennial age, the original
French suggests that Henry will place the exiles and returning
refugees in positions of power, always tending to favour the
underdog. Indeed, so often does Nostradamus use the term
exilés throughout his writings as to suggest that refugees are
likely to be a major feature of the twenty-first century.

Presage 38*   *Acclaimed as Victor-Emperor is the King;*
To tainted Church the royal deed proclaimed.
On Matthew's day they shall his triumph sing
O'er haughty race, repentant now and tamed.

In this summary verse for April 1559, the theme continues,
with the term 'haughty race' confirmed as applying to the
now-tearful Muslim invaders. St Matthew's Day is 21
September.

VI.70   *Lord over all great Chyren is acclaimed,*
Like Charles the Fifth himself feared and adored,
Well pleased the only victor to be named.
Heaven-high his fame and praise shall soon have
soared.

Henry is now triumphant. Via the Emperor's motto *PLUS
ULTRA*, Nostradamus once again likens him to the former

Charles V, following his triumphant return from the raid on
Tunis of 1535.

V.6   *On the king's head the Prophet lays his hand*
        Praying the while for peace in Italy.
        The sceptre changing then to his left hand,
        The King an Emperor of peace shall be.

Clearly, in an echo of Charles VIII in 1495,[49] we are still at
Henry's coronation. On the same basis, the 'Prophet' is none
other than the new Pope. At last the war has all but come to
an end.

X.73   *The present time and all that once transpired*
        The mighty man of God shall judge that day.
        But in the end they'll all of him grow tired,
        And legal-minded priests shall him betray.

The Pope in question is a charismatic character. One has the
feeling that he will endeavour to re-found the church on new
bases that go much nearer to the heart of true religion than
much that has passed for it previously. In this, however, his
efforts will be subverted by the surviving priesthood, who
(predictably perhaps) would much rather return to the old
theocratic bureaucracy and its worn-out doctrines in which
their power formerly resided.

IV.34   *The mighty captive's summoned from abroad*
Before King Chyren chained with gold embossed;
His host entire put to the flames and sword,
Italy's war, Milan's great battle lost.

As a final act of victory, the supreme leader of the whole
Asiatic campaign – or at very least of that in Italy – is brought
captive before the new king in his ceremonial regalia to eat
humble pie. The last two lines evidently refer not to current
events, but to the history of his defeat.

IV.77   *Lunar the King and Italy at peace,*
A Christian king a world at one shall rule.
At Blois he'll wish to rest on his decease,
Once he has freed the seas of brigands cruel.

With only a few mopping-up operations still to complete,
Henry (in an echo, this time, of Henri II of France with his
lunar banner) has become the pre-eminent world leader.
Nostradamus makes him sound distinctly Messiah-like (thus
seemingly giving rise to the persistent French royalist expectation of a pseudo-Messianic King Henri V). Now he can
contemplate his own old age and death. He decides to be buried
in or near his ancestral city of Blois, former haunt and alternative capital of the French kings. The decision seems apt.

V.79   *All sacred pomp its wings shall soon abase*
Once the great legislator starts his glorious reign.
He'll raise the lowly, far the rebels chase.
None like him shall be born on earth again.

Once again, Nostradamus makes Henry sound distinctly Messianic – unless, of course, this verse really refers to the later millennium itself, as in terms of the 'Janus hypothesis' it could equally well do.

IX.66 *Peace there shall be, unity, many a change;*
Those that were high brought low and low raised
*   high;*
The first fruit's torment travel to arrange,
To stop all war, cases at law to try.

But re-laying the foundations of a new civilisation is never easy. As at the time of the peace-promoting royal progress of Catherine de Médicis and her young son Charles IX through France in 1564[49] – during the course of which they called on Nostradamus himself at Salon – there is much administrative work to be done.

II.95 *Where once lived crowds, now nobody can live.*
The fields must be re-marked and re-defined.
Kingdoms to wise incompetents they'll give.
Great brothers dead, can feuds be far behind?

Conditions, indeed, are decidedly difficult. The war has had dreadful environmental effects. While some areas are uncultivable, others are merely deserted. Even leaders of the stature of 'Hercules' and Henry will find such conditions hard enough to cope with. How much harder, then, will they seem to their less charismatic successors!

IV.20   *Long time the place shall reap abundant peace:*
Through all its desert realm lilies shall blow.
Thither they'll bring the dead o'er land and seas
Who hoped 'gainst hope there to their graves to go.

At the same time, there will be a rather touching episode, as the bodies of former refugees are brought back to be buried in their still-deserted homelands.

II.19   *The newcomers shall find towns undefended*
And people lands that none till now could fill.
Famine, plague, war; then acres to be tended.
Meadows, fields, houses, towns they'll take at will.

Inevitably, there will be further squabbles over land-rights in these areas, but only between the settlers themselves. In all other respects they will be taking over virtually virgin country.

III.26   *Of kings and princes icons they'll adorn*
And empty auguries hold up to view.
Gilded and azure-tipped the victim's horn.
The oracles shall be explained anew.

In this verse, meanwhile, Nostradamus seems to predict a rise in public credulity and idolatry – idolatry of their leaders in the form of the so-called personality-cult, credulity in the form of a return to a form of ritualistic paganism with a pronounced emphasis on 'reading the entrails'.

V.77   *All the degrees of honour in the church*
For Jovial Quirinus they'll revise.
To Mars Quirinal priests berobed shall lurch.
Till France's monarch shall them Vulcanise.

The new lurch towards paganism is not popular with the reigning establishment, and it eventually takes vigorous steps to stamp it out. The detail is borrowed from Livy's description of the reign of the semi-legendary King Numa of ancient Rome.[49]

III.76   *In Germany strange sects shall come to be*
That almost shall the happy pagan play.
Captive their hearts, but little gain they'll see.
They shall return their proper tithes to pay.

The delights of the flirtation with paganism, however – especially in Germany – will eventually start to pall in any case, and there will be a widespread return to mainstream religion. Possibly the Catholic Nostradamus is basing himself here on the rise of Lutheranism earlier in the sixteenth century.

II.12*   *Eyes closed to all but fantasies of yore,*
True monkish habit none shall deign to wear.
The mighty king shall scourge their madness sore,
And sack their temples while they stand and stare.

Nostradamus is quite gleeful at this development.

II.8   *Of churches hallowed in old Roman manner*
            They shall reject the very fundaments,
            Making base-principles their human banner
            At many a former saintly cult's expense.

Nevertheless, the return to mainstream religion is destined to be based not on received practice, but on a return to Christian first principles – i.e. the simple, homespun practices of the early Church. Nostradamus, with his known Franciscan sympathies, clearly approves. The whole complex edifice of traditional Roman Catholicism is likely to be severely shaken, even though some of its major saintly cults are likely to survive, reflecting as they do some very deep, even pre-Christian, instincts within the human psyche.

V.87*   *The year that Saturn shall withdraw his writ*   **2034?**
            Shall Frankish lands by floods be stricken hard.
            With Trojan blood a marriage he shall knit,
            While Spaniards shall provide a bodyguard.

The end of the long period of troubles is marked by floods in France, while Henry finally marries a woman who, similarly, is of French royal blood. Saturn finally enters Leo (its opposite sign) on 28 August 2034.

X.6   *Gard and Nemausus' spring shall flood so high*
            That they shall think Deucalion returns.
            Into the colosseum most shall fly.
            In vestal tomb fire once-extinguished burns.

Nothing is ever perfect, however, and at some stage severe weather hits the south of France. Serious flooding results. Deucalion, after all, was the ancient Greek equivalent of the biblical Noah. The people of Nîmes take refuge in the famous amphitheatre, or *arènes*. On the other hand, even disasters such as this can have their bright side, as line four and the succeeding stanzas go on to reveal.

V.66 *Beneath the ancient vestal buildings deep*
Not far from ruined aqueduct so old
Sun's gold, moon's silver still all shiny sleep
And burning Trojan lamp engraved in gold.

Possibly as a result of the flooding (not for the first time), some remarkable discoveries are unearthed – in this case an ancient vault containing what (despite line four of the foregoing verse) seems to be an ever-burning lamp. The details confirm that the discovery will indeed take place at Nîmes, on the site of the ancient and now crumbling temple to Diana. Rather than being 'Trojan' (the conventional interpretation), the lamp may date from the reign of Trajan – which is the word that Nostradamus actually writes. And indeed, much damage has been done to the ancient monuments around Nîmes by treasure-seekers unsuccessfully acting on Nostradamus's prophecy!

I.27* *'Neath mistled oak struck by a lightning blast*
The hidden treasure lies, or close nearby.
Him who shall find the age-old hoard at last
They'll find struck dead, a spring stuck in his eye.

The intriguing archaeological saga continues.

287

IX.9   *When shall be found the lamp that's never-fading,*
Still burning 'midst the vestal temple's walls
(The flame found by a child through water wading),
Floods destroy Nîmes; down fall Toulouse's halls.

Whether the floods really lead to the discovery, or the discovery merely presages the floods, is not entirely clear from this verse. But then not much of Nostradamus ever is. Probably, though, the former is the correct explanation. Nîmes was certainly severely damaged by floods in 1988 – but, so far as I know, no buried treasure came to light.

IX.37   *Bridges and mills December shall throw down:*
So high the torrent of Garonne shall race,
Buildings and halls throughout Toulouse's town
Destroyed: scarce should an old girl know the place.

What *is* clear, however, is that the flooding will be extraordinarily severe at the time, not merely at Nîmes, but in south-western France too.

VIII.30   *Not far from digger's scoop within Toulouse,*
Excavating a 'palais de spectacles',
A treasure's found that all shall sore bemuse
In caches twain quite close to the Basacle.

Perhaps it is during the course of reconstruction work that yet further valuable archaeological discoveries are made. The *Basacle* is the name of the former mill area of the city, as well of the castle that protects it – and Nostradamus specifically mentions damage to mills in IX.37, above.

VIII.29　　*By Saint-Sernin's fourth pillar shall be found*
　　　　　　(Split by a 'quake when floods are at the door)
　　　　　　The pot beneath the building underground
　　　　　　Of Caepio's stolen gold; then handed o'er.

Indeed, Toulouse is destined to yield up even more treasures, this time under the celebrated basilica of Saint-Sernin. Caepio, the Roman consul who sacked Toulouse in 106 BC, somehow managed to mislay the treasures he 'liberated' there, carefully ensuring that they never reached Rome. In consequence, he was impeached and sacked from the Senate. If Nostradamus is right, the floods will at last find him out by revealing just where he hid them.

IX.12　　　*So many silver images are found*
　　　　　　Of Hermes and Diana in the lake
　　　　　　By potter seeking new clay underground
　　　　　　As him and his rich beyond dreams to make.

Meanwhile, back at the convent ... as ever, Nostradamus invokes a double image: in the original, immersion in water has its golden counterpart. Could it be his way of suggesting that every cloud has its silver lining? And can the discovery of new riches underground itself be symbolic of what humanity is now destined to discover deep within its own psyche?

X.89　　　*Brick walls they shall in marble reconstruct:*　　2037
　　　　　　Of peace seven years and fifty shall there be.
　　　　　　For humans, joy; rebuilt each aqueduct:
　　　　　　Health, honeyed times and rich fecundity.

289

This verse is clearly based on the Emperor Augustus's celebrated declaration at the end of his 57-year rule that he had 'found Rome brick and left it marble'.[15] The application of comparative horoscopy to the date of Augustus's accession to power pinpoints 2037 as the date of the possible inception of a new Augustan Age. However, the horoscopy also fits 1945, at the start of the era of post-war reconstruction that was eventually to lead to the present world – even if our own 'white marble' is more likely to be white concrete. In the current case, then, the present era of unparalleled peace and prosperity is likely to come to an end in around 2002 – which takes us right back to the start of the invasion scenario that I have spent the last three chapters outlining.

For the more distant future, similarly, as the power-symbolising edifices of the former State and Church are alike pulled down, at last the picture is one of full recovery and prosperity which will last for over half a century. True, this very fact means that the world – or Europe, at least – is eventually likely to be overtaken by war yet again. But then it is relatively rare for peace to last even that long, so presumably humanity will have to be thankful for small mercies. Certainly, a long era of conflict for the Mediterranean area and Western Europe will at last have come to an end. Humanity can perhaps look forward to a period of some centuries during which the world may not always be nice, but whose major problems and triumphs are at least likely to be of a very different order from anything that has ever been experienced before, even if (thanks to the presumed 'Janus hypothesis') they are destined to follow curiously similar patterns.

7

INTO THE FAR FUTURE

The mighty tapestry, scarce yet unrolled,
But half of future history discloses
That, from afar, seems harsh to France and cold
Till brutal war its truth to all exposes.

Propheties: VI.61*

M OST OF NOSTRADAMUS'S PROPHECIES for the far future are based not on historical events, but on St John's Revelation, on Richard Roussat's well-known predictions for the end of the world,[53] and on the vast anthology of earlier end-time prophecies collected together in the popular *Livre Merveilleux* of 1522. They are also evidently based on general conditions in the seer's own day, which to his contemporaries bore all the hallmarks of the long-threatened Last Times. Either way, however, they lacked specific dates, and so comparative horoscopy cannot be applied to them as a means of predicting exact *future* dates, either.

I.63　　*The woes once past, the world shall smaller grow:*
　　　　　With lands unpeopled, peace shall long survive.
　　　　　Through sky, o'er land and sea they'll safely go.
　　　　　Then once again shall ghastly war revive.

After the various disasters of the foregoing forty years or so there will, it seems, be a long period of peace and progress. Not that the first line should necessarily be seen (as some commentators would have us believe) as a direct prediction of improved communications links, even though Nostradamus certainly foresees routine air travel: it is just that the population of parts of Europe especially will have been so reduced by war, famine and disease – possibly in that order – that there will be little incentive to fight, and even less people left to do it. Whole areas will be deserted or – as Nostradamus puts it – *inhabitées* (far from meaning 'inhabited', as Erika Cheetham suggests,[11,13] the French word normally means '*un*inhabited'). Italy and France in particular may suffer in this way. Only after this prolonged peaceful era will the final woes eventually return that are to lead up to the final change of cycle. Prévost[49] traces back the underlying ideas in this verse to Plato's commentary on Hesiod's exposition of the cycles of universal time.

I.56　　*Both soon and late you shall see changes vast.*
　　　　　Vast horrors, vengeance cruel the signs portend,
　　　　　When as, by angel led, the moon at last
　　　　　Of heaven shall I see the trepidation end.

The advent of these final woes will, as ever, be indicated by signs in the heavens for those who have eyes to read them. In Nostradamus's day, the archangel controlling the sphere of the moon was said to be Gabriel, and at the end of the age of

354 years and four months that fell under their tutelage the heavens would (according to Roussat[53]) regain their pristine stability and the earth, too, would in Nostradamus's words 'remain stable and firm'. On Roussat's figures, this was supposed to occur in 1887!

V.32   *When all is well, and gold and silver are*
                Richly abundant, comes their ruin near.
                To dash your fortunes, hurtling from afar,
                Like the seventh stone from heaven it shall
                    appear.

If Nostradamus is to be believed, the first sign that the initial era of peace and abundance is about to end will be the appearance from the heavens of some kind of cometary body that will burn like the seventh stone of St John's Revelation in the Bible, which is described in terms of chrysolite, golden topaz or yellow olivine. Possibly, then, some heavenly body is destined to collide with the earth, bringing ruin to the more prosperous parts of the world particularly. Curiously, scientists analysing comet Hale-Bopp during late 1997 were astonished to discover that one of its constituents was indeed olivine!

IV.49*   *Before the people blood shall then be shed,*
                Amid the highest heaven it shall appear:
                Long shall it be by none interpreted.
                The mind of one alone shall make it clear.

Certainly, a celestial omen is predicted as appearing, possibly related to the end-time events related in Revelation 6:12, which describes how 'the moon became as blood'.

II.45   *Too much high heaven the Androgyne bewails*
            New-born near to this place where blood is sprayed.
            Too late that death a mighty race avails.
            Sooner or later comes the hoped-for aid.

This mysterious stanza could mean almost anything. Who is the newly-born hermaphrodite so mourned by the celestial powers – and who, for that matter, are they? Why is 'human blood' shed, let alone 'near to this sky' (as the original words actually put it)? Could this be a reference to the upper air, or even to space itself? If the Androgyne's death is designed somehow to revivify the race, why is it too late? And is the hoped-for aid an extraterrestrial saviour or merely some kind of earthly succour? Certainly the extraterrestrial explanation seems particularly seductive. It is as though a would-be helper from space has been bloodily repulsed and so prevented from carrying out some kind of redemptive mission to earth. One is reminded of Marlowe's extraordinary line in his *Doctor Faustus* of 1589: 'See, see where Christ's blood streams in the firmament!' Nevertheless, yet further redemptive initiatives of similar type will apparently be attempted.

X.99   *At length lies wolf with ox and lion with ass:*
            The timid deer shall dwell among the pack.
            Yet no more gentle manna falls, alas!
            Take care no vigilance the mastiffs lack!

In vague, misty, biblical terms Nostradamus now foreshadows a future time when the new-found order and prosperity are in danger of breaking break down again.

I.44   *Soon shall the slaughter once again return.*
            Those who resist are laid upon the racks.
            No abbots, monks, no novices to learn:
            Honey shall cost far more than candle-wax.

In an echo of his own distinctly apocalyptic times, Nostradamus foresees an era of renewed brutality, with religion once again repressed. In association with this, he also seems to foreshadow increasing inflation, particularly where the price of food is concerned. This in turn could suggest that food shortages will be starting to be experienced.

IV.24*   *Our Lady's voice, heard underground, is feigned.*
            Man's fire shall rise while light Divine shall wane.
            Then shall the land with priestly blood be stained
            And holy temples wrecked by the profane.

The sign of the new time of terror seems to be a claimed vision of the Virgin Mary, possibly along the lines of the 1858 apparition to St Bernadette in the grotto at Lourdes.

IV.67   *When Mars and Saturn equally shall burn*
            The dried-up winds shall blow those countries o'er.
            To ashes hidden fires great swathes shall turn.
            Scarce rain, hot winds there'll be, then raids and war.

Possibly we have here the reason why. A period of severe drought commences. The 'secret fires' with which it is associated could refer either to fires that nobody notices or to some kind of underground combustion or radiation. The consequent food shortages meanwhile lead, as ever, to skirmishes and conflict. Planets were said to be *combuste* (as the French original of line one puts it) when at their closest to the sun.

I.67　　*The mighty famine whose approach I feel*
　　　　First comes and goes, then reigns from east to west.
　　　　So great, so long it is that they shall steal
　　　　From trees their roots, babes from their mother's
　　　　　　breast.

Once again the theme of food shortages surfaces, with the last line indicating the dire extent of the anticipated problem – though just how literally we should take the suggested cannibalistic element, or how broad a spectrum of people or nationalities the word 'they' (*on*) is meant to cover, is uncertain. Although neither in this stanza nor in the previous one are time or place specified, it is clear that Nostradamus sees food shortages – already starkly apparent even in our own day – eventually becoming worldwide, very much in line with the famines predicted by the biblical 'little apocalypse' of Matthew 24. Nor does this seem at all unlikely on present estimates, bearing in mind the world's rapidly rising population, spreading desertification and the possible effects of atmospheric pollution. The answers, in other words, lie (as ever) largely in our own hands. One way or the other, then, Nostradamus's quatrain deserves to be taken as a dire warning to us. Such was ever the role of the true prophet.

II.75　　*The voice of an unwonted bird is heard*
　　　　On cruel cannon and on winding stair:
　　　　So high the price of wheat, that man is stirred
　　　　His fellow man to eat in his despair.

Erika Cheetham[11,13] somehow manages to read into this quatrain an unlikely story of oracular owls on chimneys and a Third World War. She also makes the poor bird 'unwanted' instead of 'unwonted' – a hilarious piece of unintended cruelty to dumb animals into which she is blindly followed by various other commentators, one at least of whom then goes so far as to read into it a future despoliation of the earth's wild species, not excluding the whales and elephants. Of such, alas, is scholarship made! If my own reading of this somewhat obscure verse is correct, however, Nostradamus is merely once again foretelling eventual food shortages, rampant inflation and their almost inevitable effects. The 'unwonted bird' image is also to be found in the *Letter to Henri II*. Whether the 'man eats man' description is meant to be taken literally or merely figuratively is not clear: it is, after all, highly unusual for starving people to experience the urge to eat each other, still less to give way to it. As ever where 'end-time' events are concerned, no date is suggested.

III.5   *When heaven its two lights long default prepares*
          ('Twixt March and April shall that time befall),
          How costly! Yet two mighty debonairs
          By land and sea shall succour bring to all.

By the 'two great luminaries' mentioned in the original text, Nostradamus is referring to the 'two great lights' of the Genesis creation account which are set in the firmament to rule the day and night – i.e. the sun and moon. While Prévost[49] argues convincingly that this prediction is in fact based on the multiple eclipses of 1540, their 'default' would appear to refer to their expected disappearance just prior to the advent of the Kingdom of Heaven on earth, as predicted by Jesus himself in Matthew 24:29 (albeit on the basis of the earlier Old Testament prophecies):

297

As soon as the woes of those days are past, the sun shall be darkened, the moon shall not give her light, the stars shall fall from heaven and the powers of heaven shall be shaken.

We may speculate on the true reasons for this extraordinary phenomenon: the most obvious explanation would be severe atmospheric pollution, however caused (in probable order of likelihood, volcanic eruptions and industrial smog – it is quite unnecessary for us to think in terms of nuclear winter). However, Nostradamus brings two new variables into the equation. First, he actually attempts to date the early signs of this event – even though not to any particular year. And secondly, he foresees some measure of hope, in that (as Prévost sees it on the basis of the 1540 precedent) the planets Jupiter and Saturn will be favourable.

III.4   *Ere sun and moon cease their appointed work*
When distant but in minuscule degree
Cold, drought and peril near the borders lurk,
E'en where the oracle first came to be.

Despite attempts by commentators to make Nostradamus's word *lunaires* refer to present-day Muslim countries by virtue of the crescent moon on their flag, the similarity of wording makes it overwhelmingly probable that this quatrain is linked (unusually) to its direct successor (above), and that the word is actually a typically Nostradamian compression of *luminaires*. Continuing the self-same story, in other words, the inevitable consequence of the masking of sun and moon by cloud and/or smoke in the upper atmosphere would indeed be cold – and possibly drought, too, as a result of a severe reduction in solar heating and a consequent weakening of the earth's weather systems. There seems, however, to be the probability of special danger 'near the borders', which might perhaps suggest (not unreasonably) that armed forays into neighbouring countries in search of food are likely to follow. The last line looks like an attempt by the seer to pinpoint the area where the problem is likely to be felt most acutely. Unfortunately, though, he does not state which 'oracle' he means. The natural interpretation would suggest Delphi in Greece, but Prévost[49] suggests a reference to the *Prophetie de Cambrai* in the *Livre Merveilleux* of 1522.

III.34   *When heavenly sun no further beams shall shed,*
            In daylight broad the monster shall appear.
            In many different ways interpreted,
            None has foreseen how it might cost them dear.

Nostradamus makes no attempt to explain this mysterious omen or apparition, be it extraterrestrial or otherwise. Line one could as easily refer to the disappearance of sun and moon at the end of time as to a simple eclipse.

I.91   *The gods to men shall make it fully clear*
            How of the mighty war they'll be the source.
            Before the sky shall clear shall sword and spear
            To leftward turn with even greater force.

Line three suggests that this quatrain belongs not long after III.4 and III.5 (pages 297–8), when the skies are at long last showing signs of clearing again, and the earth's people have consequently started to resume their old, unregenerate ways. However, the syntax is more than a little woolly. It may suggest that everything is literally in the lap of the gods, in which case there is nothing to be done. Equally, though, it may be suggesting that humanity is the ultimate source of its own woes. In the words of Shakespeare's Cassius in *Julius Caesar*: 'The fault, dear Brutus, is not in our stars, But in ourselves.'

The message – if message it consequently is – may seem gloomy, but it is potentially a highly positive one. If we are the source of our own woes, then clearly we have it within us to be the source of our own salvation, too. Whether this prediction, like those before and after it, is ever fulfilled thus depends very largely on what we choose to do about it. Nothing is irrevocable. Everything, though, hinges in this case on just who the 'gods' in the first line are meant to be. Ufologists and Erich von Däniken will naturally assume that they are once again extraterrestrials. Who knows: they may even be correct.

I.17   *Full forty years no rainbow they shall know,*
     Then forty years shall it be seen each day.
     First arid land shall yet more arid grow:
     Then mighty floods there'll be, shine though it may.

Evidently the weather will be no less contrary in the future than ever it was. Forty years of sunless and consequently rainbowless drought will be followed by forty years of rain and floods. This prediction is taken almost lock, stock and barrel from Richard Roussat,[53] who in turn is quoting a celebrated end-time prophecy by none other than the Venerable Bede (673–735).

VI.5   *A wave of plague shall bring so great a dearth*
     While ceaseless rains the Arctic Pole shall sweep:
     Samarobryn, a hundred leagues from Earth,
     Law-free themselves from politics shall keep.

300

The last two lines of this extraordinary prediction appear to describe some kind of space station 100 French leagues (i.e. 276.4 miles) above the Earth's surface – at almost exactly the orbital altitude, in fact, of the former American *Skylab*, and only slightly above that of the Soviet *Mir*. Yet the name proposed is neither *Skylab* nor *Mir*, but *Samarobryn*. This ominous-sounding term (which Nostradamus treats as a *plural*, incidentally) has long puzzled commentators, who have generally been unaware that *Samarobriva* was the ancient Gallic name for the city of Amiens in north-eastern France. Whether this is one of Nostradamus's characteristic plays on words is not entirely clear – but it is just possible that he was somewhat deviously (as was his wont) connecting the name 'Amiens' with the Greek *amiantos*, which means 'undefiled'. If so, who are these 'undefiled ones'? Could they be either astronauts or even extraterrestrials? Whoever they are, they seem to be supranational, though the law from whose effects they are immune (whether or not Nostradamus realised the fact) could well be no more than the law of gravity. This would tend to place them a good many years – perhaps even decades or centuries – in the future. The first two lines, meanwhile, suggest that some kind of major epidemic will be sweeping the northern hemisphere at the time, accompanied by the 'long rains' which in Nostradamus's own day certainly tended to produce outbreaks of the familiar plague by flushing the rats from their dens, and which seem also to have been predicted in the previous quatrain.

II.46 *The wheel's great Mover turns the wheel again:*
Great woes once past, yet greater are at hand.
Famine, war, plague and bloody, milky rain.
Fire across heaven shall trail its blazing brand.

Here, at last, Nostradamus approaches the advent of the millennium, painted in colours reminiscent of the biblical Apocalypse itself. The heavenly fire – clearly a comet – seems to represent the long-predicted great star of the Apocalypse (Revelation 8:10–11).

IX.83   *Twenty degrees of Taurus – thus the sun –*
         The crowded theatre shall an earthquake strike.
         Air, sky and sea it shall disturb, turn dun.
         Faithless, they'll call on god and saints alike!

In the month of May, seismic events are destined to strike some at least of humanity at the very moment when ultimate events are furthest from their minds. Even those who have long forgotten their religion will suddenly be inspired to return to it.

X.74   *When turns at last the mighty number seven,*
         At time of Ritual Games it shall be found
         Not long before earth cedes its sway to heaven
         That those long dead are rising from the ground.

Possibly this verse refers to the same occasion. But there is more to it than a mere earthquake. Once again, leaning heavily on familiar biblical eschatology, Nostradamus is here clearly referring to the expected general resurrection of the dead prior to the inception of the millennium – however bizarre the whole notion may nowadays seem to us, and how we may choose to understand it in rational terms. What is particularly interesting, however, is that he chooses to link it with two predictive features of his own. First, he ties it in

302

chronologically with what, in the original French, he calls the 'Hecatombic (i.e. sacrificial) Games' – almost certainly the Olympics, which were known by precisely this term. At the same time he actually puts a date on it. This culminating event for the current world order will, it seems, take place at the end of the seventh millennium after the Creation – i.e., according to Roussat's[53] version of biblical chronology, in or around the year 1887!

II.13   *The soulless corpse shall never suffer more:*
          The day of death leads on to birth anew.
          The Holy Ghost its rapture shall restore
          As soul th' eternal Word shall plainly view.

Indeed, the millennium he foresees looks to be very much a spiritual, rather than blood-and-guts affair – more earth-in-heaven, it could be said, than heaven-on-earth. Possibly, this is a reflection of St Paul's anticipated spiritual universe, which in turn mirrors the ancient Essenes' view of the matter. Certainly it reflects standard Christian dogma – for all the latter's evident contradiction of Old Testament and gospel teaching, and not least of the Lord's Prayer itself, with its clear injunction:

> Thy Kingdom come
> Thy will be done
> *On earth* as it is in heaven.

Once again, therefore, we should do well to be suspicious of taking on board too uncritically what appear to be more in the nature of conditioned Nostradamian expectations than actual Nostradamian visions. Better by far, it might be thought, for Nostradamus to stick to his last: he may have been a prophet, but that is not at all the same thing as being a theologian, let alone a reliable one.

III.2   *The Word Divine shall grant to substance crude*
All heaven and earth, all mystic gold occult.
To body, spirit, soul all power accrued
O'er earth and heaven – such is the great result.

Thus it is that (unless he is merely talking about the Catholic conception of the Eucharist) Nostradamus now sees as his ultimate vision a universe in which heaven and earth are one, man has achieved ultimate union with the divine and all humanity's great ideals – religious, alchemical and, it has to be said, political too – are finally attained.

V.53   *The laws of Sun and Venus disagree*
Touching which shall true prophecy inspire.
Never the twain shall in agreement be.
The solar law follows the great Messiah.

Finally, Nostradamus turns his attention to prophecy itself and its fulfilment. There are, it seems, two prophetic paths – those of Christianity (the Sun) and of Islam (Venus). For Nostradamus, the true Messiah will of course fulfil the Christian prophecies.

I.48   *These twenty years the moon pursues her reign.*
By year seven thousand then another's king.
When next the sun takes up his course again
My prophecy's fulfilment it shall bring.

This is perhaps Nostradamus's culminating prediction: all his prophecies, he claims, will have come true by the year seven thousand – 7000 years, that is, after the biblical Creation. Since, in his *Letter to Henri King of France the Second*, he dates this event at 4173 years before the birth of Christ (though in his various writings he offers no less than five different dates for it), it follows that his 'seventh millennium' has already happened. It began in 1827/8!

[Mathematicians please note: there was never a 'Year 0', since under the present system, devised by Dionysus Exiguus in the sixth century of our own era, 1 BC – the 'first year before Christ' – is followed immediately by AD 1 – the first 'year of our Lord'. On the other hand, in terms of the rest of the datings since established by the same system, it turns out that Jesus of Nazareth was probably born in the autumn of what we now call 2 BC – though even earlier dates are often proposed. The overall effect, then, is to leave the mathematical calculation more or less as it was, give or take four months or so.]

The first line, meanwhile, clearly dates the quatrain itself to around 1553, two years before its actual first publication, since according to Roussat[53] (and evidently Nostradamus, too) the last great astrological lunar cycle lasted from 1533 to 1887. The next 'age of the sun' is thus already in progress. Theoretically, it finishes in 2242.

FOREWARNED IS FOREARMED

Five hundred years, then more heed they shall take
Of him who was the jewel of his age.
Suddenly then shall light resplendent break
Such as that time's approval to engage.

Century III.94 (1555)

RARELY A MAN FOR FALSE MODESTY, it was with these glowing words – apparently about himself – that Nostradamus seems to have predicted the final triumph of his predictions and their recognition by society at large by about the year 2055. This would suggest that most of the major ones will have come true by then, so making their acceptance virtually inevitable, even by the inveterate sceptics.

Perhaps, indeed, that is what it will take to bring about such an unlikely *volte-face*. Until they are actually borne out, certainly most of Nostradamus's predictions seem improbable, to say the least – and all the more so for his own apparent suggestion, oft repeated, that a good many of them are not in fact inevitable at all. Much, it seems, will hinge on our reactions to events, as well as on our responses to the predictions themselves.

Especially does this apply to what appears to be Nostradamus's scenario for the future Muslim invasion of Europe, at least as I have outlined it in this book. After all, my presentation is inevitably a speculative account. I have no doubt included a good many verses that do not belong to the invasion scenario at all. I have possibly placed a 'spin' on certain verses that they perhaps do not merit, but that the words certainly allow – as Nostradamus was careful to ensure, and as he himself was not above exploiting when it suited him. It is even possible that he himself never had an overall sequence of events in mind in the first place, but simply left all such considerations to the crude operation of the 'Janus hypothesis', as governed by the as-yet unforeseen vagaries of future astrology.

Yet there can be no real doubt that such an invasion was one of his major preoccupations. It is its details that are debatable. The very operation of the 'Janus hypothesis', for example, means that its dates are not fixed. This time around, at least, our own reactions to his warnings could yet save us from the worst. And, of course, the principle itself is still not above being questioned.

That said, the projected invasion is far from being Nostradamus's only concern. The *Propheties* contain over 600 other predictions that I have not included. Most of them, though, are far more local in character and would not even make today's national newspaper headlines, despite determined efforts by modern gloom-and-doom merchants to make them apply to New York, or Sydney, or wherever their own particular countries or capitals happen to be. Most of those that I *have* included, by contrast, are prophecies on a world scale that demand our attention, our consideration and ultimately our reaction.

History repeats itself

True, oriental invasions, papal shenanigans and even Antichrists are nothing new. Neither are bloody times generally. There have been plenty of them in the past, and no doubt there will be lots more in the future, too. The 'Janus hypothesis' demands nothing less. Human nature – fortunately or unfortunately – does not change. It is not entirely unlikely, consequently, that the darker themes of history will tend to resurface repeatedly in the future much in the way that Nostradamus's predictions seem to suggest, right up until the dawning of whatever millennium eventually arrives. Nostradamus, apparently like King Solomon (to say nothing of the Hindus and Buddhists), believed as much both implicitly and explicitly.

Blaming the messenger

In reporting the fact, however, I may be accused of spreading only bad news, of actually creating the future that we most dread. But then when was news ever other than predominantly bad? The retrospective equivalent of Nostradamus's predictions, after all, would be several hundred years of newspapers. Can anyone imagine how much bad news *they* would contain? As for the accusation of creating the dark times by the very act of anticipating them, it needs to be said that the deed has been done long since. Blame the Bible, even blame Nostradamus if you must – notwithstanding the fact that it sounds suspiciously like blaming the messenger for the message (ask yourself, too, how Nostradamus can possibly be blamed for the prophetic effects of a message that, until quite recently, nobody has fully understood). But it is too late now to blame me or any other translator or commentator for the coming Asiatic invasion, if come indeed it does. The prophetic wheels, if such they were, were set spinning centuries ago, and whether in Central Asia, the Middle East or the former Yugoslavia their political and social counterparts are already stirring into motion quite independently of anything that I or anybody else can now do about it – as even the most casual glance at *today's* newspapers will soon confirm.

But if it is too late now to blame interpreters such as myself for the bad times to come, there is plenty of time yet for the dawning of the good times that I also anticipate for the distant future on the basis of Nostradamus's prophecies, once the great invasion and war are over at long last. Blame me for them, then, if you like.

Changing ourselves

Questions of blame aside, though, it actually seems quite likely (not least, once again, under the terms of the 'Janus hypothesis') that past events will indeed have their future counterparts, quite independently of whether they are predicted or not – and that these, as is the way of things, will be even bigger and better (or worse) than before. Possibly this is because the human consciousness that produces them will be the same old human consciousness as before. If so, then the only reliable way to prevent them will be to change human consciousness, not to attempt to muzzle either the prophets or their interpreters. And would-be missionaries should bear in mind that this means changing *their* consciousness, not somebody else's.

Perhaps, indeed, that was all that Nostradamus ever intended. Our own reactions are actually important. We still have some choice in the matter. We can ensure that our own thoughts and actions are not such as to bring about the events that we most wish to avoid. We can look out for advance warning-signs of the events predicted. We can choose where to live, carefully avoiding the areas worst affected (a good many of Nostradamus's predictions, it is worth remembering, are clearly designed to warn local inhabitants). We can lean on our politicians to adopt suitably prophylactic policies, draw up tentative contingency plans and respond appropriately if and when events do swing into motion. We can urge our military authorities to take suitable precautions of a fairly generalised kind. In our own homes (if we are lucky enough to have them), we can make ourselves less vulnerable to social disruption by assuring our own fuel supplies, reducing our energy-requirements, adopting alternative energy-sources, preserving our more primitive forms of heating and lighting, growing more of our own vegetables, retaining our old hand- and foot-operated machines and learning once again how to make do and mend and practise recycling in every area of our lives. Forewarned, as they say, is forearmed. And if, in the event, Nostradamus were to prove to be as wrong as he would have to be to render such precautions unnecessary, perhaps the resulting benefits for our planetary environment would not be such a high price to pay after all.

Dead prophet, then, or dead loss? Only time will tell. But if the critics really want to prove Nostradamus as wrong as they would have him be, then the best way for them to do it is not merely to *say* as much, citing in evidence the distinctly unpersuasive fact that he offends their theoretical presuppositions. Instead, they need to *prove* as much in terms of actual practice – to take a variety of steps, in other words, designed either to make the fulfilment of his predictions impossible or to mitigate their effects should they ever dare to occur. Then they could quite reasonably say 'I told you so'.

And I have no doubt that Nostradamus, for his part, would be the last to object.

REFERENCE BIBLIOGRAPHY

1. Allemand, J.: *Nostradamus et les hiéroglyphes* (Maison de Nostradamus, Salon, 1996)
2. Amadou, R.: *L'Astrologie de Nostradamus* (ARRC, Poissy, 1992)
3. Beckley (ed.): *Nostradamus's Unpublished Prophecies* (Inner Light, 1991)
4. Benazra, R.: *Répertoire Chronologique Nostradamique* (1545–1989), 1990
5. Boeser, K.: *Nostradamus* (Bloomsbury, 1994)
6. Boeser, K. (Ed.): *The Elixirs of Nostradamus* (Bloomsbury, 1995)
7. Brennan, J.H., *Nostradamus; Visions of the Future* (Aquarian, 1992)
8. Brind'Amour, P.: *Nostradamus astrophile* (University of Ottawa, 1993)
9. Brind'Amour, P.: *Nostradamus: Les premières centuries ou propheties* (Droz, 1996)
10. Cannon, D., *Conversations with Nostradamus: His Prophecies Explained*, 3 Vols. (Ozark Mountain, 1989 onwards)
11. Cheetham, E., *The Final Prophecies of Nostradamus* (Futura, 1989)
12. Cheetham, E.: *The Further Prophecies of Nostradamus* (Corgi, 1985–91)
13. Cheetham, E., *The Prophecies of Nostradamus* (Corgi, 1973)
14. Chevignard, B., *Présages de Nostradamus* (Ed. du Seuil, 1999)
15. Chomarat, M., Dupèbe, J. & Polizzi, G.: *Nostradamus ou le savoir transmis* (Chomarat, 1997)
16. Chomarat, M. & Laroche, Dr. J.-P.: *Bibliographie Nostradamus* (Koerner, 1989)
17. Dufresne, M.: *Nostradamus: Première Centurie* (series) up to

Nostradamus: Septième Centurie, 7 vols. (Chicoutimi/JCL, 1989–97)

18. Dupèbe, J.: *Nostradamus. Lettres Inédites* (Droz, 1983)
19. Erickstad, H.G.B., *The Prophecies of Nostradamus in Historical Order* (Janus, 1996)
20. Fontbrune, J.-C. de, *Nostradamus 1: Countdown to Apocalypse* (Pan, 1983)
21. Fontbrune, J.-C. de, *Nostradamus 2: Into the Twenty-First Century* (Holt, 1984)
22. Gauquelin, M.: *Cosmic Influences on Human Behaviour* (Futura, 1976)
23. Hewitt, V.J.: *Nostradamus: The Key to the Centuries* (Hutchinson, 1994)
24. Hewitt, V.J. & Lorie, P., *Nostradamus: the End of the Millennium* (Bloomsbury, 1991)
25. Hogue, J.: *Nostradamus and the Millennium* (Bloomsbury, 1987)
26. Hogue, J.: *Nostradamus: The New Revelations* (Element 1994)
27. Hogue, J.: *Nostradamus: The Complete Prophecies* (Element, 1997)
28. Ionescu, V.: *Les dernières victoires de Nostradamus* (Filipacchi, 1993)
29. Kidogo, Bardo: *The Keys to the Predictions of Nostradamus* (Foulsham, 1994)
30. King, Francis X.: *Nostradamus: Prophecies Fulfilled and Predictions for the Millennium and Beyond* (BCA, 1993)
31. Laver, J.: *Nostradamus or the Future Foretold* (Mann, 1942–81)
32. Lemesurier, P.: *Nostradamus – The Next 50 Years* (Piatkus, 1993)
33. Lemesurier, P.: *Nostradamus: The Final Reckoning* (Piatkus, 1995)
34. Lemesurier, P.: *The Nostradamus Encyclopedia* (Godsfield, 1997)
35. Lemesurier, P.: *The Essential Nostradamus* (Piatkus, 1999)
36. Lemesurier, P.: *Nostradamus Beyond 2000* (Godsfield, 1999)
37. Leoni, E.: *Nostradamus and His Prophecies* (Wings, 1961–82)
38. Leroy, Dr. E.: *Nostradamus: ses origines, sa vie, son œuvre* (Lafitte, 1993)
39. Lorie, P. (with Greene, L.): *Nostradamus: The Millennium and Beyond* (Bloomsbury, 1993)
40. Lorie, P. (with Mascetti): *Nostradamus's Prophecies for Women* (Bloomsbury, 1995)
41. Mareuil, J. de: *Les ultimes prophéties de Nostradamus* (Grancher, 1994
42. 'Moult, T.-J.': *Propheties Perpetuelles*, '1269' (assumed 1740 reprint of ditto by Friar Joseph Illyricus, c. 1530)
43. Nostradamus, M.: *Orus Apollo*, Ed. Rollet, P., as *Interprétation des hiéroglyphes de Horapollo* (Marcel Petit, 1993)
44. Nostradamus, M.: *Les Prophéties, Lyon, 1557* (Chomarat, 1993)

45. Nostradamus, M.: *Les Prophéties, Lyon, 1568* (Chomarat, 2000)
46. Nostradamus, M.: *Traité des fardemens et des confitures*, published as *Le Vray et Parfaict Embellissement de la Face*, in Plantin's Antwerp edition of 1557 (Gutenberg Reprints, 1979)
47. Ovason, D.: *The Secrets of Nostradamus* (Century, 1997)
48. Pitt Francis, D., *Nostradamus: Prophecies of Present Times?* (Aquarian, 1984)
49. Prévost, R.: *Nostradamus: le mythe et la réalité* (Laffont, 1999)
50. Randi, J.: *The Mask of Nostradamus* (Prometheus, 1993)
51. Reynaud-Plense, C.: *Les vraies Centuries et Propheties de Michel Nostradamus* (Salon, Imprimerie régionale, 1940)
52. Roberts, H.C., *The Complete Prophecies of Nostradamus* (Grafton, 1985)
53. Roussat, R.: *Livre de l'estat et mutations des temps*, 1549/50
54. Ward, C.A.: *Oracles of Nostradamus* (Society of Metaphysicians [facsimile of 1891 ed.], 1990, 1995

INDEX OF PREDICTIONS QUOTED

GENERAL INDEX